THIS HOUSE
HAS FALLEN

Nigeria in Crisis

KARL MAIER

ALLEN LANE
THE PENGUIN PRESS

ALLEN LANE
THE PENGUIN PRESS

Published by the Penguin Group
Penguin Books Ltd, 27 Wrights Lane, London W8 5TZ, England
Penguin Putnam Inc., 375 Hudson Street, New York, New York 10014, USA
Penguin Books Australia Ltd, Ringwood, Victoria, Australia
Penguin Books Canada Ltd, 10 Alcorn Avenue, Toronto, Ontario, Canada M4V 3B2
Penguin Books India (P) Ltd, 11, Community Centre, Panchsheel Park, New Delhi – 110 017, India
Penguin Books (NZ) Ltd, Private Bag 102902, NSMC, Auckland, New Zealand
Penguin Books (South Africa) (Pty) Ltd, 5 Watkins Street, Denver Ext 4, Johannesburg 2094, South Africa

Penguin Books Ltd, Registered Offices: Harmondsworth, Middlesex, England

First published in the USA by PublicAffairs™, a member of the Perseus Books Group 2000
First published in Great Britain by Allen Lane The Penguin Press 2001

1

Printed and bound in Great Britain by The Bath Press, Bath

Cover repro and printing by Concise Cover Printers

A CIP catalogue record for this book is available from the British Library

ISBN 0-713-99523-8

The resilience, the wonderfulness, the energy—Nigeria can be compared favourably with the United States of America. I put it crudely sometimes that if you know how to package shit, you can sell it in Nigeria. I want this country to be the first black superpower.

BOLA IGE

The only difference between South Africa and Nigeria is that here you have a group of blacks who don't make up ten percent of the population but control the economy, while the majority are poor.

BASHIR KURFI

This is an example of a country that has fallen down; it has collapsed. This house has fallen.

CHINUA ACHEBE

Contents

Acknowledgments   IX

Preface   XV

1   A Coup from Heaven   *1*

2   Voting Day   *23*

3   Army Arrangement   *39*

4   The Ogoni Wars   *75*

5   The Journey of a Thousand Miles . . .   *111*

6   The Faithful   *143*

7   Children of Ham   *193*

8   The Spirit of Odùduwà   *227*

9   "This Animal Called Man"   *251*

10   A Glass Cage   *269*

Epilogue   *289*

Notes   *305*

Further Reading   *311*

Index   *313*

Acknowledgments

The research and writing of this book were made possible in large part by financial support from the U.S. Institute of Peace and the Open Society Institute. Thanks also to the Centre for Defence Studies at King's College London.

Among the very many people who provided me with their time, insights, and company, I am especially grateful to Chris Alagoa, Richard Dowden, Yomi Edu, Antony Goldman, Phil Hall, Mohammed Haruna, Michael Holman, Nick Ashton-Jones, Peter Cunliffe-Jones, Bill Knight, Abidina Coomassi, Father Mathew Kukah, Dr. Suleimanu Kumo, Bashir Kurfi, Dr. Beko Ransome-Kuti, Clement Nwankwo, Nduka Obaigbena, Bayo Onanuga, Barnaby Phillips, Patrick Smith, Ulukayode Sukoya, Mathew Tostevin, Bala Usman, William Wallis and his two angels, Ken Wiwa, Simon Yohanna, and Kabiru Yusuf.

I am particularly indebted to Father Kukah and Patrick Smith for taking time out to read an initial draft, to correct errors of fact and interpretation, and to make valuable suggestions on its improvement.

Sincere thanks also go to my agent, Gloria Loomis, and the book's editor, Geoff Shandler.

As always, this book is dedicated to Sarah.

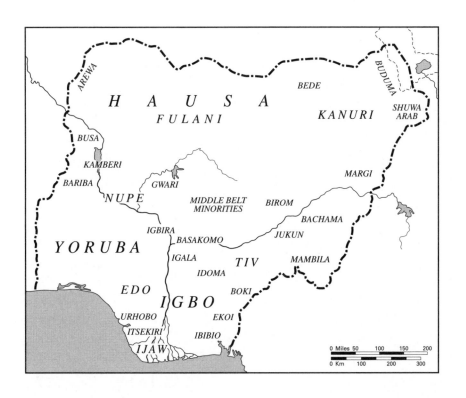

AREWA

H A U S A

FULANI

BEDE

BUDUMA

KANURI

SHUWA
ARAB

BUSA

KAMBERI

BARIBA

NUPE

GWARI

MIDDLE BELT
MINORITIES

MARGI

BIROM

BACHAMA

IGBIRA

BASAKOMO

JUKUN

YORUBA

IGALA

TIV

MAMBILA

IDOMA

EDO

BOKI

IGBO

URHOBO

EKOI

ITSEKIRI

IBIBIO

IJAW

0 Miles 50   100   150   200

0 Km   100   200   300

JIGAWA

Nguru

Dutse

YOBE

Damaturu

Potsikum

Kari

Maiduguri

BORNO

Damboa

Lake Chad

Chari

CHAD

BAUCHI

Bauchi

Gombe

GOMBE

Kumo

Biu

Mubi

Amper

PLATEAU

Yelwa

Jalingo

Yola

Miles

ADAMAWA

Benue

Lac de Lagdo

Ganye

Ibi

Bantaji

Wukari

TARABA

Katsina-Ala

Bissaula

Gembu

CAMEROON

0   50   100   150   200

0 Kilometres   100   200   300

TUNISIA

MOROCCO

WESTERN SAHARA

ALGERIA

LIBYA

EGYPT

MAURITANIA

MALI

NIGER

CHAD

SUDAN

ERITREA

SENEGAL

BURKINA FASO

DJIBOUTI

GAMBIA

GUINEA-BISSAU

GUINEA

NIGERIA

CENTRAL AFRICAN REP.

ETHIOPIA

SIERRA LEONE

IVORY COAST

GHANA

TOGO

BENIN

CAMEROON

SOMALIA

LIBERIA

SÃO TOMÉ & PRÍNCIPE

EQUATORIAL GUINEA

GABON

CONGO

DEMOCRATIC REPUBLIC OF CONGO

UGANDA

RWANDA

BURUNDI

KENYA

TANZANIA

COMOROS

ANGOLA

ZAMBIA

MALAWI

NAMIBIA

ZIMBABWE

MOZAMBIQUE

MADAGASCAR

BOTSWANA

SWAZILAND

SOUTH AFRICA

LESOTHO

Preface

---

*We have essentially relations of raw power in which right
tends to be coexistensive with power and security depends on
the control of power. The struggle for power, then, is everything and is pursued by every means.*

CLAUDE AKE

A S DUSK FADED into a hot humid night, the orange glow of multi-
ple gas flares danced across the skyline over the southeastern city
of Port Harcourt, the unofficial capital of black Africa's biggest oil industry. A major traffic jam, or "go-slow" in local parlance, gripped the
Old Aba Road near the entrance to the headquarters of the most powerful company in Nigeria, the Shell Petroleum Development
Corporation, the local subsidiary of Royal/Dutch Shell. On both sides
of the route, three lines of vehicles, ranging from motorbikes and cars
to oil tankers belching thick clouds of diesel fumes, jockeyed to
squeeze into one lane of pure gridlock. Seemingly oblivious to the
deafening cacophony of horns, young boys bobbed and weaved
through the obstacle course of metallic congestion, hawking food and
drink. Drivers switched off their engines to preserve fuel as passengers

piled out of minibuses and taxis, convinced that it would be faster to walk.

I was on my way to see a Shell public relations officer when the go-slow tightened its embrace on my taxi, a ramshackle Peugeot 504 constantly filled with smoke from a leaky exhaust pipe. The second the vehicle came to a halt in the middle of the intersection, policemen and soldiers armed with rifles emerged from the darkness and gathered around menacingly. My driver, a normally mild-mannered man named John, with the impressive title of vice president of the Airport Drivers Association, was on the verge of losing his cool. The police ordered him to move our car, but it was impossible to advance; neither fore nor aft was there a foot to spare. Suddenly a policeman in a black uniform reached through the driver's window and delivered a wicked right jab to the side of John's face. With lightning speed, John, a wiry welterweight, sprang out of the car and had the policeman by the throat, spitting mortal threats in his face. The policeman countered with a left hook that barely missed and reached for his sidearm. "I will kill you!" screamed John, outgunned but not undaunted. "I will never forget your face! Some place, I will find you when you are out of that uniform. I will kill you!"

The policeman, still groping for the pistol, called on his colleagues to haul John off to the station. The soldiers who were watching the scene stood well clear. When I requested their help, one young trooper smiled and winked as if to say there was no cause for concern; it would all blow over. After several more minutes of fire and brawling, however, the soldiers realized that the fracas was causing the go-slow to go even slower, and they moved with remarkable gentleness to separate the combatants.

John climbed back in—still hurling verbal howitzer blasts and trembling with anger—restarted the engine, and inched the car down the hill. "Stupid man! Just because he has a gun, he thinks he can treat me anyhow, without respect," he said, spittle flying from his lips. "It is like this all over Nigeria. Ignorant people with guns."

I had witnessed a similar scene the week before in Lagos, a sprawling commercial center and black Africa's biggest city, with some ten million people. In the middle of Akin Adesola Street, the broad thoroughfare that bisects Victoria Island, the posh residential and business district, two soldiers stood in front of a pair of hapless middle-aged men who were crawling on their knees with their hands behind their heads as if they were prisoners of war. The soldiers took turns punching them in the face as they shuffled along, and dirt and pebbles from the road ground into their already bloody legs. Motorists and shoppers passed by, but no one dared to upbraid the soldiers; they were a law unto themselves.

As the minutes passed, I could sense John's resentment of his own powerlessness, of the utter arbitrariness of life. He could just as easily have been gunned down in the middle of the road. Shootings of civilians by police and soldiers, as well as of police by soldiers and soldiers by police, were common. But given the level of tension in the society, I often felt surprised that confrontations were not more frequent. In Nigeria brinkmanship has evolved into an art form. "I will never forget that face," John growled. "I will find him." I did not believe him. He had a wife, two children, and, however difficult and poorly paid, a full-time job. A face-off with an armed cop was not worth the risk. Most Nigerians made the same calculation when weighing up the pros and cons of rebellion against their government.

John gradually calmed down as we rambled along in his fume-filled Peugeot to my appointment with the Shell public relations man, Bobo Brown. Bobo was the former editor of *Sunray*, a respected newspaper in Port Harcourt that had collapsed in financial troubles. With few well-paid prospects, he took a community relations job to help Shell deal with what had become a low-intensity revolt by the destitute villagers in the Niger River delta who live atop the colossal reservoirs of oil the company extracts for export to Europe and the United States.

Bobo was staying at the Shell Club, a sprawling recreational complex the company sponsors for its employees, their families, and the elite of Port Harcourt. It features living quarters, restaurants, bars, satellite television, tennis courts, and a regulation soccer field. As Bobo and I strolled on a lush lawn at the back of the club, he said with an ironic chuckle, "You see Shell spends a lot of money to build all this, so that for a while we can forget that the rest of Nigeria is out there. But of course Nigeria is always there."

We walked over to a bar by the tennis courts, and Bobo ordered two tear-inducing bowls of pepper soup and a couple of jumbo bottles of Gulder beer. Under the court floodlights, I told Bobo of John's encounter with the police—Bobo was not surprised—and that led to a broader discussion about what had gone so wrong in Nigeria. The way Bobo described it, Nigeria was suffering from a sort of national psychosis. Political and military leaders were corrupt, crime was seen by many as a legitimate avenue for advancement, and people in search of solutions were turning inwards to ethnic prejudice and religious bigotry. "There is a complete split between power and moral right, and unless you have access to power, you have nothing. Everyone is seeking instant gratification. No one is prepared to think of the future." He laughed regretfully. "Nigeria," he said, "is the land of no tomorrow."

TO MOST OUTSIDERS, the very name Nigeria conjures up images of chaos and confusion, military coups, repression, drug trafficking, and business fraud. It remains a mystery to all but a handful of academics and diplomats. The international media generally shun Nigeria because it is a difficult place to work, and it is not easy for journalists to sell the story to editors in New York, Atlanta, or London. Nigeria does not present a cut-and-dried moralistic tale of the South African type about an evil racial minority suppressing heroic resistance fighters. So from time to time Nigeria drifts across our television screens and into the world's public consciousness, only to fade back out again.

The level of ignorance and indifference about Nigeria among the world's most powerful governments can be startling. I attended a meeting of U.S. and Nigerian academics and human rights activists at the U.S. State Department in 1997. One of the Clinton administration's senior envoys to Africa strode in to make a brief appearance and said he had an important matter to address. This was at a time when senior politicians and dozens of journalists and human rights activists were in jail, and Nigeria appeared poised on the precipice of political and social catastrophe. What concerned the official, however, was Washington's fear that the military regime of the day, headed by a diminutive dictator named General Sani Abacha, might rename the street outside the U.S. embassy after Muammar Gadhafi or Fidel Castro as a way of thumbing its nose at the United States. A Nigerian human rights activist sitting next to me shook her head and said under her breath, "I don't believe what I just heard." A small incident perhaps, but it spoke volumes about the West's approach to Africa and Nigeria.

Two weeks before President Bill Clinton's historic visit to Africa in March 1998, his assistant secretary of state for African Affairs, Susan Rice, told the Senate that Washington would regard Abacha's plans to transform himself from military dictator into civilian president as "unacceptable." Then, while in South Africa, Clinton contradicted her, effectively saying that the United States would not object to the most brutal despot in Nigeria's history embarking on a course to "civilianize" his dictatorship. After all, other military leaders in Africa had done it.

These are not trivial examples. We, the outside world, ignore Nigeria at our peril, and we are ill served when our governments demonstrate such indifference. From almost any point of view, Nigeria truly matters. However deep it has sunk into a mire of corruption, repression, and economic dilapidation, Nigeria remains one of the world's strategic nations. It is the biggest trading partner the United States has in Africa. It is the fifth largest supplier of oil to the U.S. market, where its low-sulfur Bonny Light crude is especially prized because it is easily refined into gasoline. As the world's tenth most populous country, Nigeria represents an inherently sizable market that could provide trade opportunities for North American and European companies. It is a vast land, stretching from the dense mangrove swamps and tropical rain forests of the Atlantic coast to the spectacular rocky outcrops of the interior and the wide belt of savanna that finally melts into the arid rim of the Sahara desert. Its 110 million people are an extraordinary human potpourri of some three hundred ethnic groups that represent one out of six Africans. Nigeria is Africa's equivalent to Brazil, India, or Indonesia. It is the pivot point on which the continent turns.

Designed by alien occupiers and abused by army rule for three-quarters of its brief life span, the Nigerian state is like a battered and bruised elephant staggering toward an abyss with the ground crumbling under its feet. Should it fall, the impact will shake the rest of West Africa. The Liberian civil war cost tens of thousands of lives and hundreds of millions of dollars in U.S. taxpayer money. Liberia's entire population is less than half that of Lagos alone.

Nigerians from all walks of life are openly questioning whether their country should remain as one entity or discard the colonial borders and break apart into several separate states. Ethnic and religious prejudices have found fertile ground in Nigeria, where there is neither a national consensus nor a binding ideology. Indeed, the spread of virulent strains of chauvinism in Nigeria is part of a worldwide phenomenon playing out in Indonesia, the Balkans, the former Soviet Union, and a host of other African nations. This sort of politicized tribalism, a constant companion to the modern version of globalization, is the biggest threat to international peace and stability. With ever growing frequency, wars are fought not between states but within them. The conflict is neighbor against neighbor, us against them, always the menacing Other, whether the differences are racial, religious, or linguistic.

And although Nigeria shares this explosion of animosity with other states, it remains unique. It provides the story line for one of the great epics of the late twentieth century. The landscape for the unfolding human drama is a giant, heaving, multiethnic symbol of the archetypal Third World basket case. Since winning independence from Britain in 1960, Nigeria has witnessed at least one million deaths in Africa's biggest civil war, the assassination of two government leaders, six successful coups and four failed ones, and thirty years of army rule. Yet somehow the country has stayed together, despite decades of government by a clique of military and civilian elite who have behaved, to borrow a phrase from the eminent Africa historian Basil Davidson, like "pirates in power." They are modern equivalents of the African warlords of the eighteenth and nineteenth centuries who built up wealthy kingdoms by selling millions of their people to the Europeans in the Atlantic slave trade. In their current incarnation, they sell their resources—oil in the case of Nigeria—instead of human beings.

Very little trickles down. In the official arenas of international discourse—the United Nations, the World Bank, the media—Nigeria is known as a "developing nation," a phrase that conjures up images of economic progress of the sort experienced by the West or among the Asian "tigers." Nigeria, like so many countries in Africa, is patently not a developing nation. It is underdeveloping. Its people are far worse off now than they were thirty years ago. The numbers speak for themselves. Despite some $280 billion in export revenues since the discovery of oil in the late 1950s, at least half of all Nigerians live in abject poverty without access to clean water. Literacy is below that of the Democratic Republic of Congo. Gross domestic product per person is lower now than it was before the beginning of the oil boom of the 1970s. To even return to the living standards of that time, the economy would have to grow by an unlikely 5 percent per year until 2010. The value of the national currency, the naira, has fallen from $2 to a penny per naira. The foreign debt stands at $32 billion. The World Bank ranks Nigeria as the thirteenth poorest country in the world. The 1999 UN human development index gives it a slightly better though still disheartening score, 146th out of 174. The UN Center for Human Settlements (Habitat) predicts that Lagos will be the world's fifth most populous urban center by 2015, with a population of twenty-three million.

So far the West has done little to help and has often made matters worse. It is hypocritical of the West to blame Nigeria for corruption, fraud, and drug running and to demand that Nigerians own up to their foreign debt while at the same time allowing the funds garnered from such nefarious dealings to be deposited in Western banks. "A man who receives stolen goods is called a fence, but what do you call a country that is in the business of receiving stolen goods?" asked Dr. Folarin Gbadebo-Smith, a U.S.-educated dentist and businessman, while in his Lagos office one day. "They lend Nigeria money, somebody here steals the same amount of money and gives it back to them, and then they leave these poor Nigerians repaying what they never owed. The role of the Western powers has been totally disgraceful."

In May 1999, after a sixteen-year stretch of military rule, Nigeria appeared ready to turn a new page. A civilian government headed by a former head of state and war hero, retired General Olusegun Obasanjo, and his vice president, Atiku Abubakar, took office, but much damage had already been done. Obasanjo assumed the helm of an ailing ship of state almost totally lacking in morality or legitimacy. The government spends up to half of its annual budget on salaries of an estimated two million federal, state and local government workers, yet the civil service remains paralyzed, with connections and corruption still the fastest way to getting anything done. The armed forces are equally in a shambles. Up to 75 percent of the army's equipment is broken or missing vital spare parts. The navy's fifty-two admirals and commodores outnumber serviceable ships by a ratio of six to one. The air force has 10,000 men but fewer than twenty functioning aircraft.

Colonial Nigeria was designed in 1914 to serve the British Empire, and the independent state serves as a tool of plunder by the country's modern rulers. Nigerians spend a good part of their lives trying to get the better of the government for their own benefit or that of their family, their village, or their region. Rare is the head of state who acts on behalf of the entire nation. The people are not so much governed as ruled. It is as if they live in a criminally mismanaged corporation where the bosses are armed and have barricaded themselves inside the company safe. Nigeria's leaders, like the colonialists before them, have sucked out billions of dollars and stashed them in Western banks.

Millions of Nigerians, including much of the cream of the educated and business elite, have fled their country to escape impoverishment and political repression. Most live in the United States and Europe, although almost every country has a Nigerian community. Nigerian drug syndicates, aided in part by the large diaspora, have carved out a dominant share of the world market. They rank among the top importers of heroin and cocaine into the United States, and they have penetrated major African markets, such as Kenya and the nations in southern Africa. Nigeria does not itself produce such drugs, but Nigerians, brilliant traders, have stepped in to fulfill the world demand.

At the turn of the century, Nigeria was home to approximately sixty million youths under the age of eighteen, seething with frustration over the lack of academic and job opportunities that just three decades before appeared to be within reach of their parents. They represent Nigeria's equivalent to what South Africa calls its "lost generation," that huge army of frustrated youth who lack the tools to face the demands of a modern economy. In South Africa they were the products of the apartheid system and of the weapons of the struggle—school boycotts, strikes, guerrilla warfare—employed to overthrow it. In Nigeria the blame for its lost generation falls squarely on the shoulders of its people's leaders—corrupt military dictators and their civilian accomplices—who over the past quarter of a century have humbled a once proud nation through outright incompetence and greed.

Whether we know it or not, almost everyone is touched by the Nigerian crisis. The violent rebellion in the mangrove swamps of the oil-rich Niger delta region means that the gasoline sold at filling stations in the United States and Europe is almost literally stained with Nigerian blood. Nigeria reaches the most unlikely of places. The modest knitting shop where my mother works in a suburb of Louisville, Kentucky, received a form letter from a Dr. Jubril Akeh offering to share $45.5 million garnered from a corrupt business deal in Nigeria. All the knitting shop had to do was to provide the details of its bank account—but the whole deal was a con in which the swindler, once in possession of those details, would drain the account. It was the classic Nigerian confidence trick, commonly known as "419" after the statute that deals with business fraud. The extraordinary part is that someone always takes the bait. Nigerian con artists send millions of such letters to businesses and individuals around the world every year. They cost Britain up to $1 billion a year, and they probably take a similar amount from the United States.

Nigeria could, however, follow another path. Its potential is huge. Its tremendous wealth, if properly channeled, holds out the hope that a stable government could unleash the unquestioned energy and talent that pulsates through the rich ethnic mosaic. The human capital is there. Thousands of Nigerian professionals are well educated and skilled enough to drive the country forward. Anyone who has visited Nigeria's markets and witnessed its people endure the constraints of bad government and the sinking economy can testify to the country's resilience.

Nigeria was once the premier African voice, taking principled stands in the face of fierce Western opposition over important issues such as the immorality of white minority rule in Rhodesia, now independent Zimbabwe, and South Africa. It lost that position through its own inept leadership to Nelson Mandela's South Africa. In West African trouble spots such as Liberia and Sierra Leone, Nigeria has played the role of regional peacekeeper while Western nations and the United Nations have dawdled. Nigerian troops served in the Allied cause in the Second World War, and they have participated in some of the major peacekeeping efforts ever since, from the Congo crisis in the 1960s to Lebanon, Somalia, and Bosnia.

Among its writers it boasts a Nobel Laureate, Wole Soyinka; the Booker Prize winner Ben Okri; Chinua Achebe, whose *Things Fall Apart* is arguably Africa's best piece of postcolonial literature; and rising young talents such as the playwright Biyi Bandele Thomas. Nigerian professors grace university campuses across the United States and the world. Internationally renowned singers such as Sade and Seal hail from Nigeria, as do African music superstars as the late Fela Kuti and King Sunny Ade. And artistic excellence is not new to Nigeria. Terra-cotta figures discovered at a tin mine in the northern village of Nok are believed to have been produced around 450 B.C. Now they are on regular tours of museums in the United States and Europe.

In sports Nigerians regularly compete for the world's top honors. There are Nigerians playing in the National Basketball Association (NBA); the best-known of them, Hakeem "The Dream" Olajuwon, led the Houston Rockets to two championships. Nigerians can be found in the National Football League (NFL), even though football is a sport not even played in Nigeria. For me, a young soccer player named Nwankwo Kanu sums up the potential of Nigeria to turn adversity into achievement. I remember watching the tall thin Kanu bounding gracefully as he led Nigeria to victory in the under-seventeen World Cup in 1993. He went on to sign with the Dutch team Ajax, which then won two European club championships. During the 1996 Olympic games in United States, Kanu inspired Nigeria to capture the gold medal, scoring twice in the amazing 4 to 3 semifinal comeback win against Brazil. Then he joined the great Italian team, Internazionale of Milan. During a routine medical checkup, doctors detected a heart defect. Kanu would never play again, they said. Undeterred, he traveled to Cincinnati, Ohio, where doctors inserted a plastic valve in his heart. Two years later he was playing for Nigeria in the World Cup in France, and he now stars for the powerful English team Arsenal. In December 1999 Kanu was named African Footballer of the Year.

Kanu is not the only Nigerian whose courage and conduct inspires others. The world first cast its attention on Nigeria with the outbreak of the 1967–1970 Biafran civil war, in which the eastern part of the country attempted to secede. Up to one million people died. The images of starving, sticklike children brought, for the first time, the stark reality of a humanitarian disaster in Africa to living rooms around the world. Yet despite expressions of international concern about genocide, including one from the pope, the end of the war actually witnessed few massacres. Indeed, after the Biafrans' surrender, Nigeria proved that it could set new standards in compassion. The government's policy of "No victors, no vanquished" was a remarkable achievement and has played a critical role ever since in keeping the country from splitting apart. The journalist John de St. Jorre, in his excellent chronicle of the conflict, *The Nigerian Civil War*, wrote, "in the history of warfare there can rarely have been such a bloodless end and such a merciful aftermath."[1]

Chinua Achebe, in his book *The Trouble with Nigeria*, wrote,

> It is totally false to suggest, as we are apt to do, that Nigerians are fundamentally different from any other people in the world. Nigerians are corrupt because the system under which they live today makes corruption easy and profitable; they will cease to be corrupt when corruption is made difficult and inconvenient....The trouble with Nigeria is simply and squarely a failure of leadership. There is nothing basically wrong with the Nigerian character. There is nothing wrong with the Nigerian land or climate or water or air or anything

else. The Nigerian problem is the unwillingness or inability of its leaders to rise to the responsibility, to the challenge of personal example which are the hallmarks of true leadership. ...I am saying that Nigeria can change today if she discovers leaders who have the will, the ability and the vision.[2]

Sadly, this was written almost twenty years ago. Things have continued to fall apart. Of course, focusing on leadership alone misses the point. As Ishola Williams, a liberal-minded retired Nigerian general who now works with the Berlin-based anticorruption group Transparency International, notes, "A leader does not come from heaven; he comes from a group of people. If the people are good followers, they will choose the right leader." Unfortunately, so far they have not had the chance.

———

I LIVED in Nigeria as a foreign correspondent for two years, from 1991–1993, and returned often on reporting assignments. In mid-1998 I began a series of visits to gather material for this book. Nigeria has proved to be by far the most confounding, frustrating, and at the same time engaging place I have ever visited. It simply overwhelms the senses, one of those rare examples in which the sum of its parts is, at least to date, immensely greater than the whole. It is a work in progress, though one is never too sure whether it is being assembled or torn apart.

This book is by no means a comprehensive account of Nigerian history. That would involve decades and many volumes. Rather, its purpose is to portray the most intractable crisis points and the ethnic and regional tensions threatening the survival of what is perhaps the largest failed state in the Third World. Nigeria provides a stark lesson. As late as the 1980s, a long spell of good government and modest economic growth might have provided the breathing space and the common interest for Nigerians to feel it was worth continuing as one country, however artificial its origins. Now things have declined too far for that. Nigeria is on an altogether more dangerous trajectory. The only long-term solution in Nigeria to the crises that arise in a multiethnic state is for the various parties, however many they may be, to sit down and negotiate how they want to govern themselves and how they want to share their resources, and to decide whether they ultimately want to live together. Until they begin that process of internal reconciliation, at best Nigeria will lurch from crisis to crisis. At worst it will fall apart.

In chapter 1 I start with Olusegun Obasanjo's inauguration in 1999 as president and the military's withdrawal to the barracks. The ceremony itself provides an opportunity to sketch a brief history of what in fact was a colonial construct and of the rapid rise and fall of what was to be independent Africa's "showcase for democracy." This chapter highlights a major theme of this book, a theme that I believe applies beyond Nigeria to much of Africa: The primary task facing Nigeria's leaders is to convince the majority of their people that the government exists to serve rather than to prey upon them. Turning John F. Kennedy's appeal on its head, Nigerians need to know what their country can do for them, whether Nigeria itself is a worthwhile enterprise, before the country can hope to be prosperous and stable.

From the vantage point of Makoko, one of Nigeria's worst slums, the next chapter highlights Nigerian democracy in action. The recent election bringing Obasanjo to power betrays the shallow roots of democratic practice in Nigeria and shows that the vote often has little meaning other than the opportunity to promote the champion of one's ethnic group or region. This section also provides an encounter with the "lost generation" of youths who I believe provide the cutting edge of the forces of ethnic division and instability in every region of the country.

Chapter 3 centers on an encounter with the one man who epitomizes military rule in Nigeria, the retired general and former head of state Ibrahim Badamasi Babangida. In talking with Babangida, it becomes clear that Nigeria's armed forces have been transformed from a military in the conventional sense to an armed political party. From his stately mansion on a hilltop overlooking his home town of Minna, Babangida explains his involvement in every military coup since the 1970s and why he decided to annul the 1993 presidential elections, a decision that plunged Nigeria into a crisis from which it has not yet recovered.

The ongoing unrest in the Niger delta region, which calls into question the very unity of Nigeria, is the subject of chapters 4 and 5. Millions of impoverished people, mainly farmers and fishermen, live side by side, often in heavily polluted environments, with some of the world's richest oil petroleum deposits. I look at the dramatic case of Ken Saro-Wiwa, the author and playwright whose leading role in a campaign for a greater share of the oil wealth, a cleanup of the environment, and political autonomy for his minority Ogoni people ended with his execution by hanging in 1995. Since then a newer and potentially far more dangerous rebellion has erupted among the Ijaw people, the biggest ethnic group in the region, over their demands for control over their political future and the resources found on their land. Yet amid all the chaos, I visit a remarkable development project among one of the Ijaw clans that holds out hope of a model for development for the rest of the country.

The next four chapters focus on the deep ethnic and regional tensions that since independence and still today put in question Nigeria's right to exist as a single nation. Through visits with Islamic intellectuals and radicals in the north, leaders of the minority tribes in the politically explosive middle region, and the Yorubas calling for an independent republic in the southwest, I look at the various strains that are pulling Nigeria apart. In chapter 9 I visit a church on the outskirts of Lagos where a Christian preacher who claims to be able to heal everything from infidelity to AIDS has attracted a massive following. This church provides a unique window through which to view the explosion of Pentecostal churches tapping into the deep veins of human desperation.

Finally, I visit eastern Nigeria to see how enterprising Igbo businessmen have coped with the aftermath of the Biafran civil war and their perception of marginalization from the national political scene. There, on the side of a highway, I encounter a group of crippled civil war veterans who are living symbols of what can happen when politicized tribalism goes mad.

Hopefully the nation's divisions will never reach that point again. Like John, my taxi driver in Port Harcourt, Nigeria has shown an uncanny ability to pull back from the brink. And like the soccer player Nwankwo Kanu, Nigeria has the potential to rebound from adversity. As it did in the aftermath of the Biafran war, Nigeria holds valuable lessons, for good or ill. With luck, perhaps this time it might prove that a multiethnic state can survive, despite a history of corruption, violence, and poor governance, and even thrive.

The journalist Seye Kehinde, in an interview for the weekly magazine *The News*, asked me if it wasn't difficult for a foreign journalist to operate in Nigeria. Logistics, I agreed, are difficult and time consuming. Communications, even making a local telephone call, are always a problem. Water is scarce, as is often fuel, and the electricity is cut so regularly that the Nigerian Television Authority (NTA) routinely has to broadcast a warning—"We are changing our power supply. Please bear with us"—sometimes before it goes off the air altogether. But in general, I said to his obvious surprise, Nigeria is the easiest place in Africa, if not the world, for a writer to work, for the simple reason that Nigerians love to talk. Everyone has an opinion and is willing—and on occasion demands—to share it. As boisterous as the place can be, however, Nigeria's biggest problem is that Nigerians never talk to each other. Or perhaps they don't listen to each other enough. They are going to have to now.

Soyinka once described Nigeria as "the open sore of the continent."[3] But in this age of globalization, Nigeria's influence extends well beyond Africa, as the hard facts of its role in international crime and the drug trade attest. If Nigeria remains trapped in the quicksand of political malaise, economic decline, and ethnic rivalry, the world will be worse off for it.

FOR ME the journey to Nigeria began on a Sunday night in October 1991. I admit to having felt somewhat intimidated. Friends and acquaintances, especially West Africans, reveled in repeating legends about people landing at Lagos airport and being forced to bribe immigration officials to secure entry into the country. "Where's your visa?" meant where's the "dash," the cash. I had been working in Africa for the previous five years as a reporter, mainly in the countries surrounding South Africa, such as Zimbabwe, Mozambique, and Angola, when my newspaper decided it was time to cover Nigeria seriously and establish an office in Lagos. The foreign press corps was, as it is today, tiny. The British Broadcasting Corporation (BBC) and only two of the major news wire services, *Reuters* and *Agence France Presse,* ran bureaus in Lagos. The biggest U.S. news agency, the *Associated Press,* covered Nigeria with stringers and occasional brief visits by staff writers. The correspondent of the sole foreign newspaper, the *Financial Times,* had been expelled earlier in the year for reporting the disappearance of several billion dollars earned from an oil price boom caused by the Gulf War.

I arrived from Harare, Zimbabwe, flying Balkans Airlines of Bulgaria. The aircraft's sudden, slightly dizzying descent was the signal for the young woman sitting next to me to fasten her seat belt and gaze out the window at the vast panorama of light rising sharply from the ground below. She was the wife of a Nigerian diplomat stationed in Harare, and she assured me that Nigeria was nothing like Zimbabwe.

"A beautiful country," she said, returning her eyes to the window. I agreed that Zimbabwe was lovely, but she immediately corrected me. "Nigeria!" she insisted. "Zimbabwe is nice, but it is too quiet. It's not Africa, you know. Nigeria is the real Africa." It was an assertion I had heard often from Nigerian acquaintances in southern Africa. The journalist Sully Abu, who was based in Harare for the Nigerian *African Guardian* magazine in the late 1980s, used to enjoy chiding me, asking when I was going to experience the real Africa, Nigeria. By comparison, he would say, southern Africa was still too colonized, too recently free from foreign rule to represent the authentic Africa.

I left the plane and walked briskly in an undeclared race to reach immigration. The first sign of trouble appeared while I was waiting in line in the arrivals hall. Several gentlemen dressed in flowing robes demanded to inspect our passports. They were on the prowl for someone who had the misfortune of arriving in Lagos without a proper visa. When one skinny little man found nothing amiss in mine, his face immediately broke into a welcoming smile, and he offered to smooth the way for me.

It was at this point that the diplomat's wife intervened and shouted at him to "disappear from my face." The man cowered and attempted a retort, but the woman, who had metamorphosed from a gentle traveling companion into a very aggressive guardian, hissed, "Disappear!" He hastily carried out her order. Leaning over, she whispered in my ear, "Show your passport only to the man in uniform and after him to the immigration workers behind the counters. Anyone else is a tout." By *tout* she meant thief, panhandler, con artist, someone who lived by his or her wits, by receiving payment, the ubiquitous "dash," for nothing more than walking a person from A to B or simply handling travel documents before passing them on to the legitimate authority.

After filling out my landing card, I handed over my passport and ticket to an immigration official behind the counter. After a few minutes of jostling with my equally anxious fellow passengers, a woman shouted "Maier!" I presented myself sheepishly. She slapped the documents into my hand and said, "You are welcome." Giddy from the surprising ease with which I breezed through immigration, I descended the stairs to the baggage arrivals. The utter chaos of the scene took my breath away. The rest of the passengers had taken up positions around the conveyor belt, their feet planted firmly. They were fending off dozens of young men thrusting forward a bewildering array of supposedly official airport badges and pestering them for the privilege of carrying their luggage through customs. The diplomat's wife stood a few feet away embracing relatives, and within minutes she had collected her belongings and headed toward customs. As she passed me, she asked, "Do you have any money?"

"Yes."

"More than $5,000?"

"No."

"That's fine. When the customs man asks how much, you say less than 5,000. That's the limit, and they can't check you."

She paused for a moment and then asked if she should wait to see that I cleared customs all right. I assured her that I wouldn't have any problem. I had been traveling in Africa for five years, I said confidently. "Ah, yes," she smiled mischievously, "but this is Nigeria." Again, I declined her offer and thanked her for the advice. "Okay then, welcome to Nigeria," she boomed jovially and departed. Unfortunately, the customs officers must have heard her. For when I lifted my bags onto the inspection desk fifteen minutes later, they knew they were dealing with a novice.

"Anything to declare?" inquired a giant of a man as he adjusted his belt around his wide girth.

"No, nothing."

"Any money?"

"Less than $5,000," I replied with the poised smile of a seasoned Nigeria traveler. He frowned, but only briefly.

"Electronic equipment?"

An internal tremor chased the smile from my face. "Well, as a matter of fact, I have a computer; I'm a visiting journalist."

He beamed with satisfaction. "Let me see."

I hoisted my computer bag toward the counter. It never landed. Within a blink of an eye, his hand replaced mine on the handle, and my computer bag continued its journey to some unseen location behind him. "Permit? Import permit?"

"Import permit? For what?"

"Computer," he said looking through me. "It's the law."

"But the computer is old, it is for my work, and I am a visiting journalist."

"You could sell it in Lagos."

"But it is the instrument of my work. Surely I wouldn't sell it."

"The law is the law."

"But this makes no sense," I said, rather rashly in hindsight.

He frowned and barked, "Either pay for the permit or leave now. You are delaying the other passengers."

Someone bumped my leg with a suitcase, and I turned to see a line of mainly Nigerian passengers in a virtual wrestling match, desperate to push through the customs checkpoint with the greatest possible speed.

"But how much is the permit?" I asked.

Someone behind me giggled. The customs man broke into a wide grin. "Five thousand naira," he said.

I made the calculation. "But that's nearly $300," I said, incredulous. "It's an old computer, and it's not worth $300."

"Five thousand naira," he repeated, and then ordered, "Either pay or move on."

Assuring the customs man that I would return, I retreated temporarily to consider my position. Pushing through the door to the front hall of the airport, I entered another sea of bedlam. Dozens, perhaps hundreds, of people filled the room, more touts with their bogus airport badges, relatives of the arriving passengers, taxi drivers, soldiers, policemen, a complete cross section of society straining toward some ill-defined goal. Uniformed men detailed to keep order periodically surged toward the crowd and smacked their whips across the backs of a few unfortunates.

I ended up standing out of harm's way in the corner next to a barrel-chested Belgian businessman who looked upon me with sympathetic eyes. "First time?" he asked.

"Yes." I quickly explained my dilemma over the computer, and he nodded knowingly.

"The only thing you can do is get back in there and negotiate," he said. I was collecting my wits in preparation for a return when he pulled me aside. "One more thing. Is someone meeting you?"

"No."

"Well, then be sure to ask for taxi number one. Don't get into any car unless it is taxi number one—the first one in the taxi rank. On my first visit I failed to find taxi number one, and a few miles from the airport, I found myself standing on the roadside, with no money, no luggage, and no clothes. I was standing on the street completely naked. So remember, taxi number one."

By now, the queue at customs was thinning out, and with the time nearing 11:00 P.M., most of the airport was shutting down for the night. I approached the towering customs man and asked for a word. Even though I disagreed in principle, I was prepared to pay for the computer permit. But I told him that 5,000 naira was simply too high a price for an old computer that was hardly worth that amount. "How much?" he asked suspiciously.

"Five hundred naira," I said. That was more than enough for a well-used computer that was my instrument of work in the first place.

"Not serious," he retorted with a dismissive air. "Three thousand naira," he said. The negotiations had started; we had opened a line of communications.

"Eight hundred," I countered. He laughed loudly and broke into a warm, almost fatherly smile, shaking his head. I told him I was going to the currency exchange bureau and would be back in a moment.

I returned and placed 1,000 naira, about $60 at the official exchange rate, in the open palm of my hand. He slowly reached for the cash, but I took a step back. "My computer, please." He retrieved the laptop from its hiding place behind the counter and handed it to me. Again, he reached for the money. I sidestepped him and said I needed a receipt for the transaction.

"A receipt?" he asked in disbelief.

"Yes, a receipt," I said, so that in the future, I would not have to go through this process again. The fatherly smile returned.

At the customs office, the officer on duty duly wrote out a permit worth 1,000 naira for the importation of a Toshiba laptop computer. As I left the room, the customs officer was waiting.

"Need a taxi? This way." We reached the sidewalk, and the customs man handed me over to a captain in smart khaki and a green beret to act as my guide to the taxi rank. Before departing, the customs man and I shook hands as if we were longtime friends.

The captain led me to a gaggle of men who claimed to be taxi drivers, pushing and shoving each other to the point where fisticuffs appeared imminent.

"Taxi number one," I said, jerking my bags from several men who insisted on helping me. The captain looked at me impatiently. "Taxi number one," I insisted. As we reached the first car in the taxi rank, a dozen other drivers, several soldiers, and my army officer escort crowded around shouting for a "dash." One man, basing his claim on tenuous grounds, screamed, "I saw you first, I saw you first." The captain pushed them all back with both arms and pleaded, "I helped you. No dash for me?" I turned to the taxi driver with an inquisitive look, but he just shrugged his shoulders. Reaching in my pocket I pulled out a 20-naira note worth about $2 and handed it to my escort. He looked at it as if it were diseased. "Twenty naira only! Is it not an insult to the dignity of an officer?"

The captain was still shouting and staring in wonder at the paltry payment resting in his hands as the driver of taxi number one had the good sense to hit the accelerator and shoot out into the night. "First time in Nigeria?" he asked with a smirk after a few moments. I nodded to confirm the obvious. "You are welcome."

1

A Coup from Heaven

Nigeria is like being on an airplane that has just been taken over by hijackers. You do not want to compromise with the gunmen, but the prime concern is to land the plane, so there is no choice but to give in.

SULLY ABU

THE OCCASION that many in Africa and beyond feared they might never see began on what the master of ceremonies boomingly described as a "sprightly and God blessed morning." Thousands of people gathered under a blistering equatorial sun to witness the inauguration of Olusegun Obasanjo, their first civilian president in sixteen years, and to see the generals who had led Nigeria to the brink of disaster relinquish their power. For a moment it was possible to believe that Nigeria was finally taking a momentous stride toward a better future. With it, hopefully, would go the rest of Africa.

The ceremony took place in the Eagle Square stadium, especially built for the occasion, in the heart of Abuja, the ultramodern capital of glittering hotels and office towers. Huge columns of airmen, sailors, and soldiers and a troupe of school children took turns marching back and forth in fine British parade-ground tradition. Outside the complex, behind a wire fence 12 feet tall, throngs of ordinary citizens milled about, drinking, eating, dancing, and gawking at convoys of Mercedes sedans ferrying two dozen heads of state, foreign dignitaries, parliamentarians, and traditional monarchs. After years of diplomatic isolation as the "sick man of Africa," Nigeria was basking in the glow of international attention, and this time for all the right reasons. This was arguably the second most important day in Africa's recent history, after Nelson Mandela's installation as president of South Africa in 1994.

Mandela himself was on hand as a witness, along with the former German chancellor Helmut Schmidt, Britain's Prince Charles, the Reverend Jesse Jackson, and a host of African leaders. Among the honored Nigerian guests were the last civilian president, Shehu Shagari, and the soldiers who had founded the latest ruinous military reign by overthrowing him nearly sixteen years before, Muhammadu Buhari and Ibrahim Babangida, one-time military dictators whom the passing of time had transformed into venerable former heads of state. Each VIP entered Eagle Square accompanied by cars and trucks filled with plainclothes security operatives and police outriders. Within minutes the traffic swelled and the parade ground was gripped by a go-slow.

Sporadic scuffles broke out over seating arrangements as various security men cleared the way for their charges. In the end, second-tier ambassadors, foreign delegations, and businessmen trudged away, slightly embarrassed, from the places they had momentarily occupied in the VIP section. In Nigeria privilege can be fleeting. A modest gaggle of reporters and television crews encroached on the dais where the handover of power was to unfold. The master of ceremonies urged them to clear away with the warning, "Don't get embarrassed by the security officials," a rather polite way of saying that the police were prepared to unleash strong-arm tactics if necessary. The police soon would get their chance.

The mood among the gathered thousands was overwhelmingly fes-

tive. Who could blame them? Much of Nigeria, its neighbors, and anyone who cared about the fate of Africa were still heaving a collective
sigh of relief. Just a year before, General Sani Abacha had been
perched imperiously on the throne of power, running Nigeria not so
much as a country but as his personal fiefdom. Billions of dollars were
siphoned off into overseas bank accounts controlled by Abacha, his
family, or his cronies, while the masses simmered in anger at their
deepening poverty. Literally millions of Nigerians had fled into economic and political exile. Newspapers were shut down, and trade
unions were banned, while human rights activists, journalists, intellectuals, and opponents imaginary and real were jailed or, in a few cases,
eliminated by state-sponsored death squads. Among the victims were
the Ogoni rights activist and playwright Ken Saro-Wiwa, who had
been hanged, and retired General Shehu Musa Yar'Adua, a political
power broker who had died after receiving a mysterious injection in
prison. The leading political figures of the day were held incommuni-
cado. They included Chief Moshood Abiola, the Muslim millionaire
whose election as president in 1993 was halted by the military despot
Babangida, and Obasanjo, the only soldier who had ever handed power
to an elected civilian. Nigeria, many feared, would explode into a civil
war that could spark a humanitarian disaster.

All the while, the international community was left to wring its
hands in a theatrical demonstration of its impotence. There were condemnations aplenty, but little real action was taken to hurt the military. A group of thirty-four prominent Nigerians, including some who
had previously supported Abacha, wrote an open letter warning that
his persistence in succeeding himself would push Nigeria into anarchy.
Even former military dictators such as Babangida and Buhari voiced
their opposition, but nothing could dissuade Abacha from his chosen
course. When the United States tried to send a high-powered delegation to urge Abacha to institute democratic reforms, he simply refused
to let them in the country.

3

Then a series of events unfolded that was so extraordinary that it read like a work of fiction. It began on June 8, 1998, when Abacha, on his customary nightly excursion into the pleasures of the flesh, expired while in the arms of a pair of Indian prostitutes. The official cause of death was a heart attack, although unsubstantiated rumors abounded concerning his demise. Everyone had a pet theory. Some said he was murdered with an untraceable poison by army officers who realized that he was steering Nigeria toward an upheaval that would consume them all. Others, including a fair number of Western diplomats, believed he had overdosed on Viagra, taken to fortify his body for the strain of his notorious sexual appetite. But many saw what had occurred as nothing less than, in the words of one Nigerian businessman, "a coup from heaven."

Within a day of Abacha's passing, the relatively unknown Army chief of staff, General Abdulsalami Abubakar, assumed the helm and gave strong indications that the military was prepared to steer Nigeria back to the path of sanity. There was a problem, however, in the person of Moshood Abiola. Despite four years in detention, Abiola apparently had no intention of renouncing the mandate he and millions of Nigerians believed he had won in the 1993 elections, judged by local and foreign observers to have been the freest and fairest in the country's history. Abubakar indicated that he wanted to release Abiola, but the mandate was the sticking point. The military felt that a freed Abiola claiming the presidency could destabilize the country.

Abubakar called on a string of diplomatic big hitters, including UN Secretary-General Kofi Annan and Commonwealth Secretary-General Emeka Anyaoku, to meet with Abiola to try to convince him to drop his claim. So complete had been Abiola's isolation during his incarceration that he did not recognize Annan and asked him what had happened to the Egyptian. Abiola thought that Boutros Boutros-Ghali was still the UN chief. On July 7, the U.S. undersecretary of state Thomas Pickering and a delegation of U.S. officials met Abiola at a guest house in the capital, Abuja. After a few minutes, Abiola felt ill and requested a tea break to collect his thoughts. He was having trouble breathing. A physician was called, and Abiola was taken to a medical clinic. An hour and a half later he was dead. An autopsy later determined that, like his tormentor Abacha a month before, Abiola had died of a heart attack, although few Nigerians believed that.

But with both Abacha and Abiola out of the way, the coast was clear to begin an orderly transition to civilian rule. Abubakar lifted the ban on political activities; set in motion the process of holding local, state, and national elections; urged exiles to return home; and freed several hundred political prisoners from Abacha's dungeons. The release of one detainee, Obasanjo, was particularly significant. To the retired military officers who still wielded great economic and political power in Nigeria, his were a pair of trusted hands. Obasanjo was a civil war hero who had ruled Nigeria from 1976 to 1979 and who had proved his good faith by overseeing elections, giving up power to a civilian president, and retiring gracefully to the role of international statesman. Obasanjo emerged from detention on a fifteen-year sentence on charges of treason as the leading candidate for the presidency. In February 1999 he easily won an election that was largely peaceful, though it was tainted by reports of widespread vote rigging. At the time the polls were held, Nigeria did not even have a constitution, and it really had no idea what powers the presidency and National Assembly would hold.

As the groups of marchers crisscrossed the tarmac, Abubakar, his chest literally bristling with an impressive array of medals, looked on with obvious pride. He was about to do what only one Nigerian military strongman had done before: hand over power to an elected leader. The irony was, of course, that the other soldier to accomplish the feat, Obasanjo, was now the civilian destined to return to the presidency. There was a sense of déjà vu to all this. In the days leading up to the inauguration the NTA showed twenty-year-old footage of Obasanjo standing in the driving rain at another ceremony to mark the transfer of power from military dictator to elected president. Ironically, Abdulsalami Abubakar, then a lieutenant colonel, was also there, as the commander of the inauguration parade. Now that same Abubakar was about to hand the baton of leadership back.

In many ways, this day was more a celebration of the military's exit from politics than the inauguration of a new civilian president. The outgoing information minister, John Nwodo, resorted to the role of traditional praise singer in a speech on Abubakar's career, describing him as "a soldier's soldier," a man of vision. Nwodo neglected to mention that Abubakar had held the third most powerful position in the Abacha regime when all the nastiness occurred. Missing too was any allusion to the unexplained decrease, of at least $3 billion in less than six months, in foreign exchange reserves. Given the short time frame, that drop would have made even the notoriously larcenous Abacha catch his breath. Nothing was said about the disastrous state of the economy that Abubakar was handing over to the civilians, a fact that led the more cynical observers to suggest that the military was deliberately attempting to undermine the new civilian order before it even started: coup by bankruptcy, so to speak.

For the moment, all that was forgiven for the simple fact that Abubakar was about to leave office peacefully, and in Nigeria, and sadly much of the rest of Africa, such a thing was cause for jubilation. To honor his departure, the military was determined to put on quite a show, and a very high-priced one at that. Estimates of the construction cost of Eagle Square ran at about $30 million, and the bill for the fireworks display the night before was believed to be close to $5 million. In the distance sat the green domed building of the new bicameral National Assembly, built by a company owned by Abacha's Lebanese business partners, the Chagoury brothers, at a cost of some $65 million. Nigerian democracy can be an expensive business.

The marching exercises were followed by a 21-gun salute and a flyby first by three Air Force training planes and then by three jets that left trails of smoke in the national colors of green and white. In an instant, one jet returned and embarked on a spectacular steep climb just above the festivities to symbolize the military's final departure from power. As it did, a 30-foot-high video screen at the far end of the parade ground showed the beaming face of Abubakar, as if to assure the nation that this time the military really was on the way out. The crowd roared with approval. "God be with you," the master of ceremonies bellowed again, addressing Abubakar, "until we meet again!" Not one to let the significance of the moment pass, Abubakar made a short speech claiming that this day, May 29, 1999, ranked second only to independence in October 1960 in shaping the nation's destiny.

——————

WHEN AFRICA discarded the bonds of colonial rule, few could have imagined the depths to which Nigeria and the continent as a whole would sink a generation later. When the British lowered the Union Jack and freed a land they had ruled for less than a century, Nigeria was the focus of great optimism as a powerful emerging nation that would be a showcase for democratic government. Seen through the Cold War prism through which the West and particularly the United States viewed the emerging nations, Nigeria was a good guy—moderate, capitalist, and democratic.

With the benefit of hindsight, it is clear that such optimism was naive. For Nigeria, like the other modern African states with the exception of Ethiopia, was the bastard child of imperialism, its rich mosaic of peoples locked into a nation-state they had had no part in designing. Before the European conquest, Nigeria was home to an estimated three hundred ethnic groups of sometimes widely differing languages and systems of internal rule. Although its constituents had traded and often lived among each other for centuries, the land of

Nigeria had never existed as one political unit. The peoples gathered within its borders had different cultures and stood at very unequal levels of development, a state of affairs that once prompted the Yoruba nationalist leader Obafemi Awolowo to describe Nigeria as a "mere geographical expression."

For one thousand years before the British occupation, the territory was divided roughly by the three regions that have largely defined independent Nigeria: north, east, and west. In the north the main ethnic groups—the Hausas, the Fulanis, and the Kanuri—were linked culturally, religiously, and economically to North Africa, particularly after the Arabs conquered the Berbers in the seventh century. The Arabs brought Islam, as well as the transportation—the camel—and writing and mathematics skills that greatly eased communication and administration across vast territories.

The first major state within the future frontiers of Nigeria, and the initial landing point of Islam, was Kanem-Borno, in the far northeast near Lake Chad. In the northwest were the ancient Hausa city-states, such as Kano, believed to be one thousand years old. In the early 1800s these city-states fell under the control of the Sokoto Caliphate, a vast centralized Islamic state established by a jihad, or holy war, led by the Fulanis, who generations before had emigrated from the Senegal River valley. On the margins of the caliphate a myriad of pagan ethnic groups lived in scattered farming and iron-working communities on the Jos plateau in what later became known as the middle belt. Although these tiny groups were overshadowed by the political sophistication of their Muslim neighbors and were the victims of their slave raids, some of them produced the terra-cotta figures that many experts regard as great artistic works, works that were almost certainly predecessors to the Yoruba art of Ife and the Benin bronzes. This Nok culture, named after the village where the first terra-cottas were found, flourished between 500 B.C. and A.D. 200.[1]

In the west, where the Yoruba language was predominant, the Oyo and Benin empires were the preeminent powers. The Yorubas trace their origin to Ile Ife, now the site of Obafemi Awolowo University. They believe that Ile Ife was the spot where Odùduwà was sent down from the heavens by his father, the supreme god Olódùmarè, with some soil, a cockerel, and a palm nut to create the earth. The most powerful Yoruba state was Oyo, one of the great precolonial West African states that dominated much of Yoruba land. Oyo held sway over a wide territory that stretched from the Niger River though what is now the independent nation of Benin all the way to the border of Togo. The Oyo monarchy ruled through a complex system of checks and balances that involved a council of notables, the Oyo Mesi, and the secretive Ogboni society made up of eminent political and religious figures. The Oyo Mesi could depose the Alafin, the king, when their prime minister, the Bashorun, told him: "The Gods reject you, the people reject you, the earth rejects you." At that point, the Alafin was required to commit suicide. During the nineteenth century, however, partly because of Islamic pressure from the north, Oyo entered into a state of decline that set off a series of highly destructive wars among the Yoruba.

The least-centralized region was the east, which was dominated by autonomous city-states and villages of various ethnicities, ranging from the majority Igbos and the Ijaws, who dominated in the Niger River delta, to far smaller groups such as the Ibibio and the tiny Ogoni people. These communities generally shared a highly republican political tradition, with each village or city clinging ferociously to its independence.

From such a mix, Nigeria was to be born. The man who came to be known as the founder of modern Nigeria was a swashbuckling English adventurer named George Dashwood Goldie Taubman. He dreamed of establishing a British-controlled commercial empire stretching from the Niger River delta to the Nile. After traveling around North Africa, Goldie journeyed to the Guinea Coast to resuscitate a company owned by his sister-in-law's family that bought palm oil in the Niger delta. By the mid-nineteenth century, palm oil, needed to make soap and candles and to grease the machines of the industrial revolution, had replaced slaves as the main commodity of exchange between Africa and the West. In return, Britain imported into Nigeria millions of gallons of cheap gin. Goldie banded together the various English companies operating in the Niger delta, used gunboat diplomacy to subdue the African chiefs in the area and keep out the French and Germans, and obtained a royal charter from London. At the 1884–1885 Berlin Conference at which the Europeans drew their arbitrary lines across the map of Africa, the British assumed control of the Niger River basin.

But Goldie had grander ambitions. He enlisted Lord Frederick Lugard, a man of unflagging energy, with an imposing walrus mustache, whom the historian Thomas Pakenham has described as the most successful "of all the freelance imperialists."[2] Lugard, fresh from routing the French in Uganda with the Maxim gun, arrived in the Niger delta at Goldie's headquarters at Akassa. With a small army of African soldiers known as the West African Frontier Force, Lord Lugard moved up the Niger to conquer the interior. In 1914 he amalgamated the northern and southern territories in the name of the British Crown, setting the borders of what became Nigeria. The joining was not for the purposes of nation building. The simple reason was that the north's colonial budget was running at a deficit and only a link with the profitable south could eliminate the needed British subsidy. Goldie's influence on the course of events was so powerful that when it came time to name the new colony, *Goldesia*, reminiscent of Cecil Rhodes's *Rhodesia*, was considered along with *Niger Sudan* and *"Negretia."* London finally settled on *Nigeria*, a name coined sixteen years before by Lugard's future wife, Flora Shaw, in an article she wrote for the British establishment newspaper, *The Times*.[3]

The northern elite, consisting of a mainly Fulani aristocracy ruling over the Hausa-speaking commoners, enjoyed a relatively insular existence after Lugard's troops subjugated the caliphate in 1903. (The upper-class, public-school-educated British administrators sent out to Nigeria betrayed a natural admiration for the blue-blooded Fulanis.) The British administered northern Nigeria through a system called indirect rule that allowed the traditional authorities, the sultan and the emirs, to continue running things more or less as they saw fit. For the most part, the Islamic legal code, Sharia, was allowed to operate, except for cruel punishments such as amputation. The system was cheap and required few colonial officers to administer. It suited the emirs, who were allowed to maintain their power and at times even to extend it over smaller pagan communities that they had never before controlled. In turn, the British shielded the north from the advance of Christian missionaries and Western education from the south. They fanned ethnic prejudice by housing southern immigrants to the north in segregated living areas commonly known as *sabon gari*, or "strangers' quarters."

But as the date of independence approached, it dawned on the northern leaders that their people lacked the educational skills needed to compete against their southern compatriots, the Yorubas and the Igbos. The number of secondary schools in the south outnumbered those in the north by 20 to 1. In the economy, the civil service, and the military, the north feared being swamped. By 1950 southern university graduates numbered in the hundreds, compared to just one in the north.[4]

This fear continued even though the federal constitution developed in the final years of British rule gave the three regions—the Northern, Western, and Eastern—substantial powers to run their affairs autonomously. When the British finally departed, a modest and cautious northerner, Abubakar Tafawa Balewa, became the prime minister in a parliamentary democracy. Nigeria boasted one of the premier universities in the Third World, at the southwestern city of Ibadan, and had produced hundreds of graduates in law, medicine, and engineering. At independence fourteen hundred Nigerian students attended the university. By comparison, Sierra Leone had seventy-two graduates at independence, and Malawi, twenty-nine. There were sixteen in Zaire—a country the size of the eastern United States—and Burundi had none.[5] With substantial production of cocoa for exports and agriculture for domestic consumption, Nigeria's economic prospects were bright. And even more promising, in the late 1950s the multinational oil company Shell had discovered oil in the Niger delta.

But there was still a great deal of trepidation and real anxiety among some groups about domination by others. Whereas the Yorubas, rallying around Awolowo, and the Igbos, championed by the nationalist leader Nnamdi Azikiwe, had embraced Western education and pressed for independence, the political elite of the north, centered on the remnants of the Sokoto Caliphate, had seen liberation as a potential threat to their conservative, some would say feudal, way of life.

By 1964 cracks were appearing in the facade of Nigeria's federal structure. Faced with unrest among the Tiv people, a minority group in the middle belt, Balewa dispatched the army to quell the riots in the first use of the Nigerian military against civilians. Further disturbances erupted in the Western Region as rival factions of Awolowo's Action Group Party resorted to violence to resolve their struggle for regional power. Awolowo himself was jailed for treason. Two attempts to conduct a national census degenerated into a farce of widespread manipulation organized by regional leaders seeking to use inflated population figures to buttress their cases for greater power at the federal level. Massive rigging and boycotts marred a new round of national elections in 1964. By the following year, the Western Region had degenerated into near anarchy, with the Action Group factions engaging each other in "Operation Wetie," Nigeria's version of "necklacing," the murder of opponents by dousing them with fuel and setting them alight. Political chaos and reports of corruption among government officials, known as the "10 percenters" for the amount they creamed off the top of contracts, further discredited the political class in the eyes of many Nigerians.

On the morning of January 15, 1966, a group of mainly Igbo officers attempted to overthrow the civilian government. They promised radical reform and called for death sentences for a variety of crimes ranging from corruption, bribery, and subversion to rape and homosexuality. Code named Operation Damisa ("Leopard"), their coup attempt cost the lives of Tafawa Balewa, two regional premiers including the powerful northern leader Ahmadu Bello, and a federal minister. Although the coup eventually failed, the military, still controlled by Igbos, assumed power from the rump of the federal cabinet and ran Nigeria as a centralized state. The decision to abolish the regions and their powers of autonomy set into motion a constitutional crisis about how Nigeria was to be governed, a crisis that continues until today.

With the north still bitter over the killings of its political leaders and frightened by the disappearance of its autonomy, northern officers staged a revenge coup in July that was followed by a massacre of Igbos living in the north. Thousands streamed to their home area in the east, and Nigeria lurched toward civil war. Although ethnic politics provided the excuse for the conflict, the vast oil reserves of the Niger delta were the ultimate booty. The Igbos believed that the oil would ensure the viability of their Biafran state, but the rest of Nigeria refused to part with the oil-rich region.

The Biafran war effectively ended when the rebel leader Chukwuemeka Odumegwu Ojukwu fled the country and the then Colonel Obasanjo, in command of the Third Marine Division, captured Biafran Radio and broadcast a message for the Biafrans to lay down their arms. Although the wartime leader, General Yakubu Gowon, won praise for his policy of reconciliation, his delays in relinquishing power to civilians and growing reports of corruption set the stage in 1975 for the third coup in less than ten years. While Gowon was out of the country, General Murtala Mohammed, a northerner, assumed power with his deputy Obasanjo, a Yoruba. They pledged to return the country to civilian rule and to reform the economy, now booming with oil exports thanks to sharply rising prices sparked by the Middle East War. This period was arguably the Nigerian armed forces' finest hour. After only seven months, however, Mohammed was assassinated during a failed coup and Obasanjo, initially against his wishes, replaced him as Nigeria's leader with Shehu Musa Yar'Adua as his deputy.

During Obasanjo's three years in power the government was widely regarded as hardworking and effective, though at times heavy-handed in its crackdown on student protests. A Constitutional Draft Committee completed a new constitution that called for a U.S.-style executive presidency, separation of powers, and an independent judiciary. While local governments garnered more authority, they dwelled in the shadows of the federal government and the states, which had increased by nineteen from the original three regions.

The constitutional debate unleashed the potentially troublesome genie of Sharia, Islamic law. Initially championed by Islamic clerics, scholars, and lawyers, Sharia's potential as a political weapon quickly attracted the politicians. Traditional northern rulers welcomed it as a way to tighten their grip on the court system, to mollify the masses of poor desperate for better living conditions and justice, Islamic or otherwise, and to bargain for national power with the Christians of the middle belt and the south. Southern Christians saw Sharia as a violation of Nigeria's constitutional framework, while those in the middle belt feared Sharia as a reassertion of northern domination. At issue was the Muslim call for a federal court of appeal for Sharia cases. A constitutional assembly reached a compromise under which three judges versed in Islamic law could hear cases referred from the Sharia courts. But they would still be part of the Federal Court of Appeal; there would be no separate Federal Sharia Court of Appeal. The northern participants walked out of the assembly and the compromise was ap-

proved. The intervening debate had politicized religion as never before. The Sharia controversy gave birth to radical Islamic groups that
over time commanded wide sympathy among northern students and
the unemployed youth. Two decades later, the Sharia issue returned to
spark the most serious challenge to Nigeria's survival since the Biafra
war. As in 1979, Nigeria's ruler was Obasanjo, now in his second coming as a civilian.

Obasanjo ruled during a time when Africa and much of the Third
World was enamored with a nationalist ideology that held that a
strong state could promote rapid economic growth. Obasanjo's government took effective control of major media outlets, intervened in the
economy, and embarked on white elephant projects, such as the
Ajaokuta steel complex, which over the years consumed some $8 bil-
lion without producing one bar of steel. An attempt to put some order
into Nigeria's anarchic land-tenure system, the Land Use Decree of
1978, transferred control of land and mineral rights away from local
people to the state and federal governments. Not only did the decree
increase the power of the state, but it also set the federal government
on a future collision course with the residents of the oil-rich Niger
delta. The economy was entering a crisis that the oil boom revenues
only masked. Agriculture, once the economic mainstay that accounted
for 75 percent of all exports, was stalling. Importing food became more
profitable than producing it. Total land under cultivation fell by nearly
8 million hectares, more than one-third.

But Obasanjo kept his promise by overseeing the 1979 inauguration
of Shagari, a northerner who had won elections that were tainted by
the sort of vote rigging and intimidation that have marred all postindependence Nigerian polls. The civilian administration performed extremely poorly. Gross mismanagement, widespread corruption, and
continuing political and, ominously, increasing religious turmoil sent
Nigeria into a spiral of economic decline. Capital flight during
Shagari's rule, from 1979 to 1983, totaled nearly $15 billion, the foreign

debt rose to $18 billion, and the economy, buffeted by the fall in world oil prices, declined by more than 8 percent. Top government officials and the business elite enjoyed the good life while the collapse fell hardest on the urban poor, who suffered soaring unemployment and inflation of up to 50 percent per year.

The military exploited the rising public disenchantment to strike again on December 31, 1983, in a coup that put Buhari and his deputy, Major General Tunde Idiagbon, into power. Initially hailed as an antidote to the corruption and chaos of the Shagari years, the Buhari regime quickly developed a reputation for repression. It promulgated the infamous Decree 2, which permitted the government to detain opponents without trial. The commitment to deal with corrupt politicians brought dubious international fame. In one instance a former minister, Umaru Dikko, was found in London sedated and loaded in a crate destined for a Nigerian Airways flight to Lagos. (Dikko, while in control of rice distribution, had gained notoriety by dismissing reports of hunger by saying Nigerians had not reached the point of eating from dustbins.)

In 1985, to widespread acclaim, Babangida and Abacha ousted Buhari in a palace coup. Like his predecessors, Babangida pledged to embark on economic reform, a cleanup of corruption, and a transition to civilian rule. Early moves to release detained journalists and human rights activists, combined with his engaging political style and open courting of intellectuals, won him popularity. In time, however, the shine wore off his reputation. Reported levels of corruption reached all-time highs, and Nigeria became so deeply involved in the international drug trade that some observers began to describe the regime as a "narco-dictatorship." The editor of the popular weekly magazine *Newswatch*, Dele Giwa, was murdered by a parcel bomb after he mentioned to his colleagues the idea of investigating rumors that Babangida's wife Maryam was involved in the drug trade. Babangida strongly denied having had a hand in the killing, but the security services were widely believed to have been involved.

The longer Babangida stayed in office, the more it seemed he was planning to remain there. He was the only one of Nigeria's military dictators to assume the title of president. Babangida earned the nickname Maradona, after the Argentine soccer star, as the consummate tactician who could dribble the political football with bamboozling effect around friend and foe alike. He sought to engineer the political process as no leader before. He established two parties—which he made the only legal parties—that were effectively clones of each other, the Social Democrats being "a little to the left" and the National Republican Convention, "a little to the right." The state funded them, wrote their party platforms, built offices for them around the country, and banned politicians of which it did not approve. After making repeated changes to the timetable for returning the country to civilian government, Babangida finally oversaw local and state elections in 1992 and prepared for presidential polls on June 12, 1993.

Babangida's good friend and business partner Abiola ran against Bashir Tofa, a relatively unknown businessman from the northern city of Kano. As the returns streamed in from the states, it was clear that Abiola had won a handsome victory. But before the final results could be announced, Babangida canceled the election for reasons that have never been properly explained. The decision sent Nigeria into a deep political crisis. Abiola's ethnic kinsmen believed that Babangida denied him victory because the north could not accept the rule of a southerner and a Yoruba.

Under intense pressure from both the public and his military colleagues, Babangida stepped down in August 1993 after putting in place an interim civilian administration headed by the Yoruba businessman Ernest Shonekan. It never had real power, however, and in November Abacha, who had stayed on as defense minister from the Babangida administration, assumed the position of head of state.

Abacha's initial cabinet contained a number of well-known civilians, but most of them were dismissed early in the new year. The regime banned political parties and dissolved all electoral structures. In June 1994 Abiola declared himself president and was promptly arrested. The following month labor unions led by the oil workers declared an indefinite strike to demand Abiola's installation as president. By the end of August Abacha had crushed the strike and dissolved the unions. A series of bombings erupted, which the government blamed on dissidents but which many independent analysts believed were the work of the state security services. Journalists and human rights activists were the victims of repeated crackdowns, and Abacha signed a decree that specifically disqualified any court from challenging his regime's actions.

In July 1995 Abacha's Provisional Ruling Council announced the arrest of forty people, including Obasanjo and Yar'Adua, on charges of plotting to overthrow the government. Under intense international pressure, the original sentences of death were commuted to lengthy terms in prison. World outrage against Nigeria reached its peak in November 1995, when the government executed Saro-Wiwa and eight other activists of the Ogoni people in the Niger delta who had campaigned for political autonomy and reparations from Shell for environmental damages caused by its oil operations. Nigeria was suspended from the Commonwealth of former British colonies.

Abacha spread millions of dollars around Africa and Europe and in Washington to gain a sympathetic ear. His close business associate Gilbert Chagoury secured an invitation to a White House dinner by donating $460,000 to Vote Now 96, a Miami-based nonprofit voter registration group linked to the Democratic National Committee.[6] Chagoury supped with Clinton just a year after Saro-Wiwa's execution and while Abiola and Obasanjo were still languishing in jail.

Calls for economic sanctions against Nigeria of the type already imposed on Iran, Iraq, and Libya were deemed unrealistic. Mindful of Nigeria's position as the biggest U.S. trading partner and oil supplier in Africa, big business successfully lobbied against the idea of an oil embargo. Visa restrictions and other light sanctions were all the United States and its European allies could or would muster to support democracy in West Africa's regional superpower. When Abacha announced in December 1997 the arrest of his deputy, General Oladipo Diya, a Yoruba, on allegations of plotting a coup, there was hardly a murmur from the international community. Six months later, the "coup from heaven" took place.

———

AS OBASANJO mounted the dais to take the oath of office, he did not attempt to belittle the size of the task ahead. At 11:20 A.M., Obasanjo, a born-again Christian, began his inaugural address with the words: "Fellow Nigerians, we give praise and honor to God Almighty for this day specially appointed by God Himself. Everything created by God has its destiny and it is the destiny of all of us to see this day." In his plodding earthy elocution, he reminded the audience that twelve months before, no one could have imagined such an inauguration. Alluding to his time in prison, he described himself as "a man who had walked through the valley of the shadow of death."

The days leading up to the inauguration provided a timely reminder of how much divine intervention Nigeria might need in the months and years ahead. The traditional trouble spots, Lagos and the Niger delta, were once again on the boil. Riots broke out in Lagos on the night of May 17, 1999, after local thugs known as "area boys" spread rumors that Obasanjo had died mysteriously in the manner of Abacha and Abiola. In the oil-producing town of Warri in the Niger delta, a new spiral of killing between rival ethnic groups claimed up to two hundred lives.

The tone of Obasanjo's speech sounded as if he had turned the tables on the former military dictators, that his own rise to power represented another coup, this time by the civilians. "The incursion of the military into government has been a disaster for our country and for the military over the last thirty years," he said. "The esprit-de-corps amongst military personnel has been destroyed; professionalism has been lost. Youths go into the military not to pursue a noble career but with the sole intention of taking part in coups and to be appointed as military administrators of states and chairmen of task forces. As a retired officer, my heart bleeds to see the degradation in the proficiency of the military."

Corruption had reached the proportions of "full-blown cancer," he said, calling it "the greatest single bane of our society today." Obasanjo pledged to whip Nigeria into shape and to stamp out malfeasance wherever it might lurk. "There will be no sacred cows. Nobody, no matter who and where, will be allowed to get away with the breach of the law or the perpetration of corruption and evil." Nigeria must change its ways in order to "ensure progress, justice, harmony and unity and above all to rekindle confidence amongst our people. Confidence that their conditions will rapidly improve and that Nigeria will be great and will become a major world player in the near future."

As Obasanjo was speaking, it was difficult not to wonder whether he would play the role of an African Mikhail Gorbachev, who, while trying to reform a rotten system, oversaw its dismemberment. The other side of Nigeria, that of seething frustration, of police and army brutality, of sheer desperation, came into view fifty yards away from the pageantry, just behind the stands holding the VIPs. A truck pulled into the parking lot with a load of inauguration paraphernalia, such as umbrellas, T-shirts, handkerchiefs, and drinking mugs. There was an immediate uproar of hundreds of voices. A horde of civilian bystanders, policemen, and soldiers surrounded the vehicle like a swarm of bees. Dozens piled into the truck, grabbing anything they could. Initially the police and soldiers tried to do their duty and control the onslaught, but they too joined in what quickly degenerated into a no-holds-barred looting spree. The truck driver struggled to navigate clear of the boiling mass, but the presence of so many cars made an escape impossible. Fistfights erupted, and the police and soldiers used rawhide whips and their belts in a vain attempt to beat the civilians into submission. The turmoil exploded into a near riot when a policeman struggling for his share of the booty apparently lost his gun in the melee.

Not wanting to miss their chance at the loot, the crowds outside the grounds began pushing and cutting through the wire fence. The handful of police at the entrance was quickly routed, and hundreds of people streamed into the parking lot and attacked the beleaguered truck in what looked like a feeding frenzy of human piranhas. One man who had just looted an umbrella returned to the stands where I was sitting and took a place next to his young son. He was drenched in sweat from the exertion, and when his son attempted to look over the wall at the bedlam, the man told him to stay put as if to spare him the sight of such an unsavory scene.

Obasanjo, his face projected on the giant video screen, lamented the moral malaise that has made Nigeria a laughing stock in the international community while just across the way in the parking lot the orgy of looting intensified. "Where official pronouncements are repeatedly made and not matched by action, government forfeits the confidence of the people and their trust," he said in a perfect accompanying narration to his people's actions.

By now the fracas had reached the edge of the parade ground itself, with police and soldiers stealing Cokes and snacks that young women attendants tried to hand out to the assembled guests. While Obasanjo spoke about the police being "in the forefront of fighting crimes and ensuring our security," a good number of the officers on hand were busy cracking skulls and scrambling for the goodies.

As the ceremony wound down and the audience prepared to depart, the throng rushed from the parking lot into the parade ground, to be met by a very malicious response from the police, who employed whips and chains in an effort to maintain order. As the visiting delegations, nearly overwhelmed in the crush of humanity, scrambled to their vehicles to beat a hasty retreat, the crowd chanted "No more military, no more violence."

Still ringing in my ears was the plea Obasanjo made to end the occasion: "May the Almighty help us."

2

Voting Day

———

*Barring a cruel joke by Kismet (perish the thought) nothing
is likely to derail the train panting its way to the last station.
No banana peels on our way to the next republic. The doom-
sayers must be munching their own words in shame.*

"THE CHOICE WE MAKE,"
NEWSWATCH MAGAZINE EDITORIAL, MARCH 1, 1999

A N ELECTION is a remarkable event in Nigeria. Military dictators
have ruled for all but ten years since independence. The first civilian leader, Prime Minister Balewa, lasted six years before the military
murdered him and several other political leaders. The second, President
Shagari, stayed in office four years before he was tossed out. The only
other time the generals allowed presidential elections, in June 1993,
they annulled the vote when they did not fancy the man who won,
locked him up, and kept him in detention for five years until he died.

Now, on February 27, 1999, Nigeria was trying once again to elect a
new civilian president. Even when it came to democracy, however,
there was no escaping the military's influence. One of the two con-
tenders, Obasanjo, was a retired general, although he had freely given
up power to an elected government. His opponent, Olu Falae, owed his

political career mostly to service in a military regime. Partly because many Nigerians believed the outcome of the election had been already determined, or "tele-guided," as they like to say, and partly because neither candidate thrilled the masses, few people showed much enthusiasm in exercising their franchise. For the vast majority of people, the election was simply an excuse to take the day off.

To ensure that the vote went off with as little trouble as possible, the military authorities had banned all movement. The unusual silence was as pleasant as it was unsettling. For once, absolute stillness reigned supreme over the typically frenetic streets of Lagos, Nigeria's steamy high-octane commercial capital. A buzzing hive of humanity living in a seemingly endless patchwork of decaying cement houses and shacks on top of swamps and lagoons, Lagos can be most inhospitable. It is a place full of a frustration borne by millions of people who moved to the city in search of riches but only found poverty, power cuts, water shortages, and breathtaking mounds of garbage. The city's heart literally beats to pulsating rhythms and angry lyrics railing against the thieves in power from the Afro-beat musician and political activist, Fela Kuti, who died of AIDS in August 1997.

Lagosians rightly regard themselves as among the toughest people on earth, a reputation that was only boosted by their reaction to a grisly scene discovered just three weeks before the election. As Joseph Olalekan Bello was walking by a flyover near the road to Murtala Muhammed international airport one morning after attending an all-night church service, he smelled something strange and heard a voice singing "You go sweet well well today."[1] When he investigated, he discovered the aroma came from roasting human flesh. He raised the alarm and the police soon arrived to find a pile of mutilated limbs and decomposed bodies resting next to a police helmet, and Awawu Lawal, an emaciated woman who was to be the next victim. Bello had stumbled onto the lair of Clifford Orji, the Hannibal Lecter of Lagos.

Orji was known in the area as a wild man in filthy clothes, sometimes naked, who screamed at passersby, but no one seemed to know that he had been a cannibal for years. He would pick his victims from the crowds of people waiting at nearby bus stops and lure them to his den by "blowing on their foreheads." A few days after Orji's arrest on February 3, when I happened to be passing by Orji's underpass, I saw dozens of cars pulled to the side of the road and crowds of the curious milling around like tourists. A mile down the road, Lagos's street hawkers were selling calendars with photographs snapped from Orji's killing ground. Clifford the Cannibal had become a celebrity.

Normally a city that stretched the meaning of extreme to its very breaking point, Lagos was now a bastion of tranquillity. Minutes passed between seeing a single car, a truck, or any of the rusty and battered vans and minibuses that provide public transport, the notorious *danfos* and *molues* that so arrogantly mock the term *road-worthy*. There was not even a hint of the standard roar of engines, the relentless blare of horns, the grinding of worn-out gears, or the incessant cries of street-market traders that fuse into the background music of sub-Saharan Africa's monument to unbridled urban blight.

Paradoxically, Lagos is a city almost paralyzed by its perpetual motion, where street hawking provides a livelihood for millions of mainly young people. Routinely on sale are racks of cigarettes, orange drinks of uncertain origin in plastic bags, the Bible, the Koran, traditional hats, key chains, black market cassettes and CDs, pocket calculators, a Tummy Trimmer exercise machine in a cardboard box that sports a busty blond in a bathing suit, tomatoes, onions, countless pairs of shoes, car seat cushions, steering wheel grips, fan belts, sunglasses by the dozens, newspapers, magazines, and scores of other items too numerous to remember.

I looked for those most imaginative of Lagos's sellers, the youngsters who proudly hold up strings of dead or almost dead rats—sometimes they are still twitching. When I first saw them I assumed they were meant for consumption. After all, their robust country cousins, known as the "grass cutters," are considered a delicacy. But the dead vermin thrust toward your car window are part of a far more sophisticated pitch. The commodity on offer is rat poison, and the carcasses are there to testify to its effectiveness. Yet for once there was not one rat executioner in sight.

Gone too from the roadside were the swarms of beggars—the physically deformed, the blind, the indigent, and the band of tiny light-skinned children from the edge of the Sahara desert who walk from car to car singing, "God bless your mother and father; God bless your sister and your brother," before flipping their palms upward in a plea for money. Sailing through intersections renowned for their mind-numbing go-slows left one feeling positively light-headed. The only policemen around could be found sitting glumly in their stark black uniforms in the shade. The traffic wardens, affectionately known as "yellow fever" for their yellowish-orange uniforms, had not bothered to come to work. Occasionally entire streets were taken over by teams of shirtless boys playing soccer. For a day Lagos appeared to have taken a major stride toward realizing the pretentious description of itself carried on its license plate: "Center of Excellence."

The Independent National Electoral Commission (INEC) had kindly furnished me with a plastic identity card granting me the status of an international observer. Together with my longtime Lagos guide and friend, Kayode Sukoya, I decided to monitor the vote in Makoko, a giant slum of some 500,000 people. The homes are slapdash wooden shacks with corrugated tin roofs perched precariously on stilts above the marshy edge of a black lagoon that also serves as an open sewer. In a city full of impoverished eyesores, Makoko carried to a new level its assault on the senses, especially its spirited affront to one's nose. So powerful was the aroma that it took the best part of a day to block it from my mind.

As we climbed the on-ramp toward Makoko, I marveled that almost no one spoke anymore of the late Chief Abiola, the man who would have won the vote of June 12, 1993, had his good friend and business partner Babangida not canceled it. Abiola's campaign was filled with U.S.-style razzmatazz and money. Flamboyant and generous with his riches, he was a household name in Nigeria, with more than 150 traditional chieftaincy titles and a nationwide network of support. His presidency might have been the mess that many predicted it would be, but surely it would have been interesting.

In many ways Abiola was the human embodiment of the profound contradictions that continue to haunt Nigeria. Reputedly one of the richest men in Africa, his common touch and rich oratory endeared him to the masses. His was a quintessential rags-to-riches story that began in August 1937 in the southwestern city of Abeokuta, birthplace of some of Nigeria's leading personalities, such as Soyinka, Obasanjo, and the human rights activist Dr. Beko Ransome-Kuti and his brothers Fela Kuti, the musician, and Olikoye, the former health minister. In his youth Abiola proved as determined as he was as an adult. Born into severe poverty, he earned money to pay for his education by singing and drumming, and after attending Baptist Boys School in Abeokuta, he won a scholarship to study accountancy at the University of Glasgow. Upon returning to Nigeria, he took a position as chief accountant with Pfizer of Nigeria before moving on to the U.S. multinational International Telegraph and Telephone (ITT), where he rose to become regional vice president for Africa and the Middle East and chief executive of ITT Nigeria. One of his first assignments for ITT was to collect a bill of several million dollars for telecommunications equipment from the government.

When the explosion of the oil wealth was transforming Nigeria's military rulers into very rich men, Abiola was perfectly placed to join them. He started to build his fortune when he negotiated a billion-dollar contract with Murtala Mohammed's military government to install a nationwide telephone system. Close ties to the military never embarrassed Abiola, and he often explained them with a proverb: "To kiss somebody, you have to get near them; to bite them you have to get near them too." The telephone system was renowned for its grave deficiencies, and for many, Abiola symbolized the civilian elite's ruinous complicity with Western capitalism and military rule. It was with Abiola in mind that Fela Kuti composed the popular hit "ITT—International Thief Thief."

When Abiola fled the country shortly after the annulment of his election, I remember routinely calling him on his cellular telephone for a quote to fill out my story of the day. Often I caught him while he was riding through the streets of central London en route to some appointment in search of support for his presidential mandate or to a television interview to publicize his case. It was surreal speaking from my apartment in Lagos with the man many considered the president-elect while he sought salvation in the corridors of power in Britain.

When Abiola returned and declared himself president-elect in 1994, saying at a press conference, "Let the heavens fall," Abacha locked him up on charges of treason. Abiola never walked again as a free man. Over the next four years, his health failed, he was allowed only infrequent visits from his doctor, and his business empire suffered. In June 1996 gunmen allegedly operating under the command of Abacha's top security aide, Hamza al-Mustapha, assassinated Abiola's senior wife Kudirat. Through it all, however, Abiola remained a symbol of the popular desire for an elected government, especially among his fellow Yorubas.

The sudden death of his archenemy Abacha gave Abiola's family and supporters hope that his nightmare was nearing its end. But a month later Abiola too was gone. Even in death Abiola cast a long shadow over this latest contest. Both Obasanjo and Falae owed their nominations in large part to the fact that they, like Abiola, were Yorubas. But Obasanjo had little support among his kinsmen. Many never forgave him for handing over power to the northerner Shagari in 1979, and after the 1993 election debacle, Obasanjo had angered Yorubas by saying that Abiola was not a messiah. The facts that he was seen as "de-tribalized" and that he refused to champion the Yoruba cause counted against him. His detractors also cited the need to rid Nigeria of military rule to explain their opposition to him.

In fact, Obasanjo enjoyed the backing of retired army generals, including Babangida, and he was not ashamed of it. His top campaign manager was the former director of military intelligence Aliyu Mohammed Gusau. He had other prominent supporters too, among them Mandela, Jimmy Carter, and Andrew Young. Obasanjo was generally popular throughout the country, both in the mainly Muslim north where the Hausa-speaking ethnic groups dominate and in the east among the Igbos, as well as among the hundreds of minority groups. And so convinced were the majority of people that Obasanjo would emerge victorious that many Nigerians, with their penchant for humorous play on words, dubbed his People's Democratic Party, the PDP, the "Pre-determined President."

Falae had received the nomination through a series of backroom deals. First, a small caucus of the Alliance for Democracy (AD) Party picked him. Then the All People's Party (APP) jettisoned its original nominee within forty-eight hours of choosing him, and in the hope of thwarting Obasanjo, they adopted Falae, because he was a Yoruba, as the joint candidate. Falae had never been a soldier, though his detractors noted that he had served as finance minister under Babangida. They also pointed to the AD's alliance with what many regarded as the unsavory APP, whose members included prominent figures who supported Abacha, thus earning the APP the nickname "Abacha's People's Party."

Obasanjo had faced a more severe test in gaining his party's support, one that at least resembled a democratic process. The PDP nominating convention took place over a weekend ten days before the general election in the northern city of Jos. Obasanjo's strongest opposition came from Alex Ekwueme, a distinguished Igbo who had served as vice president in the Shagari administration. At the convention they vied for the loyalty of 2,439 delegates. Because politics means money in Nigeria, there was plenty of cash around. Everyone from delegates to praise singers were paid for their work. The head of one state delegation told me that his delegates had set their price for a vote at 150,000 naira, about $1,500, each. At the end of the first day I encountered a group of irate women who had danced and sung in the streets on behalf of Ekwueme. They wanted their money, 500 naira, or $5, and the poor man in charge of finances was trapped standing on top of a table in the middle of the crowd. "Pay us or we will work for Obasanjo tomorrow," shouted one woman in an eloquent display of her political loyalty.

On that first evening I ended up in the room of one of the PDP convention kingmakers, Bamanga Tukur, and over tea and biscuits he explained the difference between the two candidates. He likened Ekwueme to a chauffeur of a Rolls Royce and Obasanjo to a truck driver. Ekwueme was an excellent person, he said, but "what Nigeria needs is a truck driver." And, I suggested, someone who could deal with the highway bandits prevalent on Nigeria's political thoroughfares. "Exactly," he said. Two days later, the truck driver had won with 68 percent of the delegate vote and the nomination.

MAKOKO is about as far as away from power as it is possible to get in Nigeria. Most of its men are technically unemployed. Many cruise around in wooden pirogues like aquatic cowboys eking out a living by fishing and scavenging in the tidal lagoon waters. Others cut building planks from rafts of logs floated down from the dwindling rain forests of what was once an unbroken belt of tropical woodlands running from Sierra Leone to the Congo River. The women contribute to their families' income as their sisters throughout the city do: by engaging in petty trading in Lagos's vast informal markets. The slum of Ayetoro marks the edge of Makoko, just over the cement wall of the Yaba off-ramp. The road in is an undulating rocky track of potholes and sun-baked earth that gradually tapers off into the lagoon.

By 9:00 A.M. a small line of people had formed in the shade of a pedestrian footbridge in front of a rough-hewn wooden table named the "Act of Apostle" polling station after the local church. The expectant voters were going through an accreditation exercise to check their registration cards against a master list held by two election officials. The procedure lacked its usual importance, however, because the Electoral Commission had admitted that it had distributed nearly twenty million more voter cards than were statistically necessary for the estimated voting population.

As soon as I arrived I ran into Adeoye Ayadi, a spokesman for Ayetoro's Yoruba residents. He was standing in front of a wooden shack that sold odds and ends such as cigarettes, candles, and chewing gum. Within moments he loudly unleashed a catalogue of the community's grievances against the military government ruling from Abuja. A gang of area boys—unemployed youths, ruffians with an attitude—and a gaggle of dusty little boys and girls encircled Ayadi as he narrated how the health clinic had closed a decade ago. The nurses and doctors had deserted the place because of a lack of funds and medicines. Now the building served as the residential quarters of government workers from another neighborhood, and the closest health facility for Ayetoro's residents was a 15-minute walk away on the ominously named Cemetery Street.

Ayadi, a fisherman by trade, said business had been poor since January 1998, when a giant oil spill at offshore installations owned by the U.S. oil company Mobil had contaminated fishing waters all along the Nigerian coast. Constant power cuts by the state-run National Electric Power Company, NEPA—dubbed "Never Ever Power Always"—meant that those running the makeshift sawmills spent a considerable part of their time sitting idle. Unrest in the oil-rich Niger delta had cut the supply of logs and increased the flow of Ilaje (a Yoruba clan) refugees seeking to settle in Ayetoro. Housing was short, Ayadi admitted, but people had to make room. "They are our brothers and children," he shouted, "so of course we just take them in."

A few yards away at the polling station, the process of accreditation dragged on amid an increasingly tense argument between rival supporters of the two candidates. I sat down on a bench next to one of the election workers, Toyin Aribaba, a high school home economics teacher. Within seconds of exchanging greetings, she lowered her voice and wondered if she should have listened to her father's warning about working the election in Ayetoro. "He said Ayetoro was a bad place because these area boys are troublesome," she said as the shouting continued unabated. The 390 naira, about $4, she would earn was not worth it, he said, and if something did happen, she should not complain to him about it. The 390 naira did not sound like a lot, Toyin admitted, but considering that her teacher's salary was 3,000 naira, some $30, a month, it was not a bad day's earnings.

Well-educated and well-spoken, Toyin was from a middle-class family, although in the past fifteen years the Nigerian middle class had been hammered by an economy locked into free fall. One brother was a lawyer, a second was an optometrist, and her sister was a secretary. Her father was retired, and her mother had to engage in petty trading to pay the bills. Living with her parents was the only way Toyin could make ends meet. "They still pay for my clothes and my feeding," she said.

Toyin sympathized with the plight of Ayetoro's residents, but she knew that she and her equally nervous election coworker, Bayo Fagbuagun, also a teacher, were on the firing line. It was their duty to accredit all the voters properly, keep the vote as secret as possible, and conduct the count openly before anyone attempted to stuff the ballot box. They had been promised police protection, but by late morning none of Lagos's finest had bothered to show up. "I am frightened because everybody here is ready to make trouble," she said looking around at the rowdy crowd of youths. "I pray that everything will take place peacefully."

For most of the morning that appeared unlikely. The first trouble arose with the appearance of a heavily pregnant woman, who arrived at the station sweating and panting. The two party agents representing the APP and PDP scoured the registration papers for her name, and as soon as they found it, they erupted into an argument so bitter and angry that it seemed their very lives depended on it. The problem was that her age was listed as fifty. A pregnant woman could not be fifty, the agent for Obasanjo's PDP shouted as he wrapped his arms around the registration forms and hugged them tightly to his chest. The APP agent, screaming that it must be a mistake, leaped across the table and grabbed hold of the list. A tussle ensued, and a group of area boys surrounded the desk demanding justice. "A mistake!" they sang. After five minutes of a running verbal battle, Toyin and Bayo decided they had little choice but to accredit the woman.

Sitting calmly on the edge of the concrete pillar holding up the pedestrian walkway, Omogbemi Idowu, the leader of the anti-Obasanjo youths in the area, chuckled to himself with satisfaction as he monitored the raucous behavior of what he called "my boys." The accreditation list was filled with such errors because the voter registration was poorly done. "The government did it deliberately to help the Obasanjo cause," he said, hinting at a dark conspiracy. "The military wants to impose another military man on us. That's why we are here in force. We won't let the Obasanjo people cheat us," he said as several young men around him grunted in agreement.

When I asked about possible fraud by his people, his smile melted into a grimace and he said, "We don't need to cheat here. Everyone supports us." Another round of grunts rose from the crowd of his boys. The people of Ayetoro and the Yorubas hate Obasanjo, Omogbemi pronounced like a college professor, because he was a stooge of the northern

Muslims and the army generals. "Look what military rule has brought us. I have a university degree in political science but there is no job for me," he hissed. "I have to share a room here with a friend and make some naira sawing logs. If there is no electricity, I make nothing. Nigeria can't go on like this. There must be a change from military rule and Obasanjo is a general, just like them."

A halfhearted attempt by several bystanders to ignite the chant "No more soldiers!" quickly faded. I pointed out that it was Falae who had served more recently in a military government. "But it wasn't his government; he was powerless to help the people," Omogbemi insisted. I asked why, then, he had agreed to serve. Omogbemi turned away without providing an answer.

At that moment, he nodded to a tall, clean-cut young man in shorts and a T-shirt named Felix Ayetoba. Felix walked quietly over to the wall behind the registration table, where posters of the candidates had been placed in violation of the ban on campaign materials anywhere near the voting booths. With a mischievous gleam in his eye, he ripped down the sole Obasanjo poster. Omogbemi smiled his approval. For a few minutes no one noticed, and Felix returned to the gathering pleased with his deed. He explained his action by pulling out an ID card that identified him as a student of accountancy and public administration at Yaba Polytechnic College. "All the students in Nigeria are against Obasanjo," he said. "When he was in power, he repressed us and dismissed some university officials." Felix was speaking of events some twenty years ago, when he was seven. At the time the Obasanjo government had cracked down on students protesting tuition increases.

In the open space in front of the polling station, a new source of trouble appeared in the form of Thompson Eretan, the self-described leader of the pro-Obasanjo campaign in Ayetoro. Having noticed his champion's poster lying in shreds on the ground, he had worked himself into an almighty frenzy. His face twisted in such apparent pain and anguish that a passerby would have been justified in thinking the man's family had been burned at the stake. "Obasanjo is a Yoruba man, and I can vote for him if I want!" he screamed. When I marveled at how seriously Nigerians took politics, Toyin shook her head. "These people have nothing and they're just desperate to win at something."

A spirited shoving match moved around the polling station in a wide arc, and just when it seemed that blood would be spilled, Thompson announced that he was going home to find another poster. If anyone removed it this time, he promised, there would be a fight. One of Thompson's cohorts, a thin, shirtless, middle-aged man, turned to offer me a drink from his bottle of Guinness. When I declined, he started shouting that it was the duty of the international observers to tear down all the Falae posters. One of Omogbemi's boys ran up to the Falae posters and swayed back and forth singing, "Talk to me and I talk to you."

Omogbemi and Felix were having a good laugh over the affair when Toyin and Bayo, seeing there was no one left in the line, decided it was time to wrap up the accreditation. Their reaction was one of outrage. "Close it, how could you close it?" the youths demanded. Accreditation was due to end at 11:30 A.M., and there were fifteen minutes left. Several of the area boys start dancing and chanting "11:30-oh! 11:30-oh!" Faced with such a chorus of opposition, Toyin and Bayo quite wisely relented.

As soon as the noise died down for a minute, another rumble arose from around the corner. Thompson was back with his Obasanjo poster plastered on a small board attached to a 5-foot-long pole. He cut sharply through the astonished gathering and defiantly placed the placard against the wall. Bedlam erupted again, with everyone pushing and shoving but never quite crossing that fine line into full-fledged brawling.

Toyin and Bayo hunkered down on the table and dug into plates of rice and beans in a vain attempt to block out the pandemonium swirling around them. Felix stood calmly aloof in front of the polling station, acting as if he had nothing to do with the trouble. He turned with a smile and a wink—the perfect agent provocateur. By now even Omogbemi was tiring of all the fuss, so he wandered over and sat down under the footbridge. The accreditation was closed. Out of 650 registered voters, only one-third had showed up. "Would you come to vote with all these boys around?" Toyin asked rhetorically by way of explanation. "I wouldn't."

It was time to vote. All those not directly involved in the brouhaha over the Obasanjo poster formed a snarled line. The area boys took it upon themselves to wander up and down the line, in clear violation of the election rules, to urge voters to make the correct choice. Another small table was set to the side for the voters to mark their ballots with their thumbprint. The youths moved in close with the clear intention of seeing how their neighbors voted.

Bayo turned the clear glass ballot box upside down to show that it had not been stuffed. All the while, the shouting match raged in the background. At the head of the line stood an elderly man who introduced himself as Chief Simeon Ehuwa, the traditional leader of the Ilaje community in Ayetoro. Out of respect to his position, he was to vote first. Before he did, he bent over the table and said, "We are praying for a president to make Nigeria good again and earn respect overseas. We want someone who will help the common man." Chief Ehuwa was oblivious to the hubbub behind him and to the fact that as the traditional authority, he might have had a role in bringing his subjects to order.

Just when all hope of avoiding an altercation was vanishing in the hot afternoon air, a van pulled up and disgorged a dozen policemen. The shouting immediately died, the area boys dispersed, and the voters snapped into a disciplined line. The senior policeman approached regally with his long black walking stick and ordered his subordinates to rip down the campaign posters behind the voting station. "We came

36

on information that some of these boys were causing trouble," the officer announced. The area boys looked at each other in amazement. Trouble? What trouble? Turning to the bridge pillar, where a kaleidoscope of posters loomed over the voting table, he ruled that because the placards had been hanging there for the past several months, they could remain. The posters were too high to remove easily, so he had little choice but to leave them in place.

The policemen strutted around for a few minutes before returning to their vehicle in preparation to depart. Toyin, fearing what would happen when they did, pleaded, "Can you leave someone behind?"

The officer laughed and said, "I am giving you a husband." The assignment fell to a bull-necked policeman in dark sunglasses named Ganiyu Abudu, who approached the young toughs, regarding them as little more than cockroaches, and shooed them to the fringes of the polling area.

From then on the voting proceeded with little rancor. One by one, each person took a ballot from Toyin, moved to the small table set to the side, chose their preferred party by putting their thumbprint in the designated box, and then slipped it into the glass box. A few ancient women provided comical moments by handing their papers back to Toyin, not understanding that they alone were meant to deposit them. From time to time a group of area boys casually approached the voting table for a better view, only to have Abudu stand up and wave them away. There was little doubt, however, that they could see how the voters were marking their ballots. For those in the Falae camp, of course, this posed no problem. But the majority of Obasanjo supporters folded their ballots with extra care before dropping them in. A few were open about their choice. When one young man held his ballot aloft, dancing a jig and shouting "Obasanjo!" Officer Abudu frowned and asked, "What is wrong with you?"

At 2:30 P.M. the vote closed and the count began. Toyin and Bayo sorted the ballots into three separate piles: for Falae, for Obasanjo, and spoiled papers. Toyin then counted the votes out loud so that there would be no doubt. As expected, Chief Falae won handily, by 174 to 36, with two spoiled ballots. Toyin and Bayo slid the papers back into the glass box and started to walk the hundred yards to the collating center, where the ballots from all over Makoko were arriving for final tabulation. The area boys from the opposing camps retreated to the shade under the footbridge and continued an argument that by now was well lubricated with bottles of beer.

There was an air of inevitability about the result. "Sentiments aside, it is clear that Obasanjo is ordained to be the next president," Chief Ehuwa's thirty-five-year-old son, Kolawole Bright Ehuwa, said as he watched Bayo and Toyin depart for the collating center. "The people of Ayetoro wanted to show that they want the military out of politics. Military rule has been a disaster for Nigeria. Maybe, now that Obasanjo is a civilian, he can do something. But frankly, I am not optimistic. Those generals who brought him to power don't want him to rule on behalf of the common man. They want him there to protect their interests."

Two days later the final official tally gave Obasanjo some eighteen million votes to Falae's eleven million, an overwhelming 62 to 38 percent margin of victory. Lagos State had gone heavily for Falae, by an 88 to 12 percent margin. Nationwide the election was relatively peaceful, but it was often farcical. There were widespread reports of cheating, ballot box stuffing, phantom voting booths, and consequently an impossibly high turnout. Some districts recorded a turnout of 100 percent even though observers reported that voting had been light. In others voters turned up to find the polling station closed and all the ballots marked. Even Obasanjo's friend Jimmy Carter could not endorse the proceedings. "Regrettably," he said, "it is not possible for us to make an accurate judgment about the outcome of the presidential election."

It was, as many Nigerians say, not an election but a selection.

3

Army Arrangement

Coups succeed coups. We will never be at peace again.

MAJOR HASSAN KATSINA, JANUARY 1966

M Y JOURNEY to understand the motives of Nigeria's former military dictators began late one morning in August 1998 at a filling station on the outskirts of the northern city of Kaduna. It was the last legal source of fuel before the road joined the highway south toward Abuja, and rowdy lines of vehicles were already forming for the chance of filling up their tanks. Dozens of street hawkers wove in and out of the line pushing their wares, mainly plastic bags of water, soft drinks, peanuts, and the mildly stimulating kola nuts, the north's answer to the double espresso of Nigerians' soul mates, the Italians. The two countries share many things—the natural swagger, the passion for life, the sublime skills of their soccer stars, a certain notoriety for corruption, and especially their stomach-churning driving habits. The Italians, a local joke goes, are the Nigerians of Europe. The difference is, of course, that the Italian system basically works, and that of Nigeria patently does not. And therein lies the story.

A tall young man backed up by a 3-foot plank studded with metal spikes and a makeshift barrier cobbled together from strands of wire and rusty tire rims stood guard at the entrance to the gas station. Suddenly, as he understood our determination to enter the station, his grimace melted into a wide smile and his body began swaying to a rhythm known only to him. "I pray to chop for your hand-oh," he sang in pidgin English, meaning he wanted money for the honor of passing through the tiny area he controlled to reach the other side. He was, in his modest way, symbolic of the manner in which Nigeria's rulers had practiced governance: Stake a claim over a piece of territory, a government office, or an oil field and use your authority to obtain financial reward.

Mohammed Haruna, a colleague who was behind the wheel, turned to me in an explosion of laughter as we waited for the singing custodian of the filling station entrance to remove the wire barrier. Tiny boys bobbed past the side window with outstretched hands singing the blessings of Allah in Hausa, the lingua franca of the north. An elderly man sat on the curb a few yards in front of a roadside mosque beckoning with his wooden staff for a handout. Over at the pumps a crowd hovered like an angry swarm of bees each time a car pulled in and rose as one to inflict a mass verbal sting on anyone who tried to jump the line. Their latest victim was a minibus taxi driver, who was sulking a few yards away after his rather reckless attempt at an end run had been stopped short with a barrage of abuse. He had been ordered to the back of the line, and his fifteen passengers, knowing this could mean a day-long wait, piled out of his vehicle.

We were fortunate because Haruna, one of the best-known journalists in northern Nigeria, was a personal friend of the station owner. If the man was around, he would ensure a quick purchase, from his reserve stocks if necessary. Most of the rest of the anxious customers would have to await the arrival of the next fuel tanker—which might be that day, the next day, or possibly the next week. No one was quite sure. There simply was not enough fuel to go around. The nation's four oil refineries had been crippled through neglect and negligence, so the world's sixth biggest oil producer was in the ludicrous position of having to import fuel from abroad to meet the demands of its own people. The simple act of filling one's tank had become a privilege for the well-off few and a daily struggle for the rest.

Blame for the shortages usually fell on the cheap official price of gasoline, a true bargain at less than 50 cents a gallon. Nigeria's Western creditors and the International Monetary Fund (IMF) had been pressing the government for years to allow domestic fuel prices to rise to something near world levels. The increased revenue, the foreign experts reasoned, would both help cover government budget deficits, thus easing the state's onerous burden on the domestic credit, and ensure that individuals and businesses would have ample fuel supplies. But whereas Western economists considered the low price an inefficient subsidy, most Nigerians regarded fuel as a natural resource that must remain cheap. Because the state did nothing else for its people, the reasoning went, at least it could provide cheap gas. Historically, even small price increases proved the surest route to domestic unrest. Nevertheless, on the black market a gallon fetched anywhere between $1 and $4.

One of the principal problems in stopping this illegal trade was that the black marketeers and the agencies tasked with cracking down on them were really one and the same. Take the special "task forces," comprising members of the Army and the police and representatives of the state governments, that were set up to bring an immediate end to the fuel shortages. Instead, they routinely received 300,000 to 500,000 naira, about $3,250 to $5,400, for every tanker that was diverted to the unofficial market. Not surprisingly, that was where most of the petrol ended up. The result was that while the gas stations were starved for their product, the number of illegal fuel salesmen sitting by the sides of highways throughout Nigeria ran into the thousands. The system of corruption had become so ingrained that entire villages in northern Nigeria depended on the fuel shortages for their livelihood: The longer the lines of vehicles outside the legitimate gas stations in the big northern cities, such as Kano, Kaduna, and Zaria, the more numerous the roadside gangs of youths selling plastic jugs full of pink motor fuel.

At the time, in mid-1998, the only places certain to have ample supplies of Nigerian gasoline were outside Nigeria. Large amounts of domestic fuel disappeared across Nigeria's borders with Chad, Niger, Benin, and Cameroon, whose people paid four times as much for a gallon as did Nigerian motorists. Nearly half of Nigeria's two million barrels a day in oil production was exported to the insatiable U.S. market. The rest of the world consumed another 25 percent. Of the 400,000 barrels a day destined for domestic consumption, Nigeria's West African neighbors took a significant share. All along the coastal highway from Nigeria to neighboring Benin and beyond that Togo, black marketeers set out liter bottles filled with Nigerian gasoline for sale.

Not to be outdone in business acumen, Abacha had devised various ingenious scams to profit from the price differentials. Family members and cronies won contracts, stuffed with bloated commissions and inflated prices, to import bargain-basement gasoline, which, given its extremely poor quality, hardly merited being called gasoline. Abacha's business advisers loaded Nigerian gasoline onto ships, motored out off the Guinea Coast, then returned to port as if the fuel were arriving from abroad, and resold it to the country at the higher international import prices. Once in the domestic supply, some of the fuel then entered the black market or crossed the border for resale at even higher prices. In the end, a deficit remained in the stocks on the official market, Nigeria needed additional imports, and the wheel of corruption spun effortlessly. When Abubakar came into office, he too had promised to deal with the scarcity. But in the early months of his rule the lines only lengthened. It is somehow appropriate then that the Nigerian pronunciation of the word *fuel*—"foo-ell"—sounds more or less like an exaggerated enunciation of *fool*.

Haruna deftly eased our car around the makeshift blockade, and within fifteen minutes we pulled out again fully loaded for the two-hour journey ahead. Our destination was the town of Minna, the home of Babangida, whom some called the "Prince of the Niger." Babangida once referred to himself as the "evil genius." Most people knew him as IBB.

By now IBB had been out of the presidency for more than half a decade, but his close personal ties to the width and breadth of the Nigerian elite, military and civilian alike, together with a war chest believed to total billions of dollars, ensured his continued influence. Abacha had been his deputy when he was in power, and with his successor Abubakar Babangida maintained a friendship that had begun in boyhood. In fact, they were neighbors.

My initial attempts by telephone to set up an interview with IBB had stumbled at various hurdles. First, his office secretary assured me of an audience but said I would have to speak with the general's private secretary. He, however, wasn't around; call back tomorrow. When I reached the private secretary two days later, he likewise said that an interview was surely possible, but it had to be cleared with the chief's aide-de-camp (ADC). When I reached the ADC three days later, he was far less forthcoming, explaining that IBB was a very busy man and that I should call back the next week. The real problem was that after years of silence Babangida had recently granted several newspaper interviews. His tortured explanations in these interviews for his annulment of the 1993 polls had drawn widespread criticism for what was deemed their lack of frankness.

I could tell from the ADC's unenthusiastic tone of voice that the request to call back the following week was simply a polite brush-off. It was only then that I decided to ask Haruna, whom I had known since the early 1990s when he was the editor of the *Citizen* magazine, to intercede on my behalf. Haruna was generally known to be a confidant of IBB, earning him a place in the ranks of what the press had dubbed "the Babangida boys." He kindly made the appropriate contacts, and a week later we had an appointment fixed for midday.

During the drive our conversation centered on Nigeria's prospects since the deaths of Abacha and Abiola, the military's attitude toward withdrawing from politics, and the mediocre caliber of politicians who were emerging to try their luck in the new transition to democracy. But mostly we talked about IBB, the ultimate soldier-politician, or "militician," a smiling dictator who had been a major player in the country's political scene for the past two decades, nearly half of Nigeria's entire independence.

Coups seemed to run in his blood. His first direct experience with plotting rebellion came in 1975, when, as a colonel, he was among a group of young officers who replaced the civil war–time leader, Gowon, with Murtala Mohammed. In 1983 together with Abacha, he led the removal of Nigeria's second elected leader, Shagari, and the installation of Buhari as head of state. Two years later he teamed up with Abacha again to oust Buhari and take the seat of power himself. When he finally resigned in 1993 amid widespread social unrest over the election debacle, he left behind a human time bomb in the form of his good friend Abacha.

Babangida came into office to widespread public acclaim as a military redeemer, a man who could take the difficult decisions on the economy, throttle the robber barons, and foster a more just society. Compared to his predecessor, the strict disciplinarian Buhari, Babangida was liberal, prepared to discuss the issues and allow public debate. Abroad he was feted by world leaders, including the queen of England, as a progressive, determined African leader. At home he established a virtual military version of John F. Kennedy's Camelot, complete with study groups and intellectuals. By releasing imprisoned journalists and repealing repressive military decrees, Babangida convinced many of his compatriots and most of the outside world that in the topsy-turvy world of Nigerian politics, he was the best possible ruler: the enlightened strongman. With the benefit of hindsight, it was clear to see that he simply seduced nearly everyone.

After the harshness of Abacha's five years in power, Babangida's methods seemed rather benign. For years Babangida's tactic was, in the words of the prominent northern lawyer Suleimanu Kumo, to allow his critics "to bark and bark and bark and even to bite," while assuring they could not cause any serious wounds. Unlike Abacha, who favored strong-arm tactics against suspected opponents, Babangida employed a more sophisticated mixture of repression and "settling," the Nigerian equivalent of greasing the palms. There were many, however, who compared his rule unfavorably with that of Abacha. "I think Babangida was even worse than Abacha," I was once told by M. D. Yusufu, the highly respected former inspector general of police. "Babangida went all out to corrupt society. Abacha was intimidating people with fear. With him gone now, you can recover. But this corruption remains, and it is very corrosive to society." In this legacy, Babangida remains the dominant political character of his generation.

———

BABANGIDA'S residence sat prominently on the crest of a shoulder of hills above downtown Minna. In it, the general lorded over a city whose transformation from a dusty trading post on the railway line to a center of political and military power mirrored his own meteoric rise. Minna was born in 1915 as a melting pot of ethnic groups— Gwari, Hausa, Fulani, and Kamberi, among others—who came to sell their peanuts, yams, and cotton for export on the Jebba extension on the Lagos-to-Kano railway line. Local commerce also built up around such crops as indigo, cattle, tobacco, and, inevitably, kola nuts. Immigrants, Yorubas from the west and Igbos from the east, came in search of work on the railway and as traders and mechanics. The city's modern industries ranged from the production of woven baskets, pottery, dyed cloth, and raffia mats to the quarrying of marble and the manufacturing of bricks. The town also had a Federal University of Technology.

Driving down the wide avenues that sliced through the center of town, dominated by a huge new golden mosque, Haruna quickly located an electronics shop where I could pick up some additional microcassettes in case the general was in a talkative mood. All told, I had about three hours of tape, surely enough to complete the task at hand. From there, we climbed the leafy hill behind Minna before turning onto the final stretch, appropriately named Babangida Road, which delivered us to the general's gates. On the final ascent Haruna pointed to a well-appointed suburban home. "That's the house of the current head of state," he said, referring to Abubakar.

Abubakar grew up with Babangida. They attended the same primary school in Minna, the Native Authority School, where Babangida developed a reputation for standing up for the younger students. His nickname was Maigari, Hausa for "the owner of the house." And they both entered the armed forces, with Babangida promoting his friend's career advancement.

Unlike Abacha and Babangida, however, Abubakar was reputed to have little interest in politics. "A soldier's soldier" was the prevailing description, tempered only by constant rumors that his transitional government engaged in the favorite pastime of all Nigerian rulers to date: making money. A cautious, at times seemingly plodding man, Abubakar earned nicknames such as Baba Go-Slow and Baba No Regrets.

One hundred yards further on was the entrance to Babangida's home, which, surprisingly for a man who has so many enemies, was guarded by a lone, slightly disheveled policeman. Apparently recognizing Haruna, he waved us through, and we rode slowly up to the general's mansion. The compound was a wide circular Arabic-style structure built by the German-based company Julius Berger Plc., which had won most of the choice, multimillion-dollar contracts to build the new capital at Abuja when Babangida's signature was needed to clinch such deals. (Babangida's rule epitomized what retired General Ishola Williams has dubbed "a government of the contractors, by the contractors, for the contractors.")

We entered the right side of the building and initially found ourselves in a room filled with fifteen to twenty people, many of them in various states of slumber, who were waiting for an audience with the general, the *oga* (literally "he is big" in Yoruba but normally translated as "big man"). From their state of fatigue it was clear that the operational word was *waiting.* Luckily, an aide quickly hurried us out of the room and moved us through several chambers manned by smartly dressed young men and women sitting behind desks and busy on typewriters and computers. Our next stop was a large office where a giant television screen was blaring the latest news from CNN. A white man sat in the corner speaking alternately into a cellular telephone and a walkie-talkie. Israeli security specialists had protected the Muslim Babangida while he was in office, and it appeared they still were.

Ten minutes later we were on the move again, out through the door of the right wing, across the driveway, and into the left wing of the house, passing through several more chambers before reaching the office of the general's wife, Maryam.

Maryam, many Nigerians believed, was even more ambitious than her husband. As first lady she had created a controversial program called Better Life for Rural Women, which, amid widespread allegations of corruption and questionable priorities, quickly received the derogatory nickname Better Life for Ruling Women. Maryam's high

profile in Nigeria sparked the concept of "big-womanism" that led to
the development of a first ladies' movement among wives of African
heads of state. She once received an award from the New York–based
Hunger Project for her supposed contribution to agricultural development. When the Babangidas finally quit the presidential complex at
Aso Rock in August 1993, no one was more upset about the move than
Maryam. She was no longer the center of attention; friends and acquaintances stopped calling to seek her endorsement and advice. By all
accounts she was embittered by the experience, especially because her
rival, Maryam Abacha, usurped her role as the prima donna of
Nigeria.

Yet by the looks of her office, Maryam was keeping busy. Just down
the hill from her house was her private high school for children of the
rich, and she was clearly still involved with first ladies' movement. On
her desk was a freshly typed speech she was to deliver at an upcoming
conference on land mine victims that had been organized by the first
lady of Angola, Ana Paula dos Santos.

Haruna and I perched on a sofa, he sipping tea and I coffee, and
waited for our summons to enter the general's inner sanctum. From
time to time a buzzer sounded, and a stout security man in khaki
would disappear to attend to some request of the *oga*. Upon returning
to his station, he invariably motioned with his hand as if he were patting a small child on the head to signal that we should be patient. We
had not been forgotten.

After a couple more cups of coffee and tea, our moment arrived.
The soldier flicked his wrist to motion us toward our meeting, and suddenly energized, we stepped through the door in great anticipation.
Unfortunately, the general was nowhere to be seen. We sat down and
waited for a few minutes, casting our eyes around at the paintings and
pictures of Babangida, with his wife, with his two sons and two daughters, with various political leaders, even riding in an open car toward
Buckingham palace with the queen of England.

A side door burst open, and in strode Babangida, dressed in a flowing beige robe and sandals and offering that winning gap-tooth smile and warm handshake. Instantly charming, Babangida possessed that rare ability to make anyone in the room with him feel that they are the most important people in the world. The three of us sank into the fluffy chairs and sofas and chatted about when I had arrived in the country and the new openness in Nigeria since the death of Abacha two months before. I recounted the number of times I had requested an interview when he was in power but said that, sadly, his press spokesman at the time had never done anything about it. "Good," said Babangida with a straight face before leaning back with a wide smile. "Journalists," he sniffed, shaking his head in mock disapproval.

A cellular telephone on the table chirped to announce an incoming call. Babangida spoke warmly and wiggled his legs like a little boy expecting a treat as he and his caller swapped witticisms in Hausa. The side door burst open again and the three of us, Babangida, Haruna, and I, rose to greet the former first lady, resplendent in a dark green wrap-around gown and matching head cloth. She shook my hand and walked over to switch on the television to reveal the beginning of Oprah Winfrey's show. She turned to her husband and asked who was on the line. Babangida cupped his hand over the phone and said, "Shinkafi." It was Umar Shinkafi, the former intelligence boss, aristocrat, and northern business magnate who was preparing a run for the presidency.

"Tell him I want a donation to Mrs. dos Santos's land mine foundation," she said with a wave of her hand. Unlike the man at the gas station, she was not asking for a contribution; her tone was rather more authoritative. She turned back and just as quickly as she had entered Maryam was gone.

Babangida sat back down for a few minutes and finished his telephone conversation. All the while, his second line had been ringing, and finally losing his patience he buzzed his security man and ordered him to hold all calls. Then he turned to me and asked, "So what can I do for you?"

―――――

THE STORY OF Babangida's life reads like a political history of modern Nigeria. His generation came of age at the very dawn of independence when the leading political figures in the north, spearheaded by the Northern Region's premier, Ahmadu Bello—whose position as the Sardauna made him the most important person in the Sokoto hierarchy after the Sultan—launched a campaign to develop an educated class of professionals in an attempt to catch up with the rest of the country.

Babangida was barely a teenager when the first Army recruiters came to his Native Authority School in Minna in 1955 as part of a drive to enlist northern officer cadets into the armed forces. They asked Babangida and some of his classmates to join the Boys Company, a military academy, but his family decided that fourteen was too tender an age. Seven years after their initial approach, the recruiters showed up at Government College in Bida, where Babangida and Abubakar were studying. They paraded a dashing young northerner who would later lead Nigeria through its most difficult hour. Though a Christian, Lieutenant Yakubu "Jack" Gowon was regarded by the younger men as a shining symbol of northern potential.

"We saw a very young man dressed up in military uniform, and they said that if we worked hard we could end up like Lieutenant Jack Gowon," Babangida recalled in the high soft voice that is so at odds with his "evil genius" reputation. "That's where the enthusiasm started." Fifteen Government College students sat for the examination to gain entrance into the Nigerian Military Training College in Kaduna, and eleven passed. Both Abubakar and Babangida enrolled in the college, and there they met a small, quiet young man from Kano

who would be linked to the rest of their careers. His name was Sani
Abacha. In 1963 Babangida received his commission as a second lieu-
tenant at the age of twenty-two, and while others trained in the
United Kingdom, the United States, and Pakistan, he studied at the
Indian Military Academy.

By then, Tafawa Balewa's administration was finding governance
problematic. Political turbulence among the Tiv people in the north,
the bloody factional fighting in the southwest within Awolowo's Action
Group, the rigging and violence surrounding the 1964 elections, rising
corruption, and the failed census defined the turbulence of the times.

But the coup that took place on January 15, 1966, changed the rules
of Nigeria's political game forever. The mainly Igbo conspirators, six
majors and a captain, were led by the popular Sandhurst-trained
Major Chukwuma Nzeogwu, who personally commanded the unit of
soldiers that murdered Ahmadu Bello and his wife in their bedroom.
In addition to Tafawa Balewa and Ahmadu Bello, prominent northern
military officers such as Brigadier Zakariya Maimalari, Colonel Kur
Mohammed, Lieutenant Colonel Abogo Largema, and Lieutenant
Colonel Yakubu Pam were killed. Military coups were in vogue in the
early 1960s, and young officers in Africa believed they were better
suited than the politicians to run their countries.

"We were beginning to have a highly articulate officer corps who
went to school, were very well informed," Babangida explained.
"Seeing their own colleagues in other parts of the world, especially in
Africa, getting involved in a thing like this really motivated the officer
corps to intervene in a situation which was already very fertile for military intervention."

In the end the coup failed, but military rule became inevitable with
the murders of the prime minister and the premiers of the Northern
and Western Regions. The rump of the federal cabinet relinquished
power to the highest-ranking surviving officer, General John Aguiyi-
Ironsi, also an Igbo. The attempt at a legalistic transfer of power did

not obscure the fact that Nigeria had crossed a perilous threshold that only a few of the wiser heads understood at the time.

Babangida recalled a warning from his commanding officer, Hassan Katsina: "We were young officers. He was a major and our squadron leader, and we were all sitting together talking about the coup. He said, 'Coups succeed coups. We will never be at peace again.' That was in January 1966, and how prophetic. It's kept on and on and on to become a recurrent feature of the Nigerian political scene." Babangida said this without batting an eye, seeming not to recognize that he was one of the main contributors to this state of affairs.

Although the coup remained popular in the south, the initial enthusiasm in the north began to wane once people realized that the core of the northern political and military leadership had been decimated. Ironsi made a series of disastrous moves that lent credence to the growing suspicion that the original military strike had been an Igbo blow against the north. He failed to put the coup plotters on trial, he surrounded himself with Igbo intellectuals, his promotions favored Igbo officers, and by military decree he transformed Nigeria from a federation into a centralized state. Nigeria's various regions were no longer going to be allowed to develop at their own pace. The north's longstanding fears of being swamped by the better-educated southerners, the Yorubas and the Igbos, appeared to be becoming a reality. Students and civil servants led demonstrations demanding that the north secede.

The revenge coup in July, "Operation Araba," was an equally bloody affair, and almost all the murdered officers were Igbos. The initial goal of Operation Araba was the secession of the north, but the idea was dropped after persistent pressure by the British and U.S. ambassadors on the rebel leaders, primarily the mercurial Major Murtala Mohammed and Captain Theophilus Yakubu Danjuma. In August the highest-ranking northern officer, Lieutenant Colonel Gowon, who had so impressed Babangida in his school days, assumed the position of head of state and leader of the governing Supreme Military Council.

Riots spiraled out of control. Beginning in September, northern mobs murdered tens of thousands of easterners, mainly Igbos, living in the northern cities. Hundreds of thousands more, urged on by the military governor of the Eastern Region, Colonel Ojukwu, packed up their belongings and streamed home to the east. For the next nine months the federal authorities remained at loggerheads with the Eastern Region's government. Ojukwu refused to accept the thirty-one-year-old Gowon, an inferior in rank, as his commander in chief. In May 1967 he declared Biafra an independent republic.

Fighting between the federal forces and the Biafran secessionists broke out on July 6, 1967. What Gowon had called a police action and Ojukwu had predicted would be a rout lasted three years and claimed up to one million lives. Babangida was in the Army's One Division in command of the Forty-Fourth Infantry Battalion, known as the Rangers. "We believed we were fighting for a cause. Despite what happened before the war, we still remained a highly cohesive institution. We believed in the concept of one Nigeria, and we were fighting to keep the country together." Notwithstanding his claims, rivalry between One Division and Two and Three Divisions was so intense that they each sent separate agents to Europe to shop for arms.

The international community mounted an extraordinary relief operation comparable to the Berlin airlift. Foreign aid workers largely accepted the Biafrans' exaggerated claims of genocide and deliberate starvation by the federal forces. The official history of Oxfam, for example, admits that its statements at the time bought the Biafran propaganda "hook, line and sinker."[1]

The war ended in January 1970 when Colonel Obasanjo's Third Marine Division captured Biafran Radio and Ojukwu fled to the Ivory Coast after commandeering a plane meant for the evacuation of sick children. With booming oil revenues and Gowon's policy of "No victors, no vanquished," Nigeria set about the task of rebuilding. But the Gowon administration pursued its plans to return Nigeria to civilian rule with markedly less vigor. Some of his advisers considered the possibility of establishing a one-party military-led government with Gowon, transformed into a civilian, at its head. That idea would return to tempt future dictators, including Babangida himself and his successor, Abacha. Gowon's Nigeria also moved closer to Ironsi's dream of a unitary state, with the central government assuming responsibility for health and education and radically increasing its share of export earnings. That would sow the seeds of conflict, particularly in the oil-rich delta region, twenty years later. Because national revenues, the so-called national cake, were distributed on the basis of population and not according to where they came from, minorities in the delta had little to show for the riches literally gushing from their land.

Given that population determined revenue allocation, provision of social services, legislative representation, and the establishment of everything from schools to roads to factories to post offices, there was little hope that the 1973 census would be any more objective than the failed attempts of a decade before. It was not. Provisional figures showing that the north had increased its share of the population to 64 percent and that the inhabitants of the mainly Yoruba Western Region had actually declined were rejected as farcical. The official results were never published.

In fact, several major demographic changes were under way. Agriculture and manufacturing fell victim to neglect while the oil boom spurred imports and convinced millions of people to migrate from their villages to the cities. Nigeria was fast becoming a model of a nonproductive economy addicted to petrodollars, ruled by a coterie of army officers and bureaucrats growing fat on contract kickbacks and siphoning off the oil revenues.

Gowon's inability to tame his twelve state governors, who were widely regarded as overbearing and corrupt, or his top government officials sparked renewed rumblings in the military and the public at large. On October 1, 1974, he dropped the bombshell in his independence anniversary broadcast: The 1976 date for a handover to civilian rule was "no longer realistic." That broadcast, like the 1966 coup, proved to be a turning point.

A group of colonels and lieutenant colonels, mainly Muslim and Christian northerners headed by Joseph Garba and Yar'Adua, decided it was time "to put a stop to the slide." Babangida said Yar'Adua first broached the subject with him while they drove to a soccer match: "We entered the car to go to the stadium, and he said, 'Look, do you think the situation will continue like this?' I said no. I suspected then that what he wanted to know was how my mind was thinking—a possible convert. We went to some of our very senior officers with our appraisal of the situation and told them of our intentions. They said, 'Okay, you boys have a point.' So we asked them to look the other way when it happened, and their attitude was, 'Okay, we will turn the other way.'"

I interrupted Babangida to point out that by this time the Nigerian military was no longer interested in purely soldierly affairs. It had become a very strange institution, with its junior officers plotting coups and telling their seniors to stand aside while they moved against the government. At first he seemed perplexed, as if wondering why anyone would doubt the right of the military to meddle in politics. When his answer eventually came, it was hardly convincing.

"Don't forget the junior officers are not unconcerned about the situation in the country," he said, raising his voice defensively. "The junior ones are very much in touch with the troops. So there is no breach between us and the preponderance of the members of the armed forces." Politics in Nigeria had become, in the immortal words of the Afro-beat singer Fela Kuti, an "Army Arrangement."

The senior officers approached by the colonels included Danjuma, by then a brigadier general, under whom Babangida had served in the civil war; Obasanjo; and Murtala Mohammed, the emotionally explosive general who had so nearly led the north into secession in the aftermath of the July 1966 revenge coup. Now the plotters wanted Mohammed to serve as commander in chief of a united Nigeria. Babangida said the colonels wanted him "from day one." He accepted, but Babangida remembered him warning his subordinates that "when you get me there, I'm not going to sit in there as a stooge. I have got my own mind and you are not going to kick me around."

Mohammed was as good as his word. His administration demonstrated a military can-do dynamism in its prosecution of the most radical reform in Nigeria's history. Chinua Achebe, in *The Trouble with Nigeria*, recounted the supposedly true story of the first morning of the new regime, when the nation's notoriously tardy civil servants were at their desks at 7:30 A.M.

Yet many of Mohammed's administration's policies, however widely acclaimed at the time, proved damaging in the long run. The government expanded its powers throughout society, assuming control of the universities, primary education, and all television and radio broadcasting. The Supreme Military Council brought labor unions under stricter discipline; established a secret service, the National Security Organization; and embarked on an exercise of "cleansing" ten thousand allegedly incompetent and corrupt public servants. The purge proved to be a body blow to morale from which the civil service has never recovered, according to the then inspector general of police M. D. Yusufu: "All the old assurances that the civil service had of staying in the office—they cannot be sacked without due process—were thrown overboard."

But to this day Murtala Mohammed is revered as Nigeria's greatest leader, the paradigm of the fearless redeemer who valiantly battles the dark forces of greed, avarice, and corruption. In Lagos, that steamy hotbed of antinorthern sentiment, the international airport is named after him; that he was a former northern secessionist does not matter. Such a high level of genuine affection is due in part to the shortness of his reign. On February 13, 1976, after just six months in office, Murtala

Mohammed was assassinated in a Lagos go-slow on his way to work during a coup attempt by officers from Nigeria's middle belt. The elder brother of the coup leader, Colonel Bukar Dimka, was married to Gowon's sister.

This was the first military coup that the vast majority of Nigerians opposed, and news of the assassination sparked immediate public protests, especially among radical university students. Obasanjo reluctantly assumed the position of head of state. Unlike Ironsi, who had treated the 1966 "January Boys" with kid gloves, the Obasanjo administration executed more than thirty coup plotters, including Dimka and the minister for defense, Major General I. D. Bissalla. Because Obasanjo was a Yoruba Christian and the chief of Army staff, Danjuma, was a Christian from the middle belt, a balanced administration required that the highest-ranking northern Muslim officer, Shehu Musa Yar'Adua, serve as Obasanjo's deputy. The alliance of Danjuma, Obasanjo, and Yar'Adua proved to be a potent force that ushered in the first elected government and that would come to power again in the next elections permitted by the military, nearly two decades later.

During Obasanjo's three years in power, Nigeria appeared to be settling down. A new constitution was drafted with a U.S.-style presidency and separation of powers, and local governments were given greater autonomy. Obasanjo carried through the transition to civilian rule and accomplished something that Babangida would so famously balk at doing fourteen years later: He handed over power to an elected president. Doing so was not without controversy. Shagari of the northern-oriented National Party of Nigeria (NPN) emerged as the clear winner, with 34 percent compared to 29 percent for the Yoruba leader Chief Awolowo and 17 percent for the Igbo stalwart Nnamdi Azikiwe, who had been the first Nigerian president when the office was purely ceremonial. But Shagari apparently failed to meet the complicated constitutional requirement that the victorious candidate gain at least

25 percent of the vote in two-thirds of the nineteen states. The Supreme Court interpreted the law rather liberally by ruling that because Shagari had obtained the necessary 25 percent in twelve states and 25 percent of two-thirds in the thirteenth, he should be declared president. Obasanjo's decision to respect the court decision and thus thwart Awolowo's challenge earned him the reputation as a traitor among many Yorubas but wide acclaim both in the north and abroad.

Public disenchantment with the Shagari government set in quickly. The first wave of the religious riots that would plague the north for years to come erupted in December 1980. A radical Muslim sect led by Muhammed Marwa, commonly known as the Maitatsine ("the one who continues to curse"), mobilized the young urban poor in a series of bloody uprisings first in Kano and later in Kaduna, Maiduguri, and Yola. Several thousand people died in the uprisings. In 1982 tensions between Christians and Muslims exploded in a wave of violence that again started in Kano and spread to Kaduna state. As the flames of political unrest spread, Shagari at times responded with an iron fist. Opposition party newspapers that published critical articles were subjected to temporary closure. The number of policemen rose from 10,000 in 1979 to more than 100,000. The government established the Mobile Police, a rough-and-ready paramilitary force whose practice of shooting first and asking questions later earned it the nickname Kill and Go.

In August 1983 new elections were held, but by most accounts they were a farce, characterized by rigging, violence, bribery, and wildly inflated voter turnouts. The NPN unleashed a no-holds-barred campaign to transform Nigeria into an effectively one-party state, and the judiciary and the electoral agency, known as the Federal Electoral Commission (FEDECO), simply could not withstand the pressure.

There had been talk among military officers of ousting Shagari as early as 1981, but Babangida and his cohorts bided their time until the climate was right. Babangida's own words betrayed his motives: "We in the military waited for an opportunity. There was the media frenzy about how bad the election was, massively rigged, corruption, the economy gone completely bad, threat of secession by people who felt aggrieved. There was frustration within society and it was not unusual to hear statements like, the worst military dictatorship is better than this democratic government. Nigerians always welcome military intervention because we have not yet developed mentally the values and virtues of democracy."

"You admit you were waiting for an opportunity?" I asked.

"You see we are very smart people. We don't intervene when we know the climate is not good for it or the public will not welcome it. We wait until there is frustration in the society. In all the coups, you find there has always been one frustration or the other. Any time there is frustration, we step in. And then there is a demonstration welcoming the redeemers." At that, the evil genius broke into a deep self-mocking chuckle at the notion of the military as redeemers.

As cynical as his words might have sounded, Babangida spoke a truth that many Nigerian intellectuals have been loathe to admit: The general populace and sometimes even the most strident pro-democracy activists repeatedly applauded soldiers who overthrew governments they did not support. It happened in 1966 with the January Boys coup, in 1975 with the overthrow of Gowon's military regime, and in 1983 with the ouster of Shagari's elected administration. The pattern was to repeat itself in 1985 when Babangida himself came to power and again in 1993 when Abacha, the man later reviled as Nigeria's worst dictator, assumed control.

Businessmen, politicians, and media tycoons played a vital role in the coups. "We couldn't have done it without collaborators in the civil society—collaborators in the media, collaborators among people who have the means. Because the means were not easily available but we received some from people who were convinced it was the right thing to do."

I asked what they expected in return.

"Of course, they normally get something back. The media is satisfied that they waged a war against a bad government, fought it to a standstill, and pulled it down. The elite who participate want recognition, maybe patronage as time goes by."

It was the old story. Everyone wanted the quick fix, a strongman to put everything right, without considering the long-term consequences. Especially guilty were the politicians who lost elections and the businessmen who lost contracts. Often they were one and the same. One such man was Abiola, the soldiers' millionaire business partner who later emerged as the rather unlikely symbol of Nigeria's struggle for democracy. In 1982 Abiola was an influential member of Shagari's NPN, well out of the Yoruba mainstream that backed Awolowo's United Party of Nigeria. He used his newspaper group, Concord, to attack Awolowo. For Abiola, the NPN was his best route to the presidency. Because Shagari, a northerner, was expected to give way to a Yoruba man in the NPN presidential nomination in 1983, Abiola figured he would get the nod. The only problem was that Shagari decided to run again. Abiola quit the party.

At the time of the coup, the friendship between Abiola and Babangida went back nine years. They had met in 1974 in Lagos when Abiola was peddling British Racal radio systems to the military. Babangida, a commander in a reconnaissance regiment, was sent to evaluate Abiola's wares. "From that time, the relationship developed and he was always around."

Babangida confirmed the widely held popular belief that Abiola had supported both coups, against Shagari and later against Buhari, with money and editorial support from his Concord newspapers. "He did. He said so. Of course he was also very good in trying to mould the thinking of the media. We relied on him a lot for that. So there was both the media support and the financial support."

Babangida was at the center of the December 31, 1983, coup that installed Buhari and his deputy, Major General Tunde Idiagbon. Initially hailed, Buhari's regime quickly developed into the country's most draconian government to date. "Everybody was frustrated. People were unnecessarily jailed," Babangida said without mentioning the fact that he had been Buhari's chief of Army staff, effectively the number three man in the regime. "The society was like a police state where you didn't feel comfortable even to talk to your wife." After continuing to describe Buhari's unpopularity, Babangida made another slip: "There is a lot that was going in our favor. So we seized the moment."

The bloodless coup d'état against Buhari, however much justified on his record of repression and continued economic decline, was merely a step on Babangida's career path. "At the risk of being called immodest, if there is any military government that prepared itself before it went in, it's our government. We knew what we wanted. We knew what areas to address, especially the economy. We read the barometer of the society and we knew what the people wanted."

But what about Babangida's friendship with Buhari, I asked.

Sounding like his old friend Abiola, Babangida said with a laugh, "To be able to stage a coup you have to be close to somebody." But when I restated the question, his voice, for the first time, snapped with impatience.

"Yeah, okay. There was Buhari the man, Buhari the military officer, and Buhari my colleague, and Buhari my friend. All that was there. But immediately after the coup, we saw also another Buhari, completely different from the person. It was like Abacha. He's my friend. The other aspect of Abacha or Buhari, they bottled it up and worked within the outside of the bottle. Eventually the bottle burst and we began to see a different person altogether." He paused for a moment. "I was a very good friend of Buhari, there's no doubt about it."

On the eve of the coup against Buhari, Abacha was the commander of the strategic division in Ibadan, the sprawling Yoruba city in the southwest. If the coup were to succeed, Babangida needed Abacha. "Nobody could get him to be involved except me because of our relationship. If it were any other person, he would have gone to the side of Buhari. But when I sat him down, he said, 'You are my chief, anything you want I will do.' So the personal relationship also helped in trying to recruit people into this unholy alliance." There was that knowing chuckle again.

The unholy alliance brought Babangida, then a forty-four-year-old major general, to power on August 27, 1985, riding a wave of public acclaim. He was the charismatic "redeemer." From the start it was clear that his administration would be different and that Babangida was a master of public relations, both at home and abroad. Newspaper editorials supported him, as did most Western countries because of his stated commitment to their cherished three D's of Third World development: deregulation of the economy, devaluation of the currency, and democracy.

His first few years in office were a whirlwind of activity. Babangida was not out just to reform Nigeria; his stated goal was to revolutionize its social order. Intellectuals were brought in to fashion a new political system, one that would do away with the corrupt "old breed" politicians and restructure the economy. Journalists and human rights activists detained under Buhari were set free. Dozens of state agencies were set up to deal with unemployment, repair roads, and educate the masses in the democratic way of life.

Not content with his predecessors' position as military head of state, Babangida assumed the post of executive president, which gave him the authority to appoint the military service chiefs, the high command, and the membership of the Armed Forces Ruling Council. Until 1990 he was also the minister of defense. Total power was concentrated in his hands.

Initially Babangida proved himself the master of political machinations. The Maradona of Nigeria spoke of democracy and economic reform, and the press, especially Abiola's *Concord* newspaper, lapped it up. He promised to lead a stable transition to civilian rule and to quit office by October 1990. He held a public debate on the merits of accepting a loan from the IMF, which most Nigerians opposed because an agreement would entail severe austerity measures. Then he turned around and announced a home-grown Structural Adjustment Program (SAP), every bit as austere as the IMF recommendations, and dressed it up in nationalist rhetoric. Again, his actions initially drew public applause.

The first dark cloud had arrived in October 1986 with the assassination by parcel bomb of Dele Giwa, the *Newswatch* magazine editor. A day before his death, according to a leading human rights group, the Constitutional Rights Project, Babangida's national security adviser, Halilu Akilu, had telephoned Giwa's wife to ask for directions to their home. When the package with the bomb arrived, it was marked, "From the office of the C-in-C [short for commander in chief]". As Giwa opened the parcel over breakfast, he said, "This must be from the president." Those were his last words.

If comfortable with his subject, Babangida could be self-assured, eloquent, and witty, but when he was not, he seemed fragile and had trouble completing a sentence. When I asked what happened to Dele Giwa, Babangida stumbled for an answer.

"It was emotive. There was a lot of passion. I think one of the problems was that people, or more or less the media ... up to now nobody seemed to say okay let's look at these things dispassionately. But from the word go, the government did it. That's the first reaction. The media, his friends, and most important, the lawyers, the crusaders in this thing. Then anybody who would want to say something different from the popularly held belief, you were seen as part of it. So they succeeded in getting only one side of the story dished up. But we carried out investigations. We had leads. There were questions we asked but nobody went into this thing about these so-called questions that we asked. But the circumstantial aspects of it ... Akilu spoke to him twenty-four hours before. But somebody had to talk to somebody. Anything could happen after you wanted to talk to somebody. That's the harsh reality of life. But unfortunately nobody wanted to listen. I suspect the media, whatever, human rights groups, if they tried to look at this dispassionately like normal intelligent people would, maybe we would have gone somewhere. But people have already made up their minds that government is guilty, period. The report, they are not interested."

Haruna interrupted to ask about the existence of a report on the murder, which he, rather implausibly given his knowledge of the government, had never heard of. Again, Babangida seemed lost.

"Yes. ...It was all blown out in this frenzy by you guys the media. ...A lot of vital links and vital information were lost. So the report was not conclusive. They were almost getting there. But they wouldn't allow the police because they said the police ... the government, Akilu, killed him."

By the late 1980s Babangida found himself in the odd situation of enjoying more support abroad than he did at home. When Prime Minister Margaret Thatcher of Britain visited Nigeria in 1988, Babangida said, she suggested that he exchange his military uniform for civilian clothes and run for president. "She visited me and said, 'Look, you could get the support of the international community. You are wise, you have the structural adjustment program, the only thing that is missing is democracy. From what we see, other people have done it before.'" Babangida said that the first person to tell him to run as a civilian candidate was Abiola.

But Babangida decided he would not make a good civilian leader. "I would be operating under a different environment. I give a command, it's carried out. Then I would have to go and lobby, to go and plead." Submitting himself to democratic scrutiny was not an attractive prospect.

While Western-dominated institutions such as the World Bank were holding Nigeria up as a model of economic reform in Africa, the so-called anti-SAP riots against his policies accelerated at home. However attractive his promises of democracy and economic restructuring might have sounded to the foreign ear, there were inherent contradictions in the idea that a military regime might transform Nigeria into a democratic system at a time of severe economic hardship. Under Babangida the government's weak fiscal discipline and the presidency's direct control of the Central Bank doomed the SAP. Oil licenses were granted to indigenous companies run by IBB cronies. While rampant unemployment and rising inflation slammed the middle classes and the urban poor, a relatively small group of banks, speculators, corrupt government officials, and importers of cheap foreign goods prospered.

Religious passions were inflamed when Babangida attempted to register Nigeria as a full member of the Organization of Islamic Countries in 1986. The decision set the stage for Muslim-Christian clashes that rocked Kaduna State, Bauchi, and Kano over the next several years.

Babangida responded to these riots and rising domestic criticism the old-fashioned military way: repression. He banned former politicians as corrupt "old breeds" and vowed famously that "we have not chosen, and we have not sought to choose, those who will succeed us. We have only decided on those who would not." Claiming that the road to democracy was "a learning process," Babangida pushed the date of his promised handover to civilian rule back to October 1992. Leaders of the major human rights groups, such as the Civil Liberties Organization and the Constitutional Rights Project, had their passports confiscated. Looking back on it now, he dismissed his critics as "eggheads" and portrayed himself as a victim of "a grand media and intellectual conspiracy."

———

BABANGIDA was about to taste some of his own medicine. The wide-spread public frustration that had facilitated his various coup plots of the past was now threatening his hold on power. In April 1990 a group of young officers, mainly from the minorities of Delta State, struck. In a radio broadcast the coup leader, Major Gideon Orkar, announced an end to the northern domination of Nigeria by excising the states of Bauchi, Borno, Kano, Katsina, and Sokoto. The coup, he said, was carried out "for the marginalized, oppressed and enslaved people of the middle belt and the south with a view to freeing ourselves and our children yet unborn from eternal slavery and colonization by a clique of this country."

Had the putsch succeeded (the final outcome was very close), it probably would have followed the pattern of the January 1966 coup in sparking a civil war. The plotters' plan to excise the north from the rest of Nigeria enjoyed wide support in the south. University students cheered the news and maps were quickly printed showing the "new" Nigeria, without northern states. But it failed.

That day was the most difficult in Babangida's life, but it did not come as a complete surprise. "I expected a coup any day. From day one I was there. I knew somehow, some day there could be a coup. Because we took it over by force, somebody is going to try to take by force."

On the night of the rebellion Babangida had just gone to sleep after watching a video in his quarters at Dodan barracks on Lagos's Ikoyi Island. Maryam woke him at 2:00 A.M. after she had glanced out the window and seen soldiers moving around. He told her to go back to sleep, but she said, "No, you will want to get up. This is serious." Babangida peered through the window and saw armed troops milling about. Within minutes firing started, and his aide-de-camp, U. K. Bello, telephoned to say something was wrong. Bello came around to the house and dropped off a walkie-talkie before leaving to investigate. Babangida and Bello were in contact for a few minutes until Bello reached the rear gate of the barracks. Babangida never spoke to him again.

Shortly after aides evacuated his family, the rebels opened up with heavy barrages of mortar fire. "It was hell," recalled Babangida fidgeting nervously. The bombardment was so heavy that he decided to flee as well, and together with his small security detachment he escaped and went into hiding at a safe house.

In his version of the story, Babangida quickly established communication links with Abacha, the local brigade commander, and Raji Rasaki, the then governor of Lagos State to rally support. But that was not exactly what happened, according to one of his closest business partners. Babangida, he said, was so traumatized that he broke down in tears while at the safe house. He did contact Abacha but refused to reveal his location for fear that Abacha was behind the coup.

When I asked Babangida where Abacha was that morning, he feigned shock. "That's a very horrible question. I never thought you would ask me that." Abacha was with a girlfriend at his guest house at 70 Alexander Road, and the coup plotters knew it. Although they shot up the house, they could not find him because he was in a bedroom concealed behind a paneled wall. Abacha's driver Sule, seeing the danger, drove off to draw the rebels away and was wounded. Eventually Abacha's son, Ibrahim, retrieved his father from his hiding place and ferried him back to his official residence at Flagstaff House. There he, Babangida, and a number of officers met to organize the counterattack. By midday the attempted coup was over.

While Babangida was at Flagstaff House, an ambulance brought Bello's body. "It really shattered me," he recalled. "I never, never expected it. I fought in the war; I sat with some of my officers and soldiers and I'd see them shot right there and then. But that was the first one that really affected me."

"Some say the coup was a turning point in your government," I suggested.

"It was a turning point, I agree. Everybody agrees that from 1985 to '90, economically we were doing well."

"Maybe you should have left at that time," I said.

"That's right."

But he did not quit, and his regime began to show its darker side. At least sixty-seven officers involved in the coup were executed. The government hounded the press, seizing entire editions of magazines that published critical articles. It arrested human rights activists and student leaders and promoted divisive splits within professional organizations such as the Nigerian Bar Association. "We said we would respect human rights," Babangida explained, "but we would not abdicate our responsibility if you crossed the line. Human rights stopped where my rights started."

At this point Babangida again lost his concentration. He indulged in rather bizarre assertions that his detentions of strident government critics were humane, even when certain individuals, such as the president of the Campaign for Democracy, Dr. Beko Ransome-Kuti, were arrested in the middle of the night and taken to unknown destinations. "When we arrested people we gave them food, we gave them shelter, we allowed them to see television, we give them water, allowed members of their families to come and see them. That's even human rights in detention, you know. Others did not allow this."

"But Beko was taken away in his pajamas," I said.

"That's all right."

We turned to Babangida's reputation for corruption. A government commission headed by the economist Pius Okigbo in 1995 found that during Babangida's time in office and during the first several months of the Abacha regime, more than $12 billion could not be accounted for.

The master dribbler searched for an answer. "Common sense.

68

Again, passion, emotion." Babangida began a tortured explanation of the famous case of the Gulf War windfall, in which several billion dollars' worth of oil revenues, earned from the sudden rise in prices following the U.S. attack on Iraq, simply disappeared. He denied any wrongdoing, of course.

By 1992 Babangida had pushed back the date of a handover to civilian rule once again, this time to January 1993. The military permitted only two political parties to contest office—the National Republican Convention and the Social Democratic Party (SDP). The military government's sponsorship of them was so complete that critics described them as "parastatals."

Twenty-three candidates contested presidential primaries that like past elections proved to be scandalous in their incidence of rigging and vote buying. The mainly southern press was incensed that the three leading candidates, Shinkafi, Adamu Ciroma, and Yar'Adua, were northerners. Babangida was urged to cancel the primaries and bar the politicians involved, and when he did he received almost universal praise. "The media killed that process, but we helped them to bury it."

The banning of established politicians left the emerging political process in chaos and made the January 1993 handover date untenable. Babangida announced a new deadline, August 27, 1993, the eighth anniversary of his coup d'état against his erstwhile friend Buhari. The door was now open to a second tier of politicians, and Abiola was at the top of the new list.

Abiola sought Babangida's approval of his candidacy. "I told him people would criticize me for handing over to him. He wanted it. I told him what the problems were, he thought he could overcome them, and I gave him the go ahead." Babangida claimed to have been the biggest financial supporter of the Abiola campaign. "Not a single person in the part of the world he comes from, even his friends, gave more money to him than I did."

Abiola's opponent was a little-known northern businessman, Bashir

Tofa, who was particularly close to Babangida's security chief, Halilu Akilu. But Tofa never stood a chance. While Abiola's Yoruba background won him allegiance in the south, northerners appreciated his financial and religious commitment to Islam. Northern radicals and students believed he would reverse the military governments' tendency to starve education for resources. Still others viewed Abiola as the best means of forcing Babangida out of office.

But fears that Babangida had a hidden agenda to hold on to power gained credence with the appearance of mysterious pro-military organizations, such as the Association for a Better Nigeria and the Third Eye. These groups actively lobbied for the army to remain in office in violation of decrees outlawing any attempt to stop the transition. On the eve of the election the director of the U.S. Information Service, Michael O'Brien, issued a statement warning the government against canceling the vote. Babangida expelled him.

Overall, the electoral process, sullied by the banning of the most popular politicians, repeated changes in the rules, and general manipulation by the military government, could hardly be called democratic. Neither the political parties themselves nor the two candidates were products of anything close to the popular will. They were in fact creations of the military. Nevertheless, Nigerian and international observers judged the June 12, 1993, vote to be one of the freest and fairest ever in Nigeria.

Most Nigerians cast their ballots as a vote of no confidence in the military. As Dr. Ransome-Kuti later put it, "Before the election, there was no difference between Abiola, the military, Babangida. One viewed him as part of the problems of the country. But we had a running battle with Babangida, and he just had to go. The military had to go."

Abiola won nineteen states to Tofa's eleven, but before the final vote count could be announced, Babangida annulled the elections. He and his officials gave a number of explanations for the decision—ranging from debts the government owed to Abiola, court challenges to the vote, the National Election Commission's lack of readiness, and opposition to Abiola by senior army officers—but none of them were convincing. Most were patently absurd.

When we discussed the annulment, again Babangida suggested that he was looking for an excuse to do it. "It was difficult. But you know Moshood Abiola didn't help matters himself. And the people handling him did not help matters. So maybe that gave us the courage to do it."

Despite the fact that Abiola broke the mold of presidential politics in Nigeria by winning votes across regional and religious barriers, Babangida attempted to argue that his victory actually threatened Nigeria's unity. "The Yoruba were saying that you are all going to go; it's going to be our time. It happened even outside Aso Rock. 'This time you will not be talking Hausa in this place,'" he quoted them as saying.

But Babangida's version of events did not bear close scrutiny. It was his annulment, not Abiola's election, that threatened to tear the country apart along ethnic and regional lines. During the crisis I was in Lagos, where pro-democracy demonstrations had degenerated into riots that cost upwards of one hundred lives. I drove over to the Iddo Motor Park one morning to find hundreds of people boarding buses and taxis to flee the city. One of those waiting to leave was Udoka Okoli, a twenty-nine-year-old spare parts dealer from the mainly Igbo city of Onitsha on the banks of the Niger River. He had sent his wife and six children back home six days before, and he was in no doubt about who was to blame for the crisis. "We are leaving because Babangida refuses to hand over. If he does, there will be no problem." He predicted "a civil war" unless Babangida respected the election result. "The president said there would be fresh elections. We don't want a fresh election because the last one was clear to everyone."

Babangida also claimed that Abiola had made promises to unnamed outside interests in order to raise money for his campaign, even though Babangida, by his own admission, had himself been the single largest contributor.

Lastly, Babangida argued that Abiola would have made "a lousy president" and "would not have lasted six months." Abacha, he said, would have overthrown him. "The military would have toppled him because all the machinery for toppling was on the ground. Abacha would have been the head of state in a violent coup." Some of his advisers told him that Abacha was scheming against the elections, he admitted, but "I did not believe them because of my long-term friendship. But I also knew that at that time, he could only pull it off after I left office."

By August a wave of demonstrations, strikes, and pressure from the top military command had forced Babangida to relinquish office. On the day of his departure, he installed a toothless Interim National Government headed by the Yoruba businessman Chief Shonekan. Before leaving, Babangida decided to retire the entire military high command, but at the last minute he withdrew Abacha's name from the list of those to be retired and named him defense minister. One of Babangida's close business partners later told me that Abacha actually removed his own name from the list.

Babangida said his close relationship with Abacha influenced his decision not to retire him. "It was being loyal to a friend that's all. But the crux of the whole thing is when eventually we decided that we were going to go, I feared that there could be a younger officers' intervention in the government. I knew that this country could not afford the luxury of having lieutenant colonels and below as leaders. I felt we needed somebody senior that this country knew. The name alone could be a stabilizing influence."

With Abacha in the government, Shonekan's power was illusory. He was not even allowed to occupy Aso Rock or use the fleet of cars reserved for the head of state. On November 17, 1993, Abacha forced Shonekan out of office in a bloodless coup that was acclaimed by some human rights activists, including the maverick lawyer, Gani Fawehinmi. Some in the pro-democracy movement believed Abacha's promises that he would rule for only a short time before installing Abiola as president.

For the next five years Babangida remained in virtual exile within his hilltop Minna home, occasionally attending public functions but for the most part remaining out of the limelight. He watched as Abacha picked off leading figures one by one and even put Babangida himself under surveillance. Ibrahim Dasuki, who as the sultan of Sokoto was the spiritual leader of Nigeria's Muslims, was removed from office and jailed. Obasanjo and Yar'Adua were arrested, tried, and jailed on charges of plotting to overthrow Abacha's government—charges that Babangida called "a frame-up." Yar'Adua died in jail after being injected with some unknown substance. Abacha's agents attempted to inject Obasanjo too, but he was able to avoid the syringe. He languished for three years in a remote prison with only the Koran and the Bible until his release following Abacha's death.

By 1998 Abacha was considering eliminating Babangida himself, an Abacha confidant told me, because "he knew that Babangida opposed his plan to become a civilian president. He asked me several times, 'Should I hit him, should I hit him?'" There is even a school of thought that believes Babangida had a hand in Abacha's death, both because he feared for his life and because Abacha's plan to remain in office as a civilian could lead Nigeria to a conflict that would engulf him. Babangida would only say, "He died naturally. The autopsy said so. I cannot offer a contrary view." And of course, Abiola was detained after declaring himself president in 1994 and remained in solitary confinement until his death four years later.

By all accounts Babangida is a wealthy man, perhaps the wealthiest individual in Nigeria. And he bears a major—many Nigerians say the largest—responsibility for the crisis Nigeria finds itself in. But he remains ambitious, and it is doubtful that Nigeria has heard the last of him. He was reported to be a major financier of the Obasanjo election campaign. He has imported state-of-the-art equipment to publish a newspaper, to be known as *New Heritage*, and has begun building a new private university in Kaduna.

I asked him if he would return to public office one day. He answered, "[As] an elder statesman, yes."

"But as a politician?"

"Politics no."

"That is completely ruled out?"

"Ruled out for the time being."

Finally, I asked Babangida whether Nigeria would survive the rising political, religious, and ethnic tensions.

"I believe in what Obasanjo used to say, 'God is a Nigerian,'" he replied. "Sometimes you think the whole world is going to end. But no matter the turbulence, no matter the bumps, you realize there's always a way out."

4

The Ogoni Wars

I am a man of ideas in and out of prison—my ideas will live.

KEN SARO-WIWA

THE PIERCING VOICES of a dozen shirtless boys playing in the shade of a palm tree echoed through the family compound as I approached the house of the patriarch's youngest wife. The old man spent most of his days there cooped up in a dark room gripped by depression. "After what they did to his son," said a family friend who knocked for me, "he's just waiting to die." A few moments passed before a voice shouted, "Who is there?" rather gruffly from behind the wooden door. Eventually a tall, thin man, a remarkably spry ninety-two, emerged unsteadily onto the front porch, his eyes blinking rapidly to adjust to the oppressive light of the early afternoon. After we exchanged a brief perfunctory greeting, he returned to his silence and shuffled in his sandals through the dust toward the main house, where our meeting would take place. Leading me into a large cement-block room with a small wooden table and two chairs stationed by an open window, he gestured for me to sit down. Groups of youngsters, from tiny little boys and girls to young men in their late teens, piled into the room to form an impromptu audience.

Chief Jim Beeson Wiwa's son Ken Saro-Wiwa was the writer and political activist who led a movement to demand greater revenues from the oil pumped from the land of his Ogoni people. The campaign against the government and Royal/Dutch Shell for a greater share of oil wealth, political autonomy, and an environmental cleanup drew worldwide attention and helped to spark what has effectively become a low-level guerrilla war throughout the Niger River delta. However small and insignificant their group appeared to be within the country's immensely complex ethnic mosaic, the Ogonis constituted a threat to those who ran Nigeria. By targeting the oil industry, the fountain of more than 90 percent of Nigeria's export earnings, they had tweaked the vital artery that kept the heart of military rule beating. Their claims raised unsettling questions about the final destination of the hundreds of billions of dollars Nigeria had earned in oil revenues since becoming a world-class oil exporter. For his troubles, Saro-Wiwa was executed in November 1995, along with eight other Ogoni activists, after being convicted on murder charges by what international jurists described as a kangaroo court.

Three years later, Chief Wiwa stayed in his compound in the village of Bane unable to forget. "I have not been able to go out anywhere," he said. "This is my own house, and I stay here waiting for God's time."

I explained that this was my first trip to Ogoniland in five years. My last visit had been in August 1993, when Ogoniland was under a virtual state of siege and Ken was in the hospital recovering from a flare-up in his congenital heart condition after a month-long spell in police custody. I told Chief Wiwa that I had also met his grandson, Ken Jr., recently in London. He nodded. I asked if he could tell me about

Ken, what he was like growing up, and why he had become involved in such a tragic confrontation with the military dictatorship and one of the world's biggest oil companies.

He did not respond immediately, but his eyes betrayed a look of indifference bordering on hostility that took me aback. Visitors to this part of Africa customarily receive a warm welcome; their hosts are usually prepared to spend all day in friendly discussions. I put the lack of response down to the fact that he was not comfortable with English. But just as I turned to ask a young man sitting on the floor behind me if he could interpret, the old man perked up and said, "First, I have a question for you."

He glanced out the window and sighed. "Would you be able to say what you see with your eyes?" he asked. Of course, I said, that is my job. Initially I thought he did not hear my answer, but I quickly realized he simply did not believe me. "Two weeks ago a group of people came from the United Nations. One of them was an elderly man. I asked him if he would be able to say what he saw with his eyes. He said yes. But eventually I think he did not say what he saw. We heard that they said that everything is improving in Nigeria." He shook his head. "I told him that there is no peace in Nigeria. He who is an elderly man like myself, who came to see for himself, should not act like that." That earlier visitor was Soli Sorajee, the UN human rights investigator who traveled to Nigeria in November 1998 to gauge the situation following Abacha's death.

Chief Wiwa leaned back in his chair, muttering "Nigeria is sick" and "the Nigerian government is wicked," before snapping at the restless gathering of youngsters to keep quiet. A few minutes before he had appeared reticent to speak, but now he was in full flow. "Today Nigeria is shouting that they have made peace in Ogoni. What kind of peace? Our position today is worse. Look at our children here. See how they are. No school; they have no education. And yet, the resources of Nigeria come from Ogoni oil. Perhaps as you go you will see soldiers on the road. If we want to go to farm, we must pay them. We pay them before we can go to the market. When you are coming here, you can see the Primary Health Care Clinic there with no roof. They said it was a clinic for our children, but for the past five years it has been like that. What kind of peace is that? We leave it in the care of God who sees and knows what is going on in Nigeria. What a miserable life we have." He paused and then said, "It is a surprise that so many people who come here to ask me things, they do not say what they see with their eyes."

Our conversation ran into the late afternoon. Chief Wiwa reminisced about Ken, his determination to succeed in school, the scholarships he had won, the various books and articles he had written. Ken saw himself as the Wiayor, a mythical Ogoni character who comes down from heaven to liberate his people. "He believed that God had sent him," Chief said. "He called me two times and said, 'Papa, don't you want me to do what God has sent me for?' and I said, 'if God has sent you, then go. After all, God sent Moses to Egypt.'" He also told me of the day he learned of his son's hanging. "Somebody came into the room and told me that my son is dead. The first time they hanged him, they did not succeed. He moved his eyes around to see the others. Then he said, 'God take my soul.'"

Minutes after leaving the village of Bane and rejoining the main highway, it was clear that Chief Wiwa had not exaggerated about having to pay the security forces for the right to circulate. A group of soldiers in full battle dress, supposedly part of the local anticrime unit known as Operation Flush, was standing in the middle of the road stopping all traffic and offering drivers the inevitable option: Either they parted with some cash, or they submitted to a vehicle inspection and a round of rather unpleasant interrogation. Most of the motorists had already made their choice. A soldier stepped out in the road, a vehicle slowed, and a driver extended an arm out the window with a 20-naira bill, worth about a quarter. As we pulled up, a line formed. One by one the cars passed through the checkpoint and the soldiers on duty collected the unofficial tolls. Twenty minutes down the road the police got their own chance to fleece the passing vehicles. So it went as we headed for Port Harcourt, the exhaust-choked capital of Rivers State. Every few miles or so another group of armed men had set up operations on the road, demanding bribes from the people they were employed to protect.

A roadside billboard describing the Ogoni kingdom of Eleme as "the heart of the Nigerian economy" seemed like a bad joke. The designation was due to the presence of a petrochemical complex, a fertilizer plant, and an oil refinery, though like much of the rest of the economy, the heart appeared to be in a state of cardiac arrest. Most of the community lived in rundown mud-brick houses. Hundreds of little barefoot children and young men loitered around the road with nothing to do, while others took a dip in creeks that stank of oil. Despite the proximity of the refinery, most gas stations in Eleme and the rest of Ogoniland were closed for lack of fuel, and motorists had to drive into Port Harcourt to buy gasoline on the black market at five times the official price. Eleme's heartbeat could be seen in the giant flame, as big as a house, erupting from a flow station to the north of the road. The flame, which burns twenty-four hours a day, was a constant reminder that the resources of this area were being drained away.

———

KEN SARO-WIWA liked to think of himself first and foremost as a writer, although not many of his contemporaries rated him among such Nigerian heavyweights as Wole Soyinka, Chinua Achebe, Ben Okri, and Amos Tutuola. Yet he produced an impressive array of novels, often hilariously polemical newspaper columns, children's books, plays, and poems. In Nigeria he was perhaps best known for *Basi & Co.*, a widely popular television soap opera about scheming Lagos area boys, which he wrote and produced in the mid-1980s. Some of the most thought-provoking writing on the Biafran war can be found in his autobiographical account, *On a Darkling Plain,* and his novel *Sozaboy,* rendered brilliantly in "pidgin," a mishmash of English, Portuguese, and various African languages that is the lingua franca of coastal West Africa. Much as he liked to champion the power of the pen, however, Saro-Wiwa wielded the spoken word with equally devastating effect. A gifted orator in front of a crowd and an adept charmer of international and domestic opinion, he moved easily among foreign and Nigerian businessmen, army officers, and the leading liberal lights in the West.

His cause was Ogoniland, a minute parcel of land of about 404 square miles in southeastern Nigeria and home to close to 500,000 souls. Over the years, 634 million barrels of oil worth approximately $30 billion had been pumped from Ogoniland alone through a network of ninety-six wells hooked up to five flow stations. The Shell Petroleum Development Corporation (SPDC) ran the system with its joint venture partners the Nigerian National Petroleum Corporation (NNPC), Agip, and Elf.

In return, the Ogonis received much of the harm but few of the benefits the oil industry had to offer. Poverty is endemic in Ogoniland and the Niger delta as a whole. Education and health facilities are primitive at best, and few Ogoni homes enjoy the most basic services, such as electricity and running water. Under the government's revenue-sharing scheme, first 1.5 percent, then 3 percent, and most recently 13 percent of income earned in a particular area was supposed to be returned to that region. The fact that a succession of military governments have failed to honor these commitments is the one thing on which Ogoni radicals and Western corporate executives agree.

In a few short years, beginning in 1990, the Ogonis had formed a remarkably potent political alliance that cut across clans, class, age, and traditional and Western beliefs. In doing so, they carried the voice of an isolated ethnic group to the forefront of Nigerian and, at certain moments, international politics. For a while their Movement for the Survival of the Ogoni People (MOSOP) represented the most cogent opposition force to military rule in Nigeria. As MOSOP's spokesman, Saro-Wiwa became the darling of Greenpeace, International PEN, the Sierra Club, the UN Working Group for Indigenous People, even Western corporations with a conscience such as the Body Shop. Foreign film crews produced sympathetic—some said unquestioning—documentaries with melodramatic titles such as *The Drilling Fields, Delta Force,* and *The Heat of the Moment.* Saro-Wiwa was showered with international tributes ranging from the Right to Livelihood Award, honoring those who work "for the survival of mankind," to the Hellman/Hammett Award of the Free Expression Project of Human Rights Watch.

Yet Saro-Wiwa knew Western support only meant so much. I remember speaking with him as he was recovering at the university hospital in Port Harcourt in August 1993. It was clear that his confidence in the power of international solidarity was waning. "The West worries about elephants," he said with an air of disgust. "They stop the export of Rhino horns and things like that and yet they cannot worry about human beings dying?"

TO HIS ADMIRERS Ken Saro-Wiwa was akin to a saint, a diminutive, courageous man with a keen intellect and a mighty voice. He trumpeted the plight of a tiny ethnic group whose people, powerless victims of globalization, were pitted in an unequal struggle against a corrupt military dictatorship and an uncaring transnational oil company. To his many critics within and outside of Ogoniland, Saro-Wiwa emerged as the archetypal demagogue who exploited the real pain of his fellow Ogonis to feed an ego as big and complex as Nigeria itself. However one looked at it, the life and death of Ken Saro-Wiwa foretold the tragedy that befell the Ogoni people and ultimately the entire nation.

Reputed at one time to have been cannibals, the Ogonis were known to be fiercely independent and to regard foreigners with a healthy dose of suspicion. As long as their land, streams, and mangrove swamps could provide them sustenance, the Ogoni people wanted as little as possible to do with the outside world. As a tiny ethnic unit of six kingdoms, they jealously guarded their culture and identity by maintaining strict prohibitions on intermarriage with most of their neighbors. Their harsh environment literally served as an umbrella protecting them from the hostile intentions of outsiders. In the nineteenth century the dense forests were the perfect refuge from the slave trade, which used the nearby Bonny and Imo Rivers to transport the human cargo to the sea and the waiting ships for the onward journey to the New World. Most Ogonis retreated to the less accessible reaches of the Ogoni plain, where they made their living through agriculture, fishing, and hunting.[1]

Although Ogoniland became a protectorate of the British Empire, British troops were unable to subdue its people until 1914, the same year that Nigeria came into existence as a single entity. This marked the beginning of Ogoniland's troubles, in Saro-Wiwa's view. British colonialism "forced alien administrative structures on us and herded us into the domestic colonialism of Nigeria."[2] Yet the British had little to do with the fundamental transformations already under way by the early 1900s. A population explosion unleashed by the end of the slave trade sent waves of homesteaders ever deeper into the forests to clear new agricultural land. Without the protection of the trees, the sandy, easily leached soil quickly degraded, and the drive for new land accelerated. By the late 1950s the woodlands had virtually disappeared, just as the first significant petroleum deposits were discovered at the Bomu field in the Dere area of the Gokana kingdom.

The oil companies brought pipelines, flow stations, gas flaring, and oil spills, which, combined with the deterioration of the soil, proved a poisonous cocktail for the Ogonis' livelihood. The immense wealth that oil represented was there to see but not to touch. People felt abandoned by the newly independent government of Nigeria and the companies that removed petroleum from their land but provided scarce educational and health facilities in return. Many locals saw an almost spiritual correlation between the arrival of the oil companies and the declining fertility of the land. The seeds of future conflict had been planted, and it was only a matter of time before they bore their explosive fruit.

It has become fashionable among Saro-Wiwa's critics and supporters alike to suggest that from the first discovery of oil to the early 1990s the Ogoni people coexisted easily with the oil companies. MOSOP's opponents sought to portray the allegations of environmental degradation and oppression as simply the words of an opportunist firebrand seeking international attention. On occasion even Saro-Wiwa himself agreed with the view that before MOSOP the Ogonis had never challenged the oil companies. The evidence suggests otherwise.

Early on, Saro-Wiwa himself did not seem to harbor ill will toward Shell, and in fact he applied for a job with the company after graduating from the University of Ibadan in 1965 at the age of twenty-four. Instead, he was offered a scholarship to study in the United Kingdom. He probably would have accepted it had the civil war not intervened and interrupted what he immodestly suggested would have been a "brilliant academic career."[3]

Just three years later, however, Saro-Wiwa aired his growing hostility to the oil companies in a pamphlet entitled *The Ogoni Nationality Today and Tomorrow*. In it he called on the Ogonis to organize "to reassert ourselves side by side with all other nationalities in the Nigerian federation. We cannot let this opportunity slip past us. If we do, posterity shall not forgive us, and we shall disappear as a people from the face of the earth."[4]

83

Complaints about oil pollution also came from the conservative but still highly influential Ogoni elders. One letter sent by six chiefs to the military governor of Rivers State in 1970 said, "May it please Your Excellency to give your fatherly attention and sympathetic consideration to the complaints of your people of Ogoni Division who have suffered in silence as a direct result of the discovery and exploitation of mineral oil and gas in this Division over the past decades."[5] The letter, which demanded a greater share of the revenues from the oil extracted from Ogoni land and a program to reverse environmental destruction, sounded remarkably similar to the stance MOSOP would adopt twenty years later. Ironically, the young Saro-Wiwa was on the receiving end of that dispatch. He was serving as the Rivers State commissioner for education.

At the time Nigeria was in the process of rebuilding itself after the Biafran war. In the Igbo propaganda of the day, the resources of the delta, particularly petroleum, were assumed to belong to the fledgling Biafran state and vouched for its economic viability. But the five-million-strong eastern minorities, including the Ogonis, the Andonis, Calabaris, Edos, Efiks, Ibibios, Ijaws, Isokos, Itsekiris, Opobos, and Urhobos, did not quite see it that way. Their land accounted for half of the Eastern Region's total, contained 95 percent of its oil reserves, all of its ports, and rich agricultural and fishing resources.[6]

In the lead-up to the conflict, when the Igbos launched a great trek from Lagos and western Nigeria to return to the east, the minorities did not join them. Many, especially in Ogoniland, felt that their fate would be worse in an Igbo-dominated Biafra. "A lot of the landlords were Igbos, and everybody I've talked to, and certainly I felt a little bit of this after the war, felt that Igbos look down on Ogoni people," Saro-Wiwa's eldest son, Ken Wiwa Jr., told me in an interview in London. "The whole chauvinism made a distinct impression on the Ogonis. Ogonis were almost like slaves on their own land."

The Nigerian military leader Gowon sought to capitalize on this sentiment. In a political masterstroke on the eve of the war, he further undermined support for Biafra by granting the delta minorities two new states, Rivers and the South-East, when he split the federation into twelve states. During the civil war the bulk of the minorities either sided with the federal forces or remained largely passive, and as a result they and the Ogonis in particular were viewed by the Biafran forces as potential saboteurs.

Saro-Wiwa immediately cast his lot with the federal government. With his mother's help, he and his young wife Maria left Ogoniland in a predawn escape by canoe to Bonny, which was the major port for oil exports and which gave its name to Nigeria's lightweight crude, Bonny Light. For the remainder of the war, he served as the federal government's administrator of Bonny.

Saro-Wiwa chronicled his hostility to the Igbos and their Biafran project in his book *On a Darkling Plain*. His son attributed this hostility to two factors: his diminutive stature—he was 5 foot 2 inches tall—and his schoolboy experiences in the 1950s at the prestigious Umuahia Government College, where he had once been called stupid because the Ogonis had failed to support the main Igbo political party in the Eastern Regional Assembly elections.

"My father always sided with the underdog," said Ken Jr.

That's one of the things about him. I guess it's probably because of his height. He always mentioned it. Certainly it was there in his psychological makeup. I remember on his fiftieth birthday, I went to Lagos to the launching of his book. I can't remember who it was who stood up and gave the final closing address, but he said that "with Ken, what I remember from him from government college, was that his favorite phrase was, 'What's height got to do with it?'" So obviously, it was something that kind of drove him on. I think that gives you a sort of complex, when you see all the chauvinism in your own homeland and then when he was at the government college he was constantly being bullied because he came from a minority. That began to seep in. By the time he was old enough to intellectualize what he saw as a kid growing up, he reached the stage where he began to think, "These guys are just bullies. The Igbos are bullying the Ogoni. I am not going to stand for this." If you grow up in Ogoni where the Igbo are treating you as slaves in your homeland, and suddenly there is a putative republic which is going to break away and the Igbos are going to be the dominant ethnic group, you are going to say no.[7]

The civil war claimed the lives of tens of thousands of civilians from the eastern ethnic minorities. They were victims of the crossfire, repression by the Biafran troops, or starvation in the refugee camps. Saro-Wiwa claimed that up to 30,000 Ogonis, or one-tenth of their total population at the time, died during the conflict. "The real victims of that war," he wrote, "were the Eastern minorities who were in a no-win situation."[8]

Throughout the Biafran tragedy and the immediate postwar years, Saro-Wiwa emerged as something of a kingpin in Rivers State and Ogoniland. He helped the thousands of Ogonis returning from the Biafran refugee camps to resettle. He established friendships with military officers stationed in the area who would play major roles in Nigerian politics, such as Obasanjo, Danjuma, and Abacha.

After the war Saro-Wiwa lived with his family on Nzimiro Street in Amadi Flats on the old First Government Reservation Area in Port Harcourt. Their home was a sprawling British colonial house with gardens, peacocks, and fruit trees, and their immediate neighbors were expatriate oil workers and the local military brass. Ken Jr., then a little boy, said he used to play with the children of the army officers, including Abacha. The officers and local elite were frequent guests at the house. "I have this memory of everybody laughing and joking. So once I remember going to the door and peeping around the corner. All I saw was tall people such as Danjuma, and two very short people, one who was my father and another person a bit taciturn and generally aloof from the atmosphere. That was Abacha."

It was during his time as Rivers State commissioner for education that Saro-Wiwa's work would create a personal political constituency that twenty years later would define the fault lines of Ogoni politics. He set about aggressively organizing scholarships for young Ogonis and other minorities. "So many people were beneficiaries of his efforts. They couldn't have gone to school without Ken's help, and that's why he enjoyed this goodwill all over Ogoniland," said Ledum Mitee, the current acting president of MOSOP. "It explained why years later, when we traveled to rallies, Ken always had so much more popular support among the youth than the other Ogoni leaders [did]."

Saro-Wiwa remained in local politics until 1977, when he failed— "surprisingly," he later said—to win a seat at the Nigerian constituent assembly. He attributed his defeat to two of his favorite Nigerian bugbears: "some educated Ogoni elite" and the military government. His bitterness, Mitee said, festered below the surface and soured his relationship with the elder Ogoni stalwarts, Dr. Garrick Leton and Edward Kobani. "In that election, Kobani actually came out to pitch a protégé against Ken. The decision on who went to the conference was taken by a sort of an electoral college. The night before the vote, Kobani gathered the members in a place where they were eating well and celebrating, and the next morning Kobani brought them to vote his way. This episode carried over in their relations."

For the next six years Saro-Wiwa concentrated on expanding his business interests from the grocery store he had established in 1973. In the process, he befriended the Chagoury brothers, Abacha's Lebanese business partners and for a time the employers of Rufus Ada George, who subsequently became governor of Rivers State and one of Saro-Wiwa's keenest enemies. Saro-Wiwa's lawyer, Barry Kumbe, said of the acquaintance, "Ken got to know the Chagoury brothers when he was getting involved in his export-import business. He wasn't a very good businessman, and he was really amazed to see them moving their goods in and out of Port Harcourt with no problem. Ken was a novice in the business area." Saro-Wiwa used the profits from his new trading business to invest in property and houses, and by 1983 he had fulfilled his mother's dream of building the family compound in Bane.

When the military returned to power at the end of the year, Saro-Wiwa decided to return to his passion, writing, and the next seven years proved to be the most productive time of his life. He produced poetry, a volume of short stories entitled *A Forest of Flowers*, two novels, *Sozaboy* and *Prisoners of Jebs*, the highly popular comedy series *Basi & Co.*, which ran for five years on Nigerian television, and he began researching *On a Darkling Plain*.

Politics of a sort beckoned in 1987, when Babangida offered him a job as the executive director of the Directorate of Mass Mobilization for Self-Reliance, Social Justice, and Economic Recovery (MAMSER). MAMSER was to be the military's mechanism to promote grassroots civic responsibility and the values of hard work, honesty, and patriotism. Saro-Wiwa accepted the offer because MAMSER's stated aim was to educate the masses about their rights and responsibilities. It did not take long, however, for him to realize that civil rights and military rule were incompatible. He quit after a year to return to writing.

On a Darkling Plain received a public launch in March 1990 at the Nigerian Institute of International Affairs in Lagos, and in his address on the occasion Saro-Wiwa threw down the gauntlet: "The present division of the country into a federation in which some ethnic groups are split into several states, whereas other ethnic groups are forced to remain together in a difficult unity system inimical to the federal culture of the country, is a recipe for dissension and future wars," he declared before turning to Ogoniland. "Twenty years after the war, the system of revenue allocation, the development policies of successive Federal administrations and the insensitivity of the Nigerian elite have turned the delta and its environs into an ecological disaster and dehumanized its inhabitants."[9]

Whereas his speech antagonized Nigeria's rulers, the book itself angered large sections of the Igbo community for its portrayal of them not as victims but as perpetrators of oppression against the eastern minorities.

At the time Saro-Wiwa was writing a biting weekly column called "Similia" for the *Sunday Times*. Part of the government-owned Daily Times publishing house, the *Sunday Times* provided the perfect launchpad for Saro-Wiwa's attacks on the Nigerian way of life and for projecting the Ogoni issue. "Week after week, I made sure that the name Ogoni appeared before the eyes of readers. It was a television technique, designed to leave the name indelibly in their minds."[10]

Written in a sarcastic, conversational tone, the column showed little sign of restraint, whether discussing Nigeria's obvious ills—ethnic chauvinism, corruption, military rule, and oppression of the minorities, among many others—or pricking the tempers of his countrymen. He was irreverent, at one time ridiculing a book by Obasanjo because it "piles synonym upon synonym and reads tediously, dribbling out to an inelegant end,"[11] and at another describing Ibadan, the historical Yoruba city that was once sub-Saharan Africa's biggest urban center, as "the vomit of a tuberculosis patient."[12]

With his editors, there were early hints of later trouble. A December 1989 essay entitled "The Killing Fields," an attack on the minister of petroleum resources, Alhaji Rilwanu Lukman, was withheld from publication until the minister was sacked. Five months later another column, concerning alleged corruption by the two military governors of Rivers State and Cross River State, appeared in the early edition of the newspaper before it was axed.

His final column, entitled "The Coming War in the Delta," was a scathing, prophetic broadside against the major oil companies, with

Shell at the top of the hit list. It appeared in the first edition of the paper but was withdrawn from the second. The minority peoples in the delta, he wrote, "are faced by a Company—Shell—whose management policies are racist and cruelly stupid, and which is out to exploit and encourage Nigerian ethnocentrism." The government, he said, must

> pay royalty to the landlords for oil mined from their land and the revenue allocation formula must be reviewed to emphasize derivation. Citizens from the oil-bearing areas must be represented on the Boards of Directors of oil companies prospecting for oil in particular areas and communities in the oil-bearing areas should have equity participation in the oil companies operating therein. Finally, the delta people must be allowed to join in the lucrative sale of crude oil. Only in this way can the cataclysm that is building up in the delta be avoided. Is anyone listening?[13]

After a series of meetings among the key elders and intellectuals in Ogoniland, the Ogoni Bill of Rights, which Saro-Wiwa said he wrote, was adopted on August 26, 1990, at the village of Bori, the traditional capital of the Ogoni people. The statement was wide-ranging in its condemnation of Shell and the Nigerian establishment, declaring that "the ethnic politics of successive Federal and state governments are gradually pushing the Ogoni people to slavery and possible extinction." The proposed solution to the crisis was hardly comforting to the authorities. It included political autonomy for the Ogonis, the right to control resources, direct representation "as a right in all Nigerian institutions," promotion of Ogoni culture, and protection from environmental degradation. The document was signed by chiefs in five of the six kingdoms; the government-appointed ruler of Eleme, Ngei O. Ngei, declined.

On the heels of the Bill of Rights emerged the organization that would champion it, MOSOP. The group was formed at Kobani's house, and Leton was chosen as president. The decision to name Saro-Wiwa as publicity secretary was prudent. "The Ogoni are so far down in the well," he said shortly after MOSOP's formation, "that only shouting loudly can they be heard by those on the surface of the soil."[14] Over the next five years Saro-Wiwa shouted, and nearly everyone, friend, foe, and those who moved from one camp to the other, had little choice but to listen.

That the journey would be a difficult and violent was driven home on October 30–31, 1990 when protesters from Umuechem, an oil-producing community ten miles east of Ogoniland, held a demonstration against the Shell Petroleum Development Corporation. Shell, having learned of the impending protest, contacted the Rivers State commissioner of police requesting "security protection." In rushed the Mobile Police, which lived up to its nickname, Kill and Go. Eighty people were shot dead, and 495 houses were destroyed or damaged, according to Amnesty International. A judicial commission set up by the government described the Mobile Police action as "a reckless disregard for lives and property."[15]

A visit to the United States organized by the U.S. Information Service brought Saro-Wiwa into contact with effective environmental groups, particularly one in Denver, Colorado, working to preserve the wilderness. "What that trip did was to convince me that the environment would have to be a strong plank on which to base [MOSOP]," he later wrote.[16] Upon his return, his final media outlet, the "Similia" column, was canceled. The fact that his writing opportunities within Nigeria were collapsing convinced him to commit himself to Ogoni politics. "He left MAMSER. He was having problems financing *Basi & Co.* Nigerian Television pulled the plug on it, and Babangida was really unhappy with the criticism and the popularity of it," said Ken Jr. "Then suddenly the *Sunday Times* column was dropped for the same reason. There was a lot of pressure, and all of his outlets were being knocked off." Saro-Wiwa later attributed his decision to dedicate his life to the Ogoni cause to the Voice of the Spirit of Ogoni, a fetish god central to the Ogoni belief system: "One night in late 1989, as I sat in my study working on a new book, I received a call to put myself, my abilities, my resources, so carefully nurtured over the years, at the feet of the Ogoni people and similar dispossessed, dispirited and disappearing peoples in Nigeria and elsewhere."[17]

For nearly a year after its inception, MOSOP made little headway. The English writer William Boyd, whom Saro-Wiwa had met a few years before, suggested that he contact Amnesty International and Greenpeace, though initially they expressed scant interest in the case. But the international connection had been made, and Saro-Wiwa emphasized its importance in the August 1991 Addendum to the Ogoni Bill of Rights. "Without the intervention of the international community, the government of the Federal Republic of Nigeria and the ethnic majority will continue these noxious policies until the Ogoni people are obliterated from the face of the earth," it said.[18]

A major break came in 1992, when Saro-Wiwa traveled to Geneva to make contact with the Unrepresented Nations and Peoples Organization (UNPO) and address the Working Group on Indigenous Populations. In October *The Heat of the Moment*, a documentary on the crisis in the Nigerian delta, was aired on British television's Channel 4. The Ogoni issue was on the international map.

Within Ogoniland itself, however, tension simmered between Saro-Wiwa and the older generation of elders and politicians, who, he claimed, were increasingly ineffective leaders. During a two-day tour of the area in November 1992, Saro-Wiwa discovered a new constituency to which he could appeal: the Ogoni youth, many of whom he had helped to receive an education.

The collapse of the traditional Ogoni economy in the early 1960s spawned an army of unemployed youths with little to do but hang around aimlessly, occasionally helping their mothers and sisters on the farm, or migrate to the slums of Port Harcourt. For them the Ogoni

elders no longer had any useful answers, and MOSOP provided a renewed source of pride, an outlet to their growing frustration. "I hadn't
mixed much with the youth of Ogoni over the years, since there was
no organization which took care of all Ogoni people," Saro-Wiwa
wrote. "On that tour, I found that there was a large number of youth
angry with a society that had cheated them and who were therefore
eager to hear us, to learn."[19]

The following month Saro-Wiwa drafted a statement setting a
thirty-day deadline for the major oil companies, Shell, Chevron, and
the Nigerian National Petroleum Corporation, to accept demands for
$4 billion in damages for the destruction of the environment and $6
billion in the payment of taxes and royalties.

MOSOP reached the pinnacle of its power in January 1993 with
the massive "Ogoni Day" rallies, in which some 300,000 people, or
two-thirds of all Ogonis, participated. The Ogoni people, Leton said in
his speech at the rallies,

[have] woken up to find our lands devastated by agents of death called
oil companies. Our atmosphere has been totally polluted, our lands
degraded, our waters contaminated, our trees poisoned, so much so
that our flora and fauna have virtually disappeared. We are asking for
the restoration of our environment, we are asking for the basic necessities of life—water, electricity, education; but above all we are asking
for the right to self-determination so that we can be responsible for
our resources and our environment.[20]

Kobani, who had led a procession in a symbolic occupation of the
oil fields, particularly impressed Ken. And the day before the Ogoni
Day celebrations, Kobani delivered a speech that greatly moved Saro-
Wiwa. "Edward was a real gem when he got to the podium. 'Don't be
afraid,' he urged the audience. 'Nothing will happen to you on this
land which God gave us!' Great stuff, meant to convince everyone to

confront the authorities and the oil companies bravely."[21] On Ogoni Day itself, Kobani's speech caused Saro-Wiwa to write, "I felt ever so proud of my friend, the great Ogoni patriot he has always been."[22] Within six months Saro-Wiwa was condemning both Leton and Kobani as traitors.

Saro-Wiwa himself used the occasion to declare Shell persona non grata in Ogoniland, and he ended his speech with a call to other minority groups in the delta to "rise up now and fight for your rights." The outpouring of popular support for MOSOP sent shock waves through the ranks of conservative chiefs, who felt the Ogonis had a better chance of improving their lot by entering into dialogue with Shell and the governor of Rivers State, Ada George. In a statement issued five days after Ogoni Day, six chiefs, all signatories to the Ogoni Bill of Rights, reaffirmed their faith in the military government's goodwill and promised no further public demonstrations. But MOSOP in general, and Saro-Wiwa in particular, thought things had gone too far for that. The dissenting stance of the six pro-government chiefs would mark the first stage in the breakdown of the broad Ogoni alliance that had held since the formation of MOSOP in 1990.

Officials of the Nigerian National Petroleum Corporation had recognized signs of environmental problems as early as 1983. "We witnessed the slow poisoning of the waters of this country, and the destruction of vegetation, and agricultural land by oil spills which occur during petroleum operations," NNPC Inspectorate Division wrote at the time. "But since the inception of the oil industry in Nigeria more than twenty-five years ago, there has been no concerned and effective effort on the part of the Government, let alone the oil operators to control the environmental problems associated with the industry."[23]

By the 1990s Ogoni activists were routinely pointing out sites of oil-related pollution, one dating back thirty years, to visiting environmentalists and journalists as evidence of "ecological devastation" caused by the oil industry. They argued that fishing and farming, the mainstays of the traditional economy, had been severely disrupted by spills from leaking pipelines that run through creeks and through villages and farmlands, often above ground. The round-the-clock flaring of natural gas both contaminated the air and disturbed residents' sleep.

Shell responded to the attacks on its record by arguing that the government, not an international oil company, had the responsibility to ensure that promised revenues were delivered to local communities and that basic infrastructure was built and maintained. It also accused its critics of greatly exaggerating the amount of pollution caused by the oil industry. "We have never denied that there are some environmental problems connected with our operation and we are committed to dealing with them," Brian Anderson, the Nigerian-born SPDC managing director, said in November 1995.

However, we totally reject accusations of devastating Ogoni land or the Niger Delta. This has been dramatized out of all proportion. The total land we have acquired for operations to build our facilities, flow-lines, pipelines and roads comes to just 0.3 per cent of the Niger Delta. In Ogoni land we have acquired just 0.7 per cent of the land area. These are very small figures that put the scale of our Niger Delta operations firmly in perspective.[24]

Responding to complaints from environmentalists that the oil companies are ruining farmland and fish habitats, Shell points to a complex situation of "rapidly expanding population, over farming, deforestation and industry."[25] Shell officials pledge readiness to clean up oil spills though they blame deliberate vandalism by villagers for many of the spillages. "Sabotage remains a significant problem, despite the widespread awareness that no compensation is paid in such cases. The usual motive for sabotage is to press claims for large sums of money as compensation and/or to attract temporary employment in the subsequent clean-up exercise," the company said in its website briefing paper on oil spills.[26] Of the annual average of 221 spills per year between 1989 and 1995, Shell blamed 28 percent of them on sabotage, though since then, company officials raised that figure to over 60 percent.[27]

———

OGONI DAY had raised alarms within Shell and the military government. In February Shell officials met in London and the Hague to consider plans for countering international protests over their operations in Nigeria. It was decided that Shell officials should closely monitor the activities of the MOSOP leaders, especially Saro-Wiwa.

Violence flared on April 30, 1993, when a U.S. contracting firm hired by Shell, Wilbros of Tulsa, Oklahoma, began bulldozing crops in the village of Biara to prepare the ground for the building of a new pipeline. When the contract workers were met by protesters, they called in the security forces, who opened fire with live ammunition. After three days of protests eleven people had been wounded, and one man, Agbarator Friday Otu, had been killed.

A week later, a group of eleven conservative Ogonis, including eight chiefs and the former Biafran ambassador to London, Ignatius Kogbara, issued a statement apologizing for the protests that led to the shootings and effectively called for a military crackdown on MOSOP. The statement, which appeared in a local newspaper, *Nigerian Tide*, expressed their "anger and complete disapproval of the lawless activities of certain elements in Ogoni who claim to be operating under MOSOP" and said they would support "any action by government to protect life and property of innocent civilians."[28] The frustrated Ogoni youth whom Saro-Wiwa had discovered only months before stepped to the fore. Militants of MOSOP's youth wing, the National Youth Council of the Ogoni People (NYCOP), attacked the homes of several chiefs and forced them to flee to Port Harcourt.

The repercussions of the Wilbros incident did not end there. Almost the entire MOSOP leadership, with the exception of Saro-Wiwa, who was traveling abroad, entered into tripartite negotiations with Governor Ada George and Shell over the payment of damages to the families of those wounded and killed during the Biara protests. MOSOP emerged from the talks with an agreement in which Shell would pay a lump sum of 1 million naira to the families and would consider individual payments in return for permission to complete the pipeline. While the negotiations were under way, however, Saro-Wiwa had contacted his Lagos office to say that no agreement should be reached until an environmental impact assessment had been completed.

The Lagos office, however, failed to pass the message on to the negotiating team and instead reported Saro-Wiwa's suggestion to other MOSOP officials who were not involved in the talks. "There was a misunderstanding," said Mitee, who had been a legal adviser to the negotiators.

When we set out to discuss the agreement with the people, they almost mobbed us. They asked "one million naira only?" Emotions were running very high because people had been injured and killed. They thought we had sold them out and called us "vultures." Even my elder brother said, "Tell me, did Shell give you some money?" This was too much for Leton and Kobani. They felt they should be respected. My view was that if the people didn't accept the agreement, we should go back and start the negotiations again. But Leton and Kobani felt they would lose face if they had to return to the governor and say that the people didn't accept the agreement. They believed that Ken had deliberately set them up.

The government, in the meantime, stepped up its harassment of Saro-Wiwa. On April 18 he was detained at Port Harcourt airport for sixteen hours but was eventually released without charge. A month later police seized his passport at Murtala Mohammed International Airport in Lagos as he was preparing to fly to London. Only a late-night call to Babangida's national security adviser, Aliyu Mohammed, secured the release of his documents so he could travel the next day. On June 11, on the eve of the presidential elections, his passport again was seized as he prepared to board a flight to Europe, this time to attend a UN Human Rights Conference in Vienna.

By now the government was incensed by MOSOP's campaign, citing its writing of a national anthem and design of an Ogoni flag as evidence of secessionist intent. "You will agree with me that this approach is treasonable," the then Nigerian high commissioner to London, Alhaji Abubakar Alhaji, wrote Lord Avebury of the British Parliamentary Human Rights Group in June. "No government worthy of the name would tolerate activities which would lead to the break up of the country no matter under any pretext."[29]

Babangida had lifted the ban on politicians in 1992, and both Leton and Kobani wanted to seek positions in the Social Democratic Party, which was considered slightly more liberal than the other military-sanctioned and -financed political party, the National Republican Convention. But Saro-Wiwa argued that all senior MOSOP officials had agreed not to engage in party politics for fear of undermining the Ogoni movement. If such an agreement existed, however, it seemed to contradict a statement Saro-Wiwa himself had made just two years before: "we must support the progression to democratic rule, as it is only through democratic action that we can re-establish our rights. The duty of party politicians among us is to represent Ogoni, their constituencies; to push the Ogoni agenda within their parties."[30]

As the June 12 presidential elections approached, the dispute over whether to participate in them raged within MOSOP. Saro-Wiwa's faction succeeded in winning a MOSOP Steering Committee vote, by 11 to 6, to boycott the polls. On election day the boycott largely held in Ogoniland. Saro-Wiwa's critics attributed its success to the strong-arm tactics of the NYCOP "vigilantes"; his supporters said it was an expression of popular will.

"The Ogoni people felt it was time for a change," Saro-Wiwa's lawyer Barry Kumbe recalled. "The issue was discussed in the churches, among the teachers, in the unions. The people were asked to air their views. There was a consensus for a boycott, as long as it was passive and nonviolent." It was anything but, said Saro-Wiwa's opponents. NYCOP youths manned roadblocks and threatened violent consequences for anyone trying to vote. Such measures were deemed necessary because the government and traditional chiefs were attempting to use what are commonly known as "flying voters." In the showdown, the more radical faction of MOSOP led by Saro-Wiwa carried the day.

Nine days after the polls Saro-Wiwa was arrested, ironically, for his activities against an election that the authorities were about to cancel. His detention sparked a wave of unrest in Ogoniland. There was, Kumbe argued, an "uncoordinated spontaneous outburst of emotion" against the chiefs. The military government responded by dispatching the Second Amphibious Brigade from Port Harcourt to Bori, Saro-Wiwa's home area.

By now the split between Leton and Kobani and the Saro-Wiwa faction was irreparable. An unsigned pamphlet circulated in Ogoniland putting Leton and Kobani firmly in the "vulture" camp and alleging that Shell was paying them $4.5 million to destroy MOSOP. A shocked Kobani detected the hand of Saro-Wiwa: "He has a formidable army of trained thugs who are terrorizing the whole of Ogoniland, destroying the lives and property of those he does not like, in the attempt to emerge as the one Ogoni leader. The vile propaganda starts the process, to be followed by physical assault on the lives and property of his target victims."[31] Saro-Wiwa replied that Kobani was jealous and said, "I invite you to copy my ways and you will find that which you desire most: the Ken Saro-Wiwa image."[32] By now, long-time comrades Leton and Kobani, whom Saro-Wiwa had once called

"the great Ogoni patriot," had become "traitors" and "fifth colum-
nists" to the Ogoni cause.

They had little alternative but to resign. First Leton and then
Kobani quit MOSOP. "The establishment of a private army of storm-
troopers bent on insulting, intimidating, and marginalizing the top
leadership of the Ogoni nationality in MOSOP can only create conflict
and disunity," Kobani said in his letter of resignation. The power
struggle between the more conservative traditional elders and Saro-
Wiwa's mass politics would continue for another year before reaching
a final, cataclysmic end.

The MOSOP Steering Committee elected Saro-Wiwa president in
absentia and chose Mitee as his deputy. As Saro-Wiwa sat in his hospital bed in early August, he was receiving reports from his MOSOP colleagues of a dramatic turn in the situation. There had been a massacre
of Ogonis at the village of Kaa on the banks of the Andoni River. It
was the second such atrocity in less than a month. The first was on July
9 when more than one hundred Ogonis were slaughtered on the
Andoni River as they returned by boat from neighboring Cameroon. A
far more brutal chapter was unfolding in Nigeria's delta wars.

———

WHEN I REACHED the area three days after the attack, the village of
Kaa was a scene of destruction. Dozens of homes, shops, and school-
rooms had been sprayed with machine-gun bullets and blasted with
explosives. Scribbled on many of the walls were anti-Ogoni slogans
such as "No to the Ogoni Kingdom!" Torn parcels of food and clothes
were strewn all along the road leading from the town, unmistakable
signs of civilian flight and of looting by their pursuers. The Nigerian
government would later claim that the attack on Kaa was the result of
a mere ethnic squabble between the Ogonis and their neighbors, the
Andonis. Others, using rather convoluted logic, attributed the clash di-

rectly to Saro-Wiwa's alleged desire to capitalize on increasing tension in the region.[35] The scale of the damage to Kaa, however, betrayed a military operation rather than an ethnic tussle.

"It had to be the military, or at least elements of the security forces," the late Professor Claude Ake, a prominent academic and expert on the delta region, told me at the time. "Andonis are fishermen, and fishermen don't usually have such weapons as hand grenades and mortars. There was no real dispute between the Ogoni and the Andoni over fishing rights, territory or the like. Besides, the Andonis depended on the market at Kaa to sell their fish. What would be the purpose of destroying their own livelihood?"

At a schoolhouse in the neighboring village of Eekwe, tension and fear filled the air as hundreds of Kaa's residents met to discuss how to feed, clothe, and house themselves. They were still counting the dead —the number had reached thirty-five—and attempting to track down more than one hundred missing. Adolphus Mesuadebari, a Kaa village leader, said the attackers had landed in boats from the Andoni River. "They came from the waterside and entered the market. But when they went into town, they started shooting," he said. "If we had guns, we would have stayed and defended ourselves. But he had no weapons, so we ran away." Mesuadebari described the assailants as a mixture of civilians and Nigerian soldiers: "They had rifles, hand grenades and mortars, and there were many men in uniform."

MOSOP officials said they feared something was about to happen because the police had withdrawn Ogoni members of their force from the area a week before, presumably because they distrusted their loyalty. Dr. Olua Kamalu, a MOSOP vice president, put the blame on the military government: "What is happening in Ogoni is a deliberate arrangement by the Nigerian authorities to stop our movement. We are being killed today because we are demanding our rights."

The presumed outbreak of violence between the Ogonis and the Andonis marked a new stage in the military government's crackdown on MOSOP—destabilization by fomenting ethnic warfare. Clashes erupted in December 1993, this time involving members of the Okrika people, and again on April 3, 1994, between the Ogonis and the Ndokis, when twenty people were reportedly killed and eight Ogoni villages destroyed.[34] In each case, witnesses said that men in Nigerian military uniforms were involved in the violence. The New York–based lobby group, Human Rights Watch/Africa, reported that the commander of the Rivers State Internal Security Task Force, Lieutenant Colonel Paul Okuntimo, had told a meeting at the Ogoni village of Barako, "You are the worst type of people. You killed the Andonis. Then the Andonis let us know. So we came and chased you people. After the Andonis, you fought with the Okrikas and then with the Ndokis. So they invited us to chase you people. So we are the people who chased you from your houses and destroyed them."[35]

Four days after Babangida resigned as president on August 27, 1993, and was replaced by Shonekan's interim administration, Saro-Wiwa and Mitee flew to Abuja aboard an air force plane sent by Abacha. As chief of the joint chiefs of staff and defense minister, Abacha was the true power in the new government. Over lunch Saro-Wiwa, Mitee, and Abacha discussed a variety of issues, ranging from Nigeria's constitution, the creation of new states, ethnicity, and the specific Ogoni demands. "I think he was already planning to take over and was using the time to meet with people and sound them out on their ideas for the country," Mitee remembered. Abacha said he feared that a "sovereign national conference" demanded by opposition groups could lead to the breakup of the nation along ethnic lines. Saro-Wiwa and Mitee, however, argued that without such a gathering, secessionist tensions would inevitably grow. At one point Saro-Wiwa complained about the repeated seizure of his passport, and Abacha apologized, saying it was owing to overzealous security officers. He called his top security aide, Hamza al-Mustapha, into the room and instructed him to ensure it did not happen again.

Within three months Abacha had forced Shonekan's resignation and assumed leadership of the Provisional Ruling Council. Saro-Wiwa, like many of the pro-democracy campaigners in Lagos, actually supported Abacha's ouster of Shonekan, a fact that many of his foreign supporters chose to forget. "It's true that Ken initially welcomed the Abacha coup," said Kumbe. "It's the idea that sometimes it's necessary for an evil to get out an evil." But his initial support for the Abacha coup proved misguided. By mid-1994 Ogoniland was under a state of siege. Hundreds of people had died in ethnic clashes cum military operations, and thousands had been displaced.

The Rivers State government's strategy was laid out in a secret memorandum that Okuntimo sent to the military administrator of Rivers State, Lieutenant Colonel Dauda Musa Komo. The memorandum, dated May 12, 1994, outlined a plan of action to neutralize MOSOP and to restore Shell's activities in the area. "Shell operations still impossible unless ruthless military operations are undertaken for smooth economic activities to commence," it said. Among Okuntimo's recommendations were "wasting operations during MOSOP and other gatherings making constant military presence justifiable," "wasting targets cutting across communities and leadership cadres especially vocal individuals in various groups," and "wasting operations coupled with psychological tactics of displacement/wasting as noted above." Unauthorized visitors from Europe were to be banned in Ogoniland, and surveillance was to be stepped up on "Ogoni leaders considered as security risks/MOSOP propellers." The memorandum went on to suggest that in order "to avoid unruly interference by other superior officers," Komo, as the military administrator of the state, should directly supervise the operations. Troops and officers should be paid the same rates as received by the Nigerian contingent to the West African peacekeeping force in Liberia, ECOMOG. As to the source of the funding, the memo said, there should be "pressure on oil companies for prompt regular inputs as discussed."[36] Despite initial denials, Shell officials later admitted that they had provided field pay to Okuntimo's forces worth up to 100 naira a day, the equivalent of about two meals.

Komo had direct access to higher echelons of the Abacha regime through personal ties to Brigadier Ishaya Bamaiyi, the former Presidential Brigade of Guards commander in Abuja who later became chief of Army staff. Like Bamaiyi, Komo was a Christian from the Zuru ethnic minority in the overwhelmingly Muslim state of Kebbi. "Komo used to tell us that when you people are talking of persecution, he knew what persecution was because he remembered that at his home, if he wanted to pray, he used to have to go to the bush," said Mitee.

It helped the government that the split between Saro-Wiwa's faction of MOSOP and the more conservative elders led by Leton and Kobani had become a gaping chasm in which there was no hope of reconciliation. Indeed, the divisions played right into Okuntimo's hands. Although Saro-Wiwa continued to preach nonviolence in public, his critics argued that in private he was turning the vigilantes loose on his opponents. There were widespread reports of NYCOP youths holding kangaroo courts and of MOSOP's Conference of Ogoni Traditional Rulers (COTRA) executing "witches." Intimidation and assault were among the strong-arm tactics employed in the name of NYCOP, although Saro-Wiwa's supporters maintained that such actions were the responsibility of unemployed area boys not firmly under MOSOP's control. "The problem was that anyone could join MOSOP. The vigilantes, who were mainly area boys, created a lot of mayhem and claimed it was NYCOP, but that wasn't true," said Kumbe. "The authorities even tried to infiltrate NYCOP with area boys to discredit MOSOP. Ken in fact helped the security forces to round up some of the vigilantes." Saro-Wiwa's son, Ken Jr., admitted that NYCOP was sometimes out of control: "My father wasn't rigorous enough in getting rid of the thugs."

But the MOSOP leadership had been trying to bring its youth wing to heel since at least November 1993, when Mitee issued a public notice denouncing vigilantes who claimed to be operating on behalf of NYCOP and MOSOP. In January 1994 Saro-Wiwa himself asked the Internal Security Task Force to arrest three youths who were running vigilante gangs in the name of NYCOP. The executive of NYCOP disbanded its Gokana kingdom branch and dismissed its coordinator, Celestine Meabe, for leading a vigilante group.[37] Such measures were far from sufficient, however.

The violence reached its tragic climax on May 21, 1994. Saro-Wiwa and Mitee were traveling in separate cars to a series of rallies in Ogoniland when police stopped their vehicles at the Kpopie junction. Less than a mile away, Edward Kobani and his brother Mohammed, Chief Samuel Orage, a former Rivers State commissioner, Chief Theophilus Orage, formerly a secretary of the Gokana Council of Chiefs, and Albert Badey were meeting at the palace of *Gbenemene* ("chief") of Gokana. The soldiers ordered Saro-Wiwa to turn back. A crowd of his supporters gathered around the car as he conferred briefly with Mitee before both men obeyed the police order.

As Saro-Wiwa was heading back to Port Harcourt, another mob at Gokana stormed the palace chanting *"E-sho-be,"* a war cry meaning that blood must be spilled, and calling on the "vultures" to appear. Kobani, Badey, and the Orage brothers were beaten to death; Kobani's brother Mohammed saved himself by hiding in the shrine of the Ogoni Spirit, a sanctuary his pursuers considered too holy to violate. He waited there until the police arrived four hours later to disperse the crowd.

The following morning Saro-Wiwa and Mitee were arrested. Komo had already decided who was guilty of the crime. He told a press conference that he had ordered that everyone who participated in the murders "must be rounded up. The MOSOP leadership that was part of this game must be arrested."[38]

At Saro-Wiwa's subsequent trial, the state prosecution alleged that he had told the crowd surrounding his stopped car to "deal" with the "vultures," that is, the conservatives. Mitee denies it. "I was driving in front, and the police who were escorting us told us to stop," he recalled.

> We stopped and I came out of the car and the police told me that we couldn't go any further. They said they had taken a decision that Ken had to turn back. They said I had to go one way, and Ken another. They wanted to separate us. So I only walked to Ken's vehicle and he wound down his window. He said, "What is happening?" I said, "These people say you can't go any further" and all that, and he said, "Okay." He told the driver to turn around. I said, "I'll go home and pick up my things, and I'll meet you." He said, "All right, join me in the office." And that was it.

After the killings, Okuntimo's Internal Security Task Force ran amok in Ogoniland, raiding some sixty towns and villages between May and July. At least fifty Ogonis were executed. Human Rights Watch/Africa described the pattern in the following terms:

> Troops entered towns and villages shooting at random, as villagers fled to the surrounding bush. Soldiers and mobile police stormed houses, breaking down doors and windows with their boots, the butts of their guns, and machetes. Villagers who crossed their paths, including children and the elderly, were severely beaten, forced to pay "settlement fees" [bribes], and sometimes shot. Many women were raped. ...Before leaving, troops looted money, food, livestock, and other property.[39]

Okuntimo's recommendations in the May 12 memo had been carried out with extreme prejudice.

There can be no more eloquent description of the security forces' tactics than the one provided by Okuntimo himself, who once said he knew 204 ways to kill a person. He told a televised press conference,

The first three days of the operation, I operated in the night. Nobody knew where I was coming from. What I will just do is that I will take some detachments of soldiers, they will just stay at the four corners of the town. They ... have automatic rifles that sound death. If you hear the sound you will freeze. And then I will equally choose about twenty [soldiers] and give them ... grenades—explosives—very hard ones. So we shall surround the town at night. ...The machine with five hundred rounds will open up. When four or five like that open up and then we are throwing grenades and they are making "eekpuwaa!" What do you think the ... and they know I am around, what do you think the people are going to do? And we have already put roadblocks on the main road, we don't want anybody to start running. ...so the option we made was that we should drive all these boys, all these people into the bush with nothing except the pants and the wrapper they are using that night.[40]

Saro-Wiwa and fifteen other Ogoni activists remained in detention without charge and without access to their lawyers. In November Abacha bypassed the civilian courts and established a Civil Disturbances Special Tribunal consisting of two judges and one military officer. There was no right of appeal, the tribunal was empowered to impose the death penalty, and it was up to the Provisional Ruling Council to confirm the sentences. The first five detainees, including Saro-Wiwa and Mitee, were finally charged on January 28, 1995. The other eleven detainees were charged the following month. The accused were allowed to meet with their defense counsel only with the consent, and often the presence, of Okuntimo.

Saro-Wiwa swore an affidavit alleging that he was beaten and manacled for long periods and denied food, medical care, access to counsel, and family visits during the initial stage of his incarceration. His original defense team of human rights lawyers, headed by Chief Gani Fawehinmi, withdrew from the case in June to protest the tribunal's

slipshod handling of justice. Two of the principal prosecution witnesses against Saro-Wiwa, Charles Danwi and Naayone Nkpah, later
swore affidavits that they had been bribed to give false testimony.
Another prosecution witness was Celestine Meabe, the NYCOP leader
dismissed for running a vigilante gang.

Claiming a lifelong commitment to nonviolence, Saro-Wiwa denied the charges. In his closing statement to the Tribunal he said, "I
have no doubt at all about the ultimate success of my cause, no matter
the trials and tribulations which I and those who believe with me may
encounter on our journey. Nor imprisonment nor death can stop our
ultimate victory."[41]

No credible witness was ever produced in court to substantiate the
allegation that he had urged supporters to murder the chiefs. His opponents within Ogoniland blamed him for the deaths, however, and
one of his own defense lawyers told me he believed Saro-Wiwa bore
"moral responsibility" for the killings because of the climate of intol-
erance he had helped to foster within MOSOP. The former MOSOP
president, Leton, told the tribunal, "Saro-Wiwa must be exposed for
what he is: a habitual liar, a person who uses the travails of his people
to achieve his selfish desires and ambitions ... a person who is prepared
to engineer the elimination of his elders ... a person who in this situation cannot escape complicity in the murder of the four prominent
Ogoni leaders."[42]

Nevertheless, the workings of the tribunal drew sharp criticism
from international experts. "It is my view that the breaches of fundamental rights I have identified are so serious as to arouse grave concern
that any trial before this Tribunal will be fundamentally flawed and
unfair," Michael Birnbaum, QC, a British criminal lawyer, wrote in a
June 1995 report.[43] Six months later, after the tribunal returned its
guilty verdict, Birnbaum concluded, "The judgement of the Tribunal
is not merely wrong, illogical or perverse. It is downright dishonest.
The Tribunal consistently advanced arguments which no experienced

lawyer could possibly believe to be logical or just. I believe that the Tribunal first decided on its verdict and then sought for arguments to justify them. No barrel was too deep to be scraped."[44]

The conviction and death sentence were handed down on October 31. In his last statement to the tribunal, Saro-Wiwa said, "After all your judgment, convicting me is a mere formality. ...Today is certainly a black day for the black man. In the course of the trial, I have been brutalized, my family almost ruined. I am a man of ideas in and out of prison—my ideas will live."[45]

Abacha's ruling Provisional Council confirmed the sentence on November 8. In the early morning hours three days later, Ken Saro-Wiwa and eight other Ogoni activists, their ankles bound in chains, were taken to the gallows at the main Port Harcourt jail. Several hours later they were hanged. Antiriot police and tanks surrounded the prison. The bodies were buried in an unmarked grave and sprinkled with lye to accelerate decomposition.

The executions sparked a wave of international condemnation. Nigeria was suspended from the Commonwealth, whose leaders were meeting in Auckland, New Zealand, that very day. Western nations imposed a package of limited restrictions on travel of government officials and sales of military equipment. The only penalties that might hurt the regime, such as an oil embargo and seizing of assets, were not considered.

Wole Soyinka described the hangings as "a blatant unrepentant defiance of civilized norms. An atavistic psyche is what has characterized this regime from the beginning, so there should have been no cause for surprise. We have warned, and pleaded. Now we are paying yet another heavy price for the comatose nature of global conscience."[46] Ken Jr. said his father never truly believed the sentence would be carried out:

I think he was confident that he was big enough for nothing to happen to him. He felt very protected because of who he was, that they wouldn't come to him. What they were trying to do was intimidate his supporters and leave him alone, and then try to drive a wedge between the two. He felt untouchable ... given that Abacha was a friend and that he was talking to his security advisers.

The executions were a body blow to the Ogoni campaign. Of the other twenty Ogonis detained for involvement in the murders, one died in prison before Abubakar released them in 1998. The military clampdown drove much of MOSOP and NYCOP underground and forced into exile many of the movement's leaders, such as Mitee, the one person accused who was acquitted. And Saro-Wiwa's prediction of a "coming war in the delta" appeared prescient, as unrest spread among the Ijaws, the largest ethnic group in the delta. A Shell report said the number of incidents of civil unrest in the Niger delta more than doubled in 1998, to 325 from 150 the year before.

"It is going to get worse, I predict, because these other people are not organized, they are not disciplined. We have the discipline," said Mitee, who returned to Nigeria in late 1998. "There have been cases in which some Ogoni people stole Shell equipment while this crisis was on, and I, as the head of MOSOP, went personally to arrest these people and handed them over to the security agencies. We wanted to maintain discipline. These other communities don't have such organizations."

For Ken Jr. the conflict in the delta represented a lost opportunity, both for the local people and for oil companies such as Shell. "As my father always said, Shell will one day come to realize that he was their best friend. That what he was offering was actually a peaceful way to resolve the problem. Looking back on it, they should have taken up his offer."

5

The Journey
of a Thousand Miles...

If the delta explodes, Nigeria goes with it.

CHRIS ALAGOA

A TROPICAL STORM descended suddenly in a cleansing fury that washed tree branches and bundles of water hyacinth down the wide green rivers and streams of the Niger delta. Within minutes of the squall's passing, the sun muscled its way through a humid haze to reveal a film of dull rainbow colors riding the tidal currents toward the Atlantic. Chris Alagoa, a university-trained fisheries expert with whom I was traveling to Epebu, a remote community on the edge of the forest, extended his right arm and pointed an accusatory finger. "Oil!" he shouted over the roar of twin 40-horsepower outboard engines. "It's like this all the time. In the delta, oil spills are an everyday occurrence."

By the late 1990s, the delta was literally a cauldron of political and ethnic turmoil. By comparison, the violence in Ogoniland even at the height of the crisis seemed rather tame. Villagers had resorted to taking hostages, mainly oil company workers found in the delta, as their preferred means of venting their anger at what they considered to be years of neglect and repression by the Nigerian state. But they did not stop there. Self-organized units made up mainly of unemployed young men launched dozens of guerrilla actions, including the occupation of flow stations and the sabotage of pipelines run by whichever company was closest, Shell, Texaco, Chevron, Mobil, or Agip. The youths of various communities clashed at times with police, at times with neighboring ethnic groups, and more often than they liked to admit, with each other. In late 1998 the unrest in the delta had sliced the national oil production of two million barrels a day by one-third. In October a gruesome fire caused by seepage from a pipeline carrying gasoline had killed an estimated eight hundred people, the majority of them by incineration, in the town of Jesse. It seemed terribly symbolic.

In the forefront of these protests were the myriad clans of the Ijaws, a diverse and fiercely independent people who have made their living from fishing and trading from time immemorial. Their home region in the delta is a vast steamy maze of countless creeks and rivers feeding into what is reputed to be the world's biggest remaining area of mangrove. With the highest rainfall in West Africa, an elevation that rarely exceeds 2 yards, and an average humidity level at dawn of 95 percent, the delta is the soft underbelly of Nigeria. As the source of nearly half of the $280 billion Nigeria has earned from petroleum exports in the past three decades, it also stands as a monument to the failure of the modern African nation-state to care for its people. For the Ijaws and the host of other smaller delta groups, such as the Itsekiris, the Ogonis, and the Urhobos, decent jobs, clean water, functioning health facilities, and schools were the stuff of dreams. Theirs was a life of grinding poverty played out above some of the most lucrative fossil fuel deposits in the world. Epebu's state, Bayelsa, was the source of 40 percent of Nigeria's crude exports but had just one gas station. Almost the only time delta people saw any impact of the oil was when it was spilled into the water in which they fished and bathed.

"People feel short-changed," explained Alagoa, an Ijaw himself.

They have looked at the marginalization over the years, all the nonsense heaped on the people. It is as the saying goes, "When ideas are denied a natural expression, they become unnaturally explosive." The fuse on the Niger delta is very short, much shorter than most people think. All these explosions throughout the delta are just mini-explosions. There could be a big bang. The delta is at the base of Nigeria and it's like putting a keg of gunpowder under Nigeria. If the delta explodes, Nigeria goes with it.

The pilot of our launch, a young man named Gowon Consul, swung the vessel sharply into an oxbow and slowed the engines to a crawl as he approached the shore. His target was a footpath next to a rickety wooden-pier latrine that leaned so perilously over the muddy embankment that it seemed poised to slide into the water at any moment. The sexually segregated toilets marked the entrance to the village of Epebu. It is here and in other similar tiny settlements hacked out of the tropical forest of the delta that perhaps the most serious questions were being posed to the future of Nigeria.

We were in Epebu to follow up on an unscheduled visit that Alagoa, Consul, and several of their colleagues had made recently, not as guests but as hostages. Epebu youths, believing Alagoa and his colleagues worked for a Western oil company, abducted them on the river and held them captive for several hours. Alagoa showed no sign that he was worried about returning to see his captors. Threats and kidnapings were all part of working in the Niger delta. "They had one Dane gun which they used to point at us and say that we should follow them to the village. I don't think they even had any live ammunition in it," he said with his typically deadpan delivery. "I was their guest for a few hours, against my will it is true. But they weren't unruly; they were very civil."

The task of talking their way out of trouble had fallen to Bill Knight, a good-humored Welshman who was one of the prime architects of the community development project that he and Alagoa were working on among the Akassa clan. "I stood up and talked and talked," he later recalled, "and after forty-five minutes I think they just got bored and let us go. One of them told me that two years ago he would never have imagined that they would be taking hostages and behaving like 'crazy men.'" The villagers asked if they too could join the program in Akassa.

Consul cut the engines and scaled the steep bank that led to a flat grassy clearing, which, judging by the goal posts, served as Epebu's soccer field. Alagoa disembarked and walked across a small bridge over a creek that marked the entrance to the hamlet he had so recently entered as a prisoner. This time, as he advanced down the main road, people approached sheepishly and said "Welcome." In one compound a group of women cooked over an open fire, and in another a plump middle-aged woman was having her hair done in plaits. Everything about their behavior suggested that Epebu was a calm, rural community. The physical state of the village, however, testified to a rather different reality. Roughly one out of every three buildings had been destroyed; some dwellings were simply gutted, and others had been reduced to piles of rubble.

One hundred yards after entering Epebu, Alagoa turned left off the road and into a small community center that was surrounded by dozens of young men and boys. Sitting in a semicircle on a row of benches inside was a group of elderly village chiefs murmuring gravely among themselves. At the far side of the room, across a generation gap, an assortment of youths, ranging from athletic men in their twenties to pint-size boys, jostled for position. More people poked their heads in the doorway and the windows, contributing to a stifling atmosphere of overpowering humidity.

After a few minutes, Alagoa rose and began a monologue in Ijaw, explaining that he was back to see how the community was doing since his last visit. He carried off the address remarkably well for someone whom these same people had threatened to beat up the week before.

When Alagoa was done, a tall young man leaning against the wall stepped forward, introduced himself as Ezekiel Stanley Oninabharobasi, and announced that he would speak for the community. He proceeded to deliver a statement detailing the village's grievances against the Italian company Agip and describing the government's disregard of the community and Nigeria in general. Agip ran two wells in the vicinity but was neither paying proper compensation for the right to operate in the area nor providing enough jobs for community residents. After the people of Epebu demanded their rights, Stanley alleged that Agip paid their neighbors, the Madike community, to attack their village. At 5:00 A.M. on July 13, 1998, two speedboats, with new twin 75-horsepower engines, Stanley noted, came ashore, and delivered a gang of men armed with machetes, rifles and dynamite. They razed half the town and killed six people, he said, including a woman. "A pregnant woman," someone from the crowd shouted. "Yes, the woman was pregnant."

Petitions and delegations sent to the Ogbia local government, and the authorities in the capital of Bayelsa State, Yenagoa, brought no response. "We have been crying to the government about it, but nothing has been done for five months, now going into its six month. No one from the government has even visited here." Their only recourse was direct action—kidnaping. "Since the government is not paying attention to us, the only way we can make the world know about this situation that we are in is to capture a boat."

Stanley continued for a while longer, outlining the village's accusations against the government and the oil companies, complaints that could be heard in almost every village the width and breadth of the Niger delta. The exact figures might have remained a mystery to these villagers, but they knew that oil worth more money than they could dream of was being taken from their home region. They believed the revenues were being sent up north to Abuja to pay for its luxurious hotels and office buildings, to the sprawling commercial center Lagos, or to foreign bank accounts.

"For the past fifteen years the government has done nothing for us," Stanley shouted. While the state did pay the meager salaries of the teachers and medical assistants, the people of Epebu themselves had to build the one-room mud-walled health clinic, now in ruins, and the high school. Fishing catches were down, owing mainly, the villagers believed, to oil pollution, and the prevailing agitation in the area meant that it was too dangerous to hunt and forage in the forest for food. "There are still further attacks and our people are starving," Stanley said. Everyone in the room moaned and nodded their heads in agreement.

The chiefs offered a round of soft drinks, and then the gathering poured out of the building to inspect the damage caused by the raid. Stanley and I walked with Chief Ombu Daufa, the village's second-ranking elder. Scores of buildings in the heart of the village lay in ruins. Chief Daufa stared blankly at one pile of rubble, which was all that remained of his house. The attackers had used sticks of dynamite to level it, he said. Shops, "chop houses" (restaurants), bars, and a church were in similar condition.

The procession took a half-hour to reach the edge of the soccer field, where the two local teams, the Super Dragons and the Escma Rocks, played each weekend. We scaled back down the shore to the launch. As Consul pushed the boat from shore and put the engines into gear, half the village stood waving as if they were bidding good-bye to tourists visiting their rural idyll.

It was getting late in the day, and Consul opened the engine throttles in a race to reach Akassa before nightfall. Occasionally he stopped to ask a passing fisherman if there were any boats nearby filled with gangs of youths on the prowl for kidnap victims. Satisfied that there were not, he roared off again, taking great care not to swamp the man's wooden pirogue. Years of uncontrolled felling of trees by the logging industry and by the fishermen themselves had stripped the delta of its hardwoods. The giant trees needed to carve out a pirogue were especially scarce, and boat builders had to trek ever deeper through the swamps to find them. Overturning a hardwood canoe and sending it, inevitably, to the bottom could cost a driver up to 20,000 naira in damages, about $200, or a year's wages.

An expert guide in the delta, Consul whipped through a series of narrow creeks and canals, some of them barely twice the width of the boat, that appeared seemingly out of nowhere. As we plunged deeper into the delta, the panorama was one of striking monotony; as far as the eye could see, the eerie mangrove trees with their aerial spiderlike roots dipped down, sucking sustenance from the muddy tidal waters.

We were still fifteen minutes outside Akassa when our boat passed a deserted fishing village that had been burnt to the ground. "Balatima," Alagoa shouted. "One hundred people—all killed or driven away." The *Amayanabo*, or paramount chief of the Akassa clan, His Royal Highness, I. N. Antony Ikonibo I, had told me about Balatima's bloody end when I met him in Port Harcourt the previous day. A woman from the neighboring village of Liama had asked a Balatima man to repay a debt; he murdered her instead. The Liama villagers demanded that the authorities punish the man, but Nigeria's notoriously corrupt police did nothing. "The police came and took the opportunity to collect bribes from both sides," Chief Antony said. "So the people of Liama said okay, jungle justice. They went and completely wiped off that village. Up till now, there is no human being living there."

The case of Balatima had nothing directly to do with the oil business, but it was a tragic indicator of the level of violent disorder in the Niger delta. "The rule of law has been thrown to the wind," Alagoa said. "Everywhere people just act as if there were no government per se. There are communal clashes, people fighting themselves, people fighting constituted authority. One community at the throat of another community, fighting oil companies. It is always fight, fight, fight to the extent that there is just no peace. The delta is on fire today."

The damp blanket of warm evening air was pitch black by the time Consul's daredevil navigation landed the launch, with characteristic flourish, at Kongho's wooden pier. Kongho is the main settlement of the Akassa clan, whose 30,000 people are spread across eighteen permanent villages and dozens of fishing ports. At the first distant sound of the engines, a small crowd of young men had gathered at the dock as an informal watchdog committee to ensure that the boat was not carrying oil company workers or troublesome rivals from a neighboring clan.

Our launch was painted orange, like dozens of others that the oil companies either used themselves or handed over to particular communities so that they would protect their installations from rival villages. Speedboats had become almost a currency in the delta. Just up a creek next to the pier was an identical orange craft that the Akassa youths had captured from Agip. It was one of two company boats that the youths were holding until Agip paid Akassa compensation for an oil spill. As soon as the youths spotted Consul—Akassa's youth leader—at the helm, however, they relaxed.

Alagoa supervised the unloading of the various parcels and baggage and then turned back toward the river to gaze at several points in the distance where a bright orange glow danced across the black sky. "Gas flares from the oil wells," he said after a moment. "The delta even looks as if it is in flames."

———

OIL BEGAN to fan the flames of turmoil in the Niger delta more than a century ago in the lead-up to the gathering of Europeans in Berlin to carve up the continent in their so-called scramble for Africa. The oil in question was not a fossil fuel, however. Rather, it was the thick oil derived from boiling palm nuts. The Atlantic slave trade and the New World plantations had furnished the capital needed to embark on the industrial revolution, and now the Europeans needed to lubricate their machinery. Palm oil emerged as the pioneer commodity in Africa's modern commercial relationship with the developed world—the export of cheap raw materials.

The Niger delta was the biggest source of palm oil in Africa, and early on, the delta chiefs and Liverpool traders were the dominant players. The Africans kept a tight grip on the trade as middlemen by preventing direct contact between the Europeans and the actual producers of palm oil in the hinterland. Like their counterparts up and down the West African coast, the African merchants were shrewd men of considerable means who had grown wealthy from the slave trade, first with the Portuguese beginning in the fifteenth century and later with the British.

When the Portuguese explorers first arrived in the delta, the Ijaws inhabited small, dispersed fishing villages. They traded among themselves or with their neighbors in the interior to the north, the Igbos. They exchanged fish and salt panned from the creeks for vegetables and iron implements. When the Europeans came shopping for slaves, however, the Ijaws adapted quickly, moving from trading with the Igbos to selling them. The supply of Igbo slaves to the delta ports was controlled not by outsiders but by the cream of Igbo society, the Aro. Their command of the most powerful oracle in the east, Long Juju, which was believed to be linked to the supreme deity Chukwu, guaranteed the Aro universal respect and fear. They shipped the slaves to the delta ports, where middlemen sold them to the Europeans, either for work on plantations on the island of São Tomé or for the mines and farms of the New World. Once-modest settlements were transformed into major slave ports, such as Bonny, New Calabar, Okrika, and Brass.

When the Atlantic slave trade was abolished in the nineteenth century, the delta chiefs found new opportunities in exporting palm oil, and they adapted accordingly and thrived. Whereas the African middlemen demonstrated strict discipline in fixing prices, the British companies operating in the region were a squabbling lot, each ready to undercut the other in the hope of gaining greater market share.

Onto the scene stepped George Dashwood Goldie Taubman, fresh from traveling around North Africa (with a beautiful Egyptian mistress, whom he discarded). He came to the Guinea Coast to discover the pecuniary illness of Holland Jacques, the company owned by his brother's in-laws. The diagnosis was simple: too much competition from wealthy African traders and, potentially even more worrisome, from the French and the Germans. Goldie took immediate action to rectify the situation. He successfully banded the various palm oil companies in 1879 into the United African Company, which subsequently became the National African Company. Fired with imperialist ambitions, Goldie lobbied London for a royal charter to make a reality of his dream of establishing a British-controlled commercial empire from east to west Africa.

As the company's main port, Akassa became the beachhead of British colonial occupation of the Niger delta and ultimately of Nigeria itself. By 1884 Goldie had secured thirty-seven treaties with local chiefs and maintained a fleet of twenty gunboats to punish any Africans who challenged his company's authority. Settlements at Brass, Patini, and Asaba all tasted the power of Goldie's cannons. A year later he used the treaties to bolster Britain's case for control over the delta at the Berlin Conference, which he attended as a delegate. He succeeded, and much of the delta was declared the Oil Rivers Protectorate.

The chiefs who signed treaties with Goldie and the British consul of the day, Major Edward Hewett, often did not understand that they were effectively ceding their sovereignty to the British Crown.

Sometimes their signatures or marks were forged or obtained under duress. Other times the British simply lied to them. When Jaja, the former slave turned king of Opobo, negotiated an agreement with Hewett, he specifically asked the consul to define the word *protectorate*. Hewett responded that "The queen does not want to take your country or your markets, but at the same time she is anxious that no other nation should take them. She undertakes to extend her gracious power and protection, which will leave your country still under your government: she has no wish to disturb your rule."[1]

In 1886 Goldie received his coveted royal charter, which gave the company political authority over the chieftaincies with which he had concluded treaties. The charter specifically ruled out the establishment of a trade monopoly in the region, but Goldie ignored this stipulation and deliberately sabotaged the business dealings of independent African merchants, Liverpool traders, and the French. Communities that remained outside the charter's authority, such as the once powerful slave-trading kingdom at Brass, were forced to pay exorbitant duties for the privilege of engaging in palm oil trade. African traders within the company area had to accept miserly prices for their product, or they were undercut altogether by company boats traveling upriver to make purchases at their source in the interior. Among the stronger chiefs who resisted were King Jaja and Chief Nana, both of whom the British defeated and deported. Chief Nana was sent to the Gold Coast colony, now the modern nation of Ghana, and King Jaja was exiled to the West Indies until 1891, when he was finally allowed to return home. He died on the way.

The resentment of the company's monopoly among the people of Brass reached its peak in 1895, when King William Koko took the offensive. Fortified by their belief in the Ijaw god of war, Egbesu, one thousand Nembe clan warriors painted with white chalk set out in war canoes. They used the cover of night to avoid British patrols and launched a dawn attack on Goldie's company headquarters in Akassa.

King Koko's force killed at least seventy-five employees, though none of them were European, and ate a fair number. "If we Brass people die through hunger," he vowed, "we had rather go to them and die on their sords [sic]."[2] Eventually, though, even King Koko succumbed to British military power, and the delta resistance faded away. Within a generation the inhabitants of the delta, no longer in control of their fate, fell into a tight grip of economic stagnation from which they have never recovered. "May this evil of palm oil not get to our children" was a popular prayer of the time.[3]

In 1893 the Oil Rivers Protectorate became the Niger Coast Protectorate, which included those adjacent areas not already under the rule of the Niger Company. The Niger Coast Protectorate was later merged with Lagos into the Protectorate of Southern Nigeria. Lord Lugard had moved from Akassa up the Niger River into the interior, and with his West African Frontier Force he occupied territories in the far north, including the Sokoto Caliphate. In 1914 Lugard amalgamated the northern and southern territories in the name of the British Crown—a development that the Ijaws and the other minorities of the delta never fully accepted.

In the 1950s, with the approach of Nigeria's independence, the Ijaws and other minority groups throughout the delta revived their argument that the nineteenth-century treaties signed with the British gave London no legal right to hand them over to the new nation-state. As Sir Henry Willink's Commission on Minority Groups found in 1957, the chiefs believed that

> [t]he British crown undertook to provide protection and to deal with foreign powers, but the treaties did not provide that the chiefs should surrender to the British Government a sovereignty which could be transferred to any other authority. If Her Majesty's Government saw fit to end the treaties, then the Chiefs of this area were morally entitled to revert to their original status.[4]

The Willink commission rejected both independence for the delta communities and granting them the status of a state within Nigeria. But it recognized, in a foreshadowing of the complaints of today, that among the peoples of the delta "lay a deep-rooted conviction that the difficulties of this difficult stretch of country were not understood at headquarters of the government."[5] The commission called for "the declaration of the Ijaw country as a Special Area," which would draw "public attention to a neglected tract and give the Ijaws an opportunity of putting forward plans of their own for improvement."[6]

The chiefs did not know it then, but as the Willink commission was gathering its evidence, the future of the delta had taken a dramatic turn, one that meant that an independent Nigerian government would be loathe to loosen its control of the region. In the Ijaw community of Oloibiri, Shell had discovered oil.

By a turn of fate, Oloibiri was also the birthplace of a man who would go down in Nigerian history as a lunatic Ijaw revolutionary or a visionary, depending on one's point of view. At the time of the oil discovery, Isaac Boro was preparing to follow in the footsteps of his father, a mission school headmaster, and become a teacher. His career in education was brief, however, and he decided to join the police after being attracted by the power they showed when putting down riots in the delta over falling standards of schools. Three years later Boro quit the force, and in 1961 he enrolled in the University of Nsukka to study chemistry.

His first foray into politics brought the taste of defeat and exposed him to what he considered to be ethnic politics. Boro and another Ijaw lost a student council election to an Igbo. From that, Boro concluded that in Nigeria the minorities were strictly second-class citizens. Together with his close associates, Sam Owonaru and Nottingham Dick, Boro set about furthering the Ijaw cause by establishing a self-help organization called Integral WXYZ that was dedicated to promoting employment and political education. One arm of Integral WXYZ was the Niger Delta Oil Council. Its mission was to take up with the Western oil companies "their continued atrocities to our people and their wicked reluctance to improve the lot of the people they were bound to be associated with for long. The council was also to make out estimated bills for payment by the oil companies with respect to inadequate damages paid to natives for cash crops and economic trees destroyed during their operations."[7]

The life of Integral WXYZ was aborted by the January Boys' coup d'état in 1966. Although the major ethnic groups, the Igbos and the Yorubas, resented Prime Minister Balewa's administration as symbolizing northern domination, the Ijaws had supported the government because it had treated the delta as a special zone. The coup convinced Boro and his associates that it was time for drastic action. "If we did not move then, we would throw ourselves into perpetual slavery. The only protector of the Ijaws, Sir Balewa, was gone."[8]

The revolution started with £150 and a red flag bearing a crocodile. Within several weeks 160 young men had joined the army, which was named the Niger Delta Volunteer Service but was commonly known simply as the Service. The Service's first military action was rather modest: the nighttime capture of a canoe smuggling illegal gin.

For spiritual fortitude the Service revived seven oracles and the cult of Egbesu of King Koko's era. To this day Egbesu is believed to protect the faithful from bullets and to punish anyone who defies the cult. The oracles are consulted to root out evil in the community and to empower warriors for military battle. In his autobiographical account, *The Twelve Day Revolution*, Boro tells the story of a group of government soldiers who attempted to destroy an oracle shrine near Kaiama by pulling on the scepter and damaging the drums. The soldiers, he reports, later drowned.

In February Boro declared an independent republic and a state of emergency in the Niger delta. He announced that all oil contracts were null and void, ordered oil companies to negotiate directly with the new republic, and required all "aliens," or non-Ijaws, to report to the Volunteer Service within twenty-four hours. On February 23 the Service went into action. Three separate operations culminated in the capture of Yenagoa, whose small police garrison fell easily. The Service fighters then went on a looting spree. "The new laws were being obeyed," Boro later crowed. "The area had been purged of non-natives. There was already jubilation everywhere."9

The celebrations proved to be short-lived. By the second day government reinforcements were beginning to arrive. Boro and his men watched the army move into position using pontoon boats provided by Shell, a pattern that would be repeated years later when the oil transnational would finance the security forces in their operations against protesters in Ogoniland in the 1990s.

By the third day ammunition shortages forced the Service to withdraw. The secession of the Niger delta quickly collapsed. Boro later explained his decision to call off the revolution because of government repression against the civilian population. His wife Georgina was threatened. On March 7 Boro turned himself in. He, Samuel Owonaru, and Nottingham Dick were eventually charged with treason and convicted, but their death sentences were later commuted. Boro died in the Biafran war fighting as a federal soldier to put down the Igbo secession.

Thirty years after Isaac Boro's uprising, oil pollution, uncontrolled logging, and overfishing spread the misery and the feeling of alienation among the Ijaws and neighboring minority groups. Following Ken Saro-Wiwa's hanging in November 1995, the baton of resistance passed to radical Ijaw youths, as the history of the delta came full circle. Once again the Nigerian security forces, like their British colonial predecessors a century before, battled militants demanding their rights to self-determination and a fair share of the wealth produced by their ancestral land.

This newer phase of the Ijaw struggle exploded in March 1997 around the oil city of Warri. The Ijaws were locked in a dispute over who should control the city with two neighboring ethnic groups, the Urhobos and the Itsekiris. Warri is home to one of Nigeria's four oil refineries, a petrochemical plant, a steel mill, and a deep-water river port. Violence among the three groups erupted when the then military administrator of Delta State, Colonel John Dungs, moved the headquarters of the local government from the Ijaw town of Ogbe-ijoh to Ogidigben in the Itsekiri area. Dungs's decision was explosive because the siting of local governments, as the primary channels for patronage and jobs from the authorities in Abuja, are always hotly disputed.

Neither the Ijaws nor the Itsekiris were happy with the arrangement. The Ijaws lost the headquarters, but the Itsekiris had only two of nine new wards. After the Itsekiris burned down the house of a prominent Ijaw, Chief Edwin Kiagbodo Bekederemo-Clark, radical young Ijaws mobilized throughout the delta, arming themselves with machetes, assault rifles, and, in a few cases, rocket launchers.

Like King Koko and Isaac Boro before them, the Ijaw youths revived Egbesu. Cult priests began recovering the seven oracles from the sacred places where they had remained hidden since the collapse of Boro's rebellion. The revival of the cult was dramatic testimony to the turmoil within Ijaw communities. The oracles reappear rarely and only when a broad consensus develops across clans and age groups that the very survival of society is at stake.

Faced with the growing threat of rebellion, the military government adopted a carrot-and-stick approach toward the Ijaw militants. "Government will not tolerate any acts of lawlessness by youths and others in these areas," Abubakar warned at a press conference in September 1998. Although the government was "sensitive" to the region's desire for improved living standards, the disruptions of the oil company operations had degenerated into "kidnapping, extortion and willful damage to pipelines and facilities," he said.

Abubakar announced the establishment of a committee chaired by the chief of air staff and member of the Provisional Ruling Council,

Air Vice Marshall Nsikak Eduok, to reorganize the Oil Minerals Producing Areas Development Commission (OMPADEC). The commission, which was designed to fund development projects in the delta, had a reputation for corruption and mismanagement and enjoyed minimal public confidence.

On December 11 hundreds of Ijaws, said to represent five hundred communities and forty Ijaw clans, gathered at Kaiama, the home village of Boro's family. They issued a declaration demanding that

> all oil companies stop all exploration and exploitation activities in the Ijaw area. We are tired of gas flaring; oil spills, blowouts and being labeled saboteurs and terrorists. It is a case of preparing the noose for our hanging. We reject this labeling. Hence, we advise all oil companies staff and contractors to withdraw from Ijaw territories by the 30th December, 1998 pending the resolution of the issue of resource ownership and control in the Ijaw area of the Niger Delta.[10]

The Kaiama meeting agreed, however, that the Ijaws would "remain within Nigeria...to demand and work for self government and resource control for the Ijaw people."

After the Kaiama declaration came Operation Climate Change. Its goal was to pressure the oil companies to cease work and withdraw from Ijaw territory, to extinguish all gas flares, and to open negotiations with the Ijaw youth leaders, according to Oronto Douglas, an environmental lawyer and Ijaw Youth Council (IYC) leader.[11] Douglas denied that the IYC had declared war on the oil companies and accused the Abubakar administration of responding with "violence, war, fear and absolute intimidation."[12]

Violence erupted on December 30, when hundreds of Ijaw youths took to the streets of the Bayelsa state capital, Yenagoa, and other communities to implement the Kaiama declaration stipulation that oil companies withdraw immediately from Ijaw territory. The security forces fired into crowds of protesters. In a week of violence, dozens of people were killed.[13] The state administrator, Lieutenant Colonel Paul Obi, imposed a one-week state of emergency in Bayelsa. In Kaiama the security forces engaged in running battles with the youths, taking time out for an occasional looting spree. One target of their peacekeeping activities was St. Mark's Anglican Church, where the soldiers smashed Reverend Atari Adou's television set, broke open two church safes, and carted away the communion vessels.

A consultative assembly of Ijaws and two neighboring groups, the Isokos and the Ndokwas, denounced the government crackdown in early January, saying, "The decision of the government of General Abdulsalami Abubakar to kill defenseless Ijaw youths amounts to a declaration of war."[14] The statement was signed by Bello Orubebe, a barrister who was described as the coordinator of the Niger Delta Volunteer Force, a name reminiscent of the one Isaac Boro had given to his secessionist army in 1966.

———

THE IMAGE of the Niger delta on fire seemed absurd as I strolled down a mud footpath along the Nun River estuary one sunny afternoon with a young man in shorts and flip-flops named Tomoworio "Mecks" Gooden. The adjacent Akassa villages of Kongho and Bekekiri seemed more like tourist resorts than the front line of a low-intensity secessionist war.

But though quiet now, the volatile past of the delta ran right through the heart of Akassa, and Mecks was giving me a tour of the historical sights. Along the trail it was easy to spot corroded nineteenth-century British cannons lying around, the very artillery pieces that were turned on the forces of King Koko and other defiant African chiefs.

Bekekiri's English translation is "the area of the whites," and indeed much of the brickwork and corrugated iron of the United African

Company's installations are still intact, though they bear the scars of time. The company's two-story sleeping quarters now serve as a makeshift laundry for local residents, and one of the warehouses echoed to the pounding of muscle-bound men salvaging scrap metal. No one seemed to enter one eerily silent block building that Mecks described as a Portuguese holding room for slaves.

Mecks led me to an overgrown graveyard for the company's European employees behind Akassa's only elementary school, Bishop Crowther Memorial, built in 1947 by Christian missionaries and named after Samuel Crowther, the first Nigerian clergyman. The school had finished for the day. Mecks asked a group of children in blue-and-white uniforms milling about in the shade if they would mind clearing a path into the burial ground. Several of the younger boys readily agreed, and within minutes they were hacking away with machetes at stout thickets of thorn bushes.

Most of the names on the tombs were clearly British—Henry the son of Captain John Russell Hecks and Eliza, who died in 1895; D. McKenzie, who passed away in 1898; and John Stanley Owen, who passed away in 1890 at the age of eighty. One man, whose name, Josue Zwefel, betrays a Portuguese heritage, died in 1885. His 4-foot headstone bore the inscription "This monument has been erected by his friends in the Nigerian territories." The little boys stood watching in awe, not at the presence of European ghosts but at the resilience of their marble tombstones. "They built things a lot better in those days," Mecks said after chatting with the youngsters in Ijaw. "Modern buildings fall down after only a few years."

There was plenty of evidence to back up his observation. Of the ten blocks that had once comprised the government high school, only two remained intact. The rest had fallen into ruin a few years back after a tropical squall tore off their roofs. The government never bothered to repair them. Their walls were collapsing, and in the middle of the empty shells of classrooms that once nourished young minds, weeds grew chest high. Conditions were so poor that the headmaster of the school had sent his own children away to study in Yenagoa. The school was one of many symptoms of the stunted development in Akassa since independence. Health facilities were rudimentary, clean water was scarce, and the only electricity came from a handful of private generators owned by a few businessmen and traditional chiefs.

As we advanced along the trail, Mecks pointed out a flat two-room building that was meant to serve as Akassa's police station. A couple of men in civilian clothes milled about the entrance, but there was no sign of a constable in uniform. "They do nothing here and they are even frightened to wear their uniforms," Mecks said with a chuckle. The apparently off-duty policemen were the only sign of the government's presence in Akassa. Police matters were generally handled by the community itself, either through the Akassa Council of Chiefs or by the youths, who tended to take matters into their own hands. Earlier in the year a boat had arrived from the nearest government outpost at Brass with a couple of immigration officers, who were notorious for harassing people to secure bribes. Chief Antony warned them to be out of town within ten minutes. They had not been back since.

It was a testament to the feeling of utter neglect by the government and the oil companies that some in Akassa looked back with nostalgia to the time of the United African Company (UAC), the corporate right arm of Britain's colonial administration. The price for palm oil might have been low and working conditions brutal, but at least local traders and laborers could earn a living. "I would say honestly that the UAC had a more positive impact on the people than the oil companies have," Chief Antony told me. "The UAC approached various communities where they settled, signed an agreement with them, and then did their oil trading. They employed the locals, and the locals participated in the business, either as agents or labor." That was no longer true. Since Akassa was considered a "non–oil producing area," the vast majority of the clan received almost nothing from the petroleum industry, except of course pollution.

It was an explosive situation that worried even traditional leaders who had profited handsomely from the oil business. Chief Antony, for example, was a wealthy subcontractor for the industry. His Ikonibo company compound, just a few blocks away from the headquarters of Royal/Dutch Shell in Port Harcourt, was equipped with computers and a private radio network with direct links to Akassa and Lagos. But now he was worried about the burning frustration in the delta. "Everybody is just fed up," Chief Antony said. "After forty years of independence, there is not one single thing to show for it, except for a few primary school buildings and white elephant projects. Everyone just wants the basics, clean water and light. We don't have them."

Beyond the pervasive disillusionment with the government and the oil companies, over the years something far more disturbing had happened to the psychology of the people of Akassa and the delta as a whole: People had lost the ability to trust each other. In fact, as recent events in Epebu, Balatima, and countless other settlements showed, more often than not they were at each other's throats. Ijaw society could be forcefully democratic at times but rampantly anarchic at others.

In Akassa there was a saying that went something like "Although oil pollution can be cleaned up, the pollution of the community cannot." The remark was a reference to the millions of dollars that the companies and the government had spent over the years on dubious schemes and on compensation for oil spills that had disappeared into the pockets of the elite. It also highlighted the fighting between villages over the spoils of the little revenue that came their way. This explained in part why one *poro*, or extended family compound, was often quick to fight a neighboring *poro* for the right to compensation from an oil company rather joining its neighbor to present a united front.

"There has been little co-operation," admitted Chief Antony. "The only time people came together was when there was a festival or when somebody managed to catch a big shark or swordfish in his net. Then the whole community would gather on the shore and cut it up."

By the mid-1990s economic conditions had deteriorated so far that local people could not even afford to purchase the fish and shrimp caught in Akassa's waters. The fishermen sold the bulk of their catches to outside buyers, who offered better prices. Justina Digitemie, a prominent local leader, and a group of women decided to take action. Akassa is a matrilineal society, with all property being handed down through the wife's side of the family, and women have a powerful voice in community affairs. The community women called a meeting to discuss the problem and demanded that the Council of Chiefs order the fishermen to sell part of their catch locally. It was a small but important step by Akassa to take its destiny in its own hands.

Then, quite unexpectedly, an oil company stepped in with an offer of help. Statoil-BP, a joint venture between Norway's Statoil and British Petroleum, was beginning to prospect for offshore fields. Because of the international controversy that the Saro-Wiwa execution and the Ogoni campaign had generated, Statoil-BP wanted to fund a showpiece development project to promote its reputation both in the delta and in the eyes of its shareholders.

Statoil-BP approached two nongovernmental organizations with experience in the region, Pro Natura International and the Niger Delta Wetlands Center, and asked them to draw up a plan for Akassa. They sent in a small team of expatriates and Ijaws, including Knight, who had a couple of decades of development experience in Nigeria, and Alagoa, a fisheries lecturer at the Rivers State University of Science and Technology.

With Chief Antony providing housing and moral support, the team linked up with a group of local activists to visit the communities one by one and ask people what problems they wanted to address. The answers, not surprisingly, were poverty, lack of education, poor health facilities, declining fishing catches, environmental degradation, scarce supplies of clean water—"everything that adds up to life in this place," said Mecks, a project "facilitator."

Another enthusiastic recruit to the program was Justina, a mother of nine who was elected chairperson of the Akassa Community Development Council, an umbrella body that provides clanwide oversight. The involvement of people like Justina and Mecks was critical if the project was to win public confidence. Skepticism about development projects ran deep because of past experience with what are known as benefit captors, that is, corrupt government officials or middlemen who siphon funds meant for development into their own pockets. "People are really afraid of anyone above them," said Knight. "There is a complete lack of trust."

At the base of the program was the *ogbo,* a traditional institution that organized interest groups—traders, snail gatherers, and fishermen, for example. The obvious attraction of the *ogbo* was that people knew and trusted it. Because a shortage of capital was the main hindrance to investment, the project transformed the *ogbo* into a clanwide savings scheme. The members of each *ogbo* placed their savings in a common pool, and together they decided what to do with it. The only requirement was that individual members who borrowed from the pool pay it back, which they were inclined to do since in effect they were repaying themselves and their close neighbors. By October 1998 the capital in the system totaled 1.5 million naira, about $15,000, and there were 196 outstanding loans worth on average about $35 each.

Early one morning Mecks and I accompanied the Akassa nursing officer, Esther Digitemie, Justina's thirty-two-year-old daughter, on a trip to make her first delivery of medical supplies to remote fishing villages. We met at her office, the clan's run-down health clinic in Bekekiri that consisted of a virtually empty cement block building. The clinic was supposed to serve 30,000 people.

Esther had wanted to be a nurse since she was a little girl, ever since her mother Justina used to leave her little brother in her care while she went off to teach in the primary school. When Esther graduated from high school, she enrolled in the School of Nursing in Port Harcourt. By 1995 she was back in Akassa in charge of the health center.

On average Esther and her two assistants saw six patients a day.

Malaria, measles, and tuberculosis were the most threatening illnesses, and eye infections and diarrhea were common. Akassa needed at least one doctor and some qualified nurses, she said. "If a person needs an operation, we send them to the hospital in Brass. It has facilities, but not everything. There is only one resident doctor."

In the past, basic medicines such as aspirin were scarce, and the distant fishing villages depended on the drug hawkers who visited from time to time. Even then the medicines, outdated and spoiled by exposure to the sun, often did more harm than good. "If anybody was sick," Esther recalled, "they had to be brought from very far, where you had to paddle for two or three hours before you can find a painkiller to buy. People died from ordinary diarrhea or fever."

When the Akassa development project started in 1997, a doctor from Port Harcourt decided that the only way to overcome the problems caused by the vast distances was to establish in each village health posts that could treat simple illnesses and refer more serious cases to the nearest hospitals in Brass and Yenagoa. The project set up an arrangement to obtain cheap drugs from a special government department called the Petroleum Trust Fund and to replenish stocks with the revenues from sales of medicines in the communities.

The new health scheme sounded promising, but as we learned on a visit to one of the eighteen target villages, there were problems. After a forty-five-minute ride from Bekekiri by motorboat, we landed in Hawartimio, a tiny fishing camp of perhaps fifty open-sided wooden huts built on stilts a few yards from the water's edge. An impromptu soccer match was under way in a clearing in front of the village.

As soon as we disembarked on the shore and plunged ankle-deep in the thick, odorous *chicoco* mud of the mangrove, it was apparent that Esther's love of caring for people was matched by the short temper of a drill sergeant. She was not impressed with the lack of preparation at the health post. The installation of a plastic tank to catch rainwater was not complete, the health post hut itself still needed work, and the box where the medicines were to be kept was not yet finished.

We entered the one-room health post, which was filled with the smoke of burning red mangrove sticks. They smelt remarkably like sandalwood and were meant to keep away the minute but aggressive sand flies. Several elderly chiefs gathered for the parley, including one senior man with the colorful name of Hitler Wilson. After a round of friendly greetings, Esther delivered a stinging lecture about their lack of readiness. Eventually she began pulling out the various utensils and pills and produced an inventory that they were meant to sign. At first they demurred, not wanting to take responsibility, but after another round of goading from Esther they were only too ready to make their marks.

Hitler and his colleagues explained their reticence by saying there were "people here who want to overthrow us because of our involvement in the program." There was a perception among some of their rivals that because they had been in the forefront of establishing the health post, somehow they were enjoying personal gain. Mecks perked up to repeat one of his favorite sayings, "There's a Judas in every twelve," and the old men let out a chorus of affirmation, "eh eh!" After the presentation was over, Esther proffered some words of encouragement and warned forcefully that she would be returning and that they had better be prepared. The look of anxiety in their eyes suggested they would.

As we boarded the motorboat for the ride back to Bekekiri, Esther was still shaking her head. "That village was supposed to be supplied with the medical supplies five or six months ago but even up to today they have not completed the work," she said. "They don't compromise and work together. Some people want to work, but others don't. They say, 'well if it is not my own, then let it be.'"

Esther's obvious frustration with the people of Hawartimio reflected the change of spirit that had come over Akassa in the past two years. In places such as Kongho and Bekekiri there were so many gatherings to discuss the array of issues facing the community that

Akassa had the feel of being one giant, vibrant school. Esther's mother, Justina, spent so much time in meetings concerning her women's group, the *ogbo*, and the Akassa Development Council that she barely had time for her household chores. Esther confided that her mother was so busy that her father, Chief G. T. Digitemie Eriga, had to prepare supper. "He definitely cooks more than my mother," she said, giggling. "Most of the time my mother is out coordinating the various projects and before she returns home, he has dinner ready."

I attended a gathering on resources management that was held in one of the two functioning rooms at the high school. The turnout was low, about twenty participants, because people from all over the clan area were down at the pier awaiting the arrival of officials from Texaco to discuss compensation for an oil spill of four months before. Fishermen were particularly eager to win some cash, and I was reliably told that old, long-disused fishing nets were being trotted out to convince the Texaco representatives to part with their money.

Despite the low turnout, the meeting had to go on, and after a short prayer the discussion centered on the rapidly disappearing forests. Doing much of the explaining was Mike Weeks, a British volunteer worker. Together with Chief J. E. Claude-Eze, Weeks had studied the forests of Akassa, and his findings were alarming. Nigeria had less than 5 percent of her rain forests left, about 1 million hectares, he said, and uncontrolled tree felling in Akassa meant that its forests were on the brink of extinction. The big trees needed for dugout canoes were almost totally exhausted. The forest was so depleted that loggers, principally outsiders, were felling young trees for a single cubic, as the standard 12-foot by 9-inch by 4-inch board is known. Cutting down younger trees contributed to a vicious cycle making replenishment impossible. Furthermore, the people of Akassa were earning a pittance for their trees. A cubic that went for 140 naira, about $1.75, in Akassa was sold in Port Harcourt for about twice that price. Once it reached places like Makoko in Lagos, the cubic fetched between ten and fifteen times the original price. In London, he pointed out, "African mahogany toilet seats fetch the equivalent of many hundreds of naira."

He said the issue was simple. If this continued, in a few years Akassa would have no more forests. The Akassa Council of Chiefs had already imposed a moratorium on the felling of trees for anything other than canoes and paddles. Weeks suggested that Akassa make the moratorium local law. It would represent the first time that a local community in Nigeria took control of its environment. Weeks's presentation was received warmly. The participants were to consider his proposal and take a decision at their next meeting.

Next up was Sabina Waribungo, an Ijaw researcher on fisheries at the Rivers State University for Science and Technology. Her evaluation of the condition of the fisheries was equally somber. Everyone knew about the harmful impact of oil pollution and the presence of large trawlers that were illegally fishing in the estuary. But Akassa's local fishermen were to blame as well. They were both fishing indiscriminately and catching small fish and fry, thus destabilizing the population.

One man stood up and said the human population increase of the Akassa was to blame. Perhaps the only thing they could do was "ask Jehovah for more fishes," he said. After a pause, he shouted, "We could even beg!" Sabina considered his suggestion for a moment, desperately fighting back a grin, and then said that in normal times the fish population should increase more rapidly than that of man. As far as God was concerned, she quoted him as saying, "I made these animals for you, so don't come to me when you mismanage them."

Although still in its infancy, the project seemed to have given Akassa's people some hope that there was a future here. "Improvement in living standards is not seen immediately because it's only been two years," said Chief Antony. "But I will tell you that the intention of the youths to drift to cities like Port Harcourt or Yenagoa is not there any more. They are looking to apply themselves to something in this area."

The novelty of Akassa Community Development Program went

beyond the fact that the intended beneficiaries were being asked what they wanted. That did make it rather unique in the delta, where Western oil companies have foisted on the communities countless projects such as the building of unwanted piers, schools without teachers, and health clinics without doctors and medicines. The true innovation was that the people determined how they wanted to solve the problems and then carried out the solutions themselves. "It won't work any other way," said Knight. "Unless the community runs the program themselves, unless they feel they 'own' it, nothing will happen."

All around Akassa, however, were clear signs that the potential for conflict was increasing. The oil companies' policy of "adopting" so-called oil-producing communities was making matters worse. Among the Akassa clan, for example, Texaco adopted two Akassa communities, Sangana and Fishtown, because they were located near its production facilities. Texaco paid local youths from the two settlements to protect their installations from potential attackers, but the rest of Akassa felt left out. "Our people have one father and one mother," said Mecks. "How can you take care of one while not taking care of another? That is the whole problem, and it causes conflicts among our people." In other areas companies such as Shell and Agip provided youth groups with speedboats and cash salaries to act as guards. As a result, the delta had the feel of Somalia about it, with gangs of youths cruising up and down the creeks and canals in high-powered boats reminiscent of the clan fighters riding through the streets of Mogadishu in their "technicals."

Chief Antony was reminded of the "divide and rule" policies of the British. He gave an example. In June 1998 Agip brought in a rig and asked one community to protect its work from their neighbors. But, he said,

A rig costs $80,000 per day just for the work, and what they get out of it is far more than that. But for these communities even $50,000 in compensation is a huge amount of money. Instead of doing that, they tried to settle with one community and told the other community to get out. Then they asked the first people to stay as guards over the rig. The people who were left out blamed their neighbors for depriving them of their means of livelihood.

Alagoa and other local observers believed that with the money these communities received, their youths were buying arms. He accused the oil companies of "just postponing an evil day, buying temporary peace, which is not good for them in the long run, which is not good for us as a people, or this country. How could they arm a section of a community to police another section of the same community? It is immoral, it is wrong, it is evil."

Despite the obvious dangers, Chief Antony felt that the people of Akassa had made an important start that could carry lessons for the rest of the delta, perhaps all of Nigeria. "People are thinking far ahead now. They spend time discussing how to improve either health or education, even their farms. You know the proverbial to kill a goose to get all the eggs. It's not like that now. We want to keep the goose alive."

Alagoa liked to say, "the journey of a thousand miles begins with one step" when discussing Akassa's revolutionary experiment in participatory development work. "That is why we are doing something. Around us the whole place is exploding, but not Akassa. I wouldn't want to roll out our own drums and beat them. But right now this place is peaceful and maybe there's a way forward in what is done here."

Yet no one harbored any illusions about the encouraging start. In a sea of anarchy this represented a small island of relative stability that could be engulfed by another crisis with one of the oil companies or an upsurge elsewhere in the delta.

The violence continued during and after Obasanjo's inauguration. In late June 1999 a group calling itself Enough Is Enough held hostage a helicopter belonging to a Shell subcontractor and its two foreign crew members.[15] The ongoing disturbances forced Shell to declare a force majeure in July, saying it could not meet its export commitments for the month. Obasanjo made several moves designed to calm passions in the delta, but they were not enough. The new constitution approved in the dying days of the Abubakar government stipulated that "at least 13 percent" of the oil revenues would remain in the region. In June Obasanjo presented a bill to the National Assembly to set up a Niger Delta Development Commission to promote economic growth in the region. The new bill included a $500-million endowment for reparation for environmental damage. Nevertheless, most Ijaw activists dismissed the new commission as a repackaged version of the notoriously corrupt OMPADEC.

In August five Britons were kidnaped in two different operations. Two of the men were aboard a hijacked ship, the *Askalad,* and three were working for a subcontractor of the U.S. company Texaco.[16] All five were eventually released. On August 18 an estimated thousand youths attacked the offices of Texaco in Warri. The assailants smashed office windows and glass doors, locked the staff inside, and left a symbolic coffin outside the entrance.[17]

In November Obasanjo faced his first Niger delta emergency in the town of Odi, and his response, the deployment of armed troops, ended in disaster. The roots of the crisis dated to the electoral process at the end of 1998 and early 1999, which saw representatives voted into office at the local, state, and federal levels. In Bayelsa State, as in other parts of the country, no proper elections ever took place. Massive rigging included stuffing ballot boxes and intimidating potential voters, and candidates of all three parties were guilty of hiring young hoodlums to fix the election results.

One particularly effective gang, led by Ken Niweigha, the son of a former policeman, had worked for Diepreye Alamieyeseigha, who was elected governor of Bayelsa State. Facing unemployment after the polls, the thirty-strong gang took over the "black market" slum area in Yenagoa, the state capital, and embarked on a campaign of carjackings and armed robbery. After several confrontations with the security forces, which left one soldier dead, the state authorities decided to drive the youths out of Yenagoa and into the nearby town of Odi, the hometown of Niweigha's father.

Soon local residents of Odi began complaining that the gang was responsible for a reign of terror that included illegal roadblocks, extortion, and the indiscriminate firing of automatic rifles. "The security situation is, to put it mildly, frightening, disturbing and horrifying," the traditional leader of Odi, King Thunder Efeke Bolou II, wrote to Governor Alamieyeseigha on November 1.

At the same time, ethnic clashes between Yorubas and Ijaws were breaking out in the Lagos slum of Ajegunle, and there was growing pressure within the IYC to respond. "There was a great deal of pressure from the grass roots to stand up for the Ijaws in Lagos," Dimueari von Kemedi, a prominent IYC leader, later recalled. "It got so bad that we had to ban the discussion of guns from all meetings. The leadership could not disagree, but our tactic was to keep delaying a decision, to say that we had to plan well, before taking any action." Niweigha's gang, although not part of the IYC, adopted the rhetoric of the council and began mobilizing other Ijaw youths to travel to Ajegunle and engage the Yorubas militarily.

On November 4 seven policemen, including the Yoruba officer who had led the initial drive against the youths in Yenagoa, traveled to Odi in an attempt to thwart Niweigha's plans. Niweigha's gang abducted and murdered them, and over the next several days five more policemen were killed. The murders were strongly condemned by the IYC and Governor Alamieyeseigha. President Obasanjo responded with a letter that criticized the governor for failing to take action and threatening to declare a state of emergency if the killers were not arrested within two weeks. Obasanjo failed to recognize that the state governor had no authority over the police (a failure he repeated two months later during a flare-up of violence in Lagos State). That responsibility rested in the president's hands, through his inspector general of police in Abuja.

Four days before the deadline, on November 20, a heavily armed column of several hundred army troops advanced into Odi. On the outskirts of the town, Niweigha's gang ambushed the troops and engaged them in a brief firefight. The troops, apparently enraged by the ambush, embarked on a scorched-earth campaign. Over the next two weeks they razed Odi with mortars and heavy-caliber machine guns. The soldiers killed dozens of civilians and destroyed every building in town except a bank, a health center, and an Anglican church.

The Nigerian Red Cross estimated that some fifteen thousand people had fled the area. "My home has been completely destroyed," said Professor Turner Isoun, a former vice chancellor of the University of Science and Technology in Rivers State University, who maintained a weekend home in Odi. "It is clear that the house was set on fire, and we think that mortar bombs and grenades were used." The operation was so brutal that had an army leader, rather than the new civilian president, been responsible, it would have provoked worldwide outrage. During a visit to the town a week later with reporters and several senatorial colleagues, a shocked Senate president Chuba Okadigbo said, "The facts speak for themselves. There is no need for speech because there is nobody to speak with."

With the crisis spreading, the Niger Delta began to resemble a giant crack in an aging windshield that was relentlessly fanning outward because nobody had made the effort to repair the initial modest damage. In the Islamic north, the ethnically diverse middle belt, the Yoruba west, and—to far less extent, ironically—the mainly Igbo east, tiny fissures were bursting into gaping cracks. Each region had a unique context reflecting its various cultural and religious beliefs and its particular history, but common threads ran through them. Politicians were prepared to champion chauvinism in the name of ethnic or religious solidarity in order to mobilize people desperate for, if not a better opportunity, then at least the hope of one. And those same politicians were threatened with being swept away by a groundswell of popular hostility.

6

The Faithful

A kingdom can endure with unbelief,
but it cannot endure with injustice.

SHEHU USMAN DAN FODIO

W HEN THE EXPLOSION came, no one could profess surprise,
though few could have foreseen that the sheer scale of the violence would pose a real threat to Nigeria's continued existence as a nation. But holy wars are almost by definition bloody affairs because they
spring from the very depths of the human soul. The combatants in-
voke the name of God to justify their cause but by doing so they question their enemy's place in the living world. The addition of ethnicity
and power politics to the religious frenzy invariably produces an
inflammable cocktail. In Nigeria, so it has proved.

   Northern Nigeria entered the new millennium seething with resentment. The political elite was angered over a perceived pro-southern and pro-Christian bias in the Obasanjo administration. "The
north," a catch-all term to mean anyone who is Muslim and whose

family traces its ancestry to northern Nigeria, had taken a bashing in the southern press for being responsible for all of the country's ills. Obasanjo's army purge of at least one hundred senior officers saw most top posts go to soldiers from the middle belt and the south. Measures to curb corruption and bring past human rights abuses out into the open naturally fell hardest on northern officials who had enjoyed power in the Abacha and Babangida regimes. Abacha's own son, Mohammed, was on trial for murder.

"Sure the northern leaders are angry," M.D. Yusufu, the former police chief and Arabic scholar from the northern city of Katsina, told me when we met in January 2000. "It's natural. Anyone who has the feeling of power and then loses it will not take it happily." The teeming, impoverished masses of the north harbored a quiet rage over more mundane matters, such as their falling living standards, their lack of clean water, decent schools, health clinics and jobs. As much as their counterparts in the Niger Delta or the slums of Lagos, they saw the hoped for benefits of civilian rule passing them by.

Then religion took center stage. Relations between Muslims and Christians had been strained at the best of times, but since late 1999 when several northern state governors moved to impose the full weight of the Islamic legal code, Sharia—including its penalties of amputations and floggings, its strict code of sexual segregation—tensions had risen to hazardous levels. Calls for Sharia had been sweeping the north for months. Local politicians, bereft of serious political programs, latched on to Sharia as an easy tool to win support from a population desperate for an end to years of frustration, corruption, and more than anything, hopelessness. The first to go for Sharia was the remote state of Zamfara. Then Babangida's home state of Niger announced it was adopting Sharia. A host of others were preparing to follow suit.

Muslims, rich and poor, educated and illiterate, flocked to the cause. Those Muslims who doubted the wisdom of pressing for Sharia largely remained silent. Living under Sharia is believed to be an intrinsic right and duty of the Islamic faithful, and any Muslims who oppose it are deemed to be lacking in true belief. The Muslim argument that Sharia would not affect non-Muslims, however, was clearly false since its ban on alcohol, cinemas, and integration of the sexes in most spheres of life would affect everyone.

The mainly Christian opponents of Sharia tried to argue that it threatened the supposedly secular constitution, though the document's preamble describes Nigeria "as one indivisible and Sovereign Nation under God." They pointed to section 10 of the constitution, which states, "The Government of the Federation or of a state shall not adopt any religion as state religion." Their second contention that, if allowed to continue, Sharia would effectively establish two legal systems in the country also had flaws. The constitution already recognizes a role for three legal systems: British Common law, Sharia, except for what was considered cruel punishments, and mainly traditional African Customary law. President Obasanjo, perhaps worried that his born-again Christian faith and his southern Yoruba ethnicity would disqualify him as a neutral arbiter in the dispute, dawdled and hoped that the brouhaha would fizzle. It didn't.

That the inevitable confrontation erupted in the normally drowsy former colonial town of Kaduna was no shock to anyone who watched Nigeria closely. Kaduna is one of the few cities that truly encapsulates the religious, ethnic, and class diversity that defines Nigeria. Mosques and churches, beer parlors and Koranic schools literally elbow each other for room. Hausa-speaking Muslims from all over the north, and Christians and animists from the south and the middle belt immigrated to Kaduna for its job opportunities and schools. Kaduna had experienced religious and ethnic violence in the early 1990s. The news that the state government was considering the Sharia question once again raised the political temperature to the boiling point.

After several Muslim rallies calling for the introduction of Sharia, the Christians decided it was their turn to voice the dissenting view. The often militantly anti-Muslim Christian Association of Nigeria (CAN) had apparently applied twice to the police for a permit to hold a rally but was turned down on security grounds. Frustrated, CAN decided to go ahead anyway. At Sunday masses throughout Kaduna on February 20, clergymen read out a CAN message requesting Christians to attend an anti-Sharia rally the next day.

Trouble began on Monday morning with a demonstration of 5,000 Christians carrying banners such as "Rest in Hell Sharia" and "Sharia is not Y2K compliant." A group broke away from the rally and attacked the state governor's offices. By late morning, skirmishes had broken out between the Christian demonstrators and Muslim bystanders. Both sides armed themselves with axes, machetes, and in some cases, guns. The violence spread quickly across the city. Dozens of shops and office buildings, mosques and churches were razed. Victims were shot, burned alive, and beheaded. Longtime neighbors fought each other to the death.

The street warfare continued into the night and for the next two days until Obasanjo dispatched army troops to restore a semblance of order. Nigeria was sliding toward the abyss, and had the army troops ignored Obasanjo's call, the long-feared nightmare might finally have descended on the land. But the troops did obey their president's orders and established a modicum of peace. Kaduna, however, would never be the same. The death toll was estimated to be at least 2,000. Bodies littered the streets. Entire neighborhoods had been "religiously cleansed."

Like a brushfire carried by the wind, the violence quickly shifted hundreds of miles to the southeast. Many of the victims in Kaduna had been Igbos, and when their corpses started arriving in the Igbo heartland, enraged gangs of youths vented their revenge on any northerners they could find. The worst violence hit the town of Aba, where an estimated 400 died, but there were reports of killings in other southeastern towns such as Owerri and Onitsha.

During the first day of the slaughter in Aba, the Catholic Bishops Conference of Nigeria captured the mood in a statement urging the government "to take vigorous action to halt this mad rush to national suicide."[1] The next day, Obasanjo summoned northern governors to his office in Abuja for an emergency meeting. Afterwards, vice president Atiku Abubakar announced that the governors had agreed to shelve Sharia for the time being "in order to restore order and create confidence among all communities." Within twenty-four hours, however, officials of Kano state revealed their governor had signed a Sharia bill on February 27, two days before the emergency meeting.

On March 1, Obasanjo used his first nationwide television address on the crisis to tell Nigerians that they had lost all "sense of outrage and moral sensitivity" to what he described as "mindless killings and maimings."[2] He blamed the scale of the bloodshed on "so many years of tyranny and mindless violence, encouraged and practiced by the state itself." Obasanjo also used his speech to reassure the international community of Nigeria's stability, but his choice of words seemed oddly insensitive to the scope of the catastrophe. "Let me say for the benefit of investors in our economy that this tragic event is a hiccup which is not unusual for a nation like Nigeria which has been oppressed and suppressed by its rulers in recent years. The hiccup will be put behind us and we will, Insha Allah (God Willing), move full steam ahead."

There seemed little chance that Nigeria would recover easily from such a "hiccup," however, and there was growing concern that an apparently out of touch Obasanjo was moving too slowly to check Nigeria's implosion. As Wole Soyinka put it, "The roof is already burning over his head. He thinks it is not. He thinks that some accidental rain which is the act of God or Allah will put out the fire but he had better understand that he has the responsibility of putting out the fire before it spreads."[3]

In subsequent days and weeks, it was clear that the Sharia controversy would not go away. Several prominent northern leaders, such as former heads of state Shehu Shagari and Muhammadu Buhari, dissented from the decision to freeze Sharia. On March 22, Buba Jangebe became the first man to have his right hand amputated after a sharia court convicted him of stealing a cow. Then the governor of Zamfara State, Ahmed Sani, disputed vice president Abubakar's assertion that the governors had even agreed to put Sharia on hold. "We will not withdraw. We will discuss with the federal government how best we can implement, how we can adjust our arrangement," he said. "Sharia is Islam. There is no distinction."[4] Once again, the lid was balanced precariously on the cauldron that is Nigeria. But the question was for how long.

While visiting Nigeria in January 2000, I had asked many people, Muslims and Christians, about the secret of Sharia's widespread appeal. There were many answers, ranging from the desire to re-establish the north's battered pride through Islam to a plot to destabilize the Obasanjo government. But the best one I found was provided by Abba Kyari. Kyari, who comes from the northeastern state of Borno, where Islam has thrived for nearly one thousand years, is the Cambridge-educated managing director and chief executive of the United Bank of Africa, one of Nigeria's biggest banking institutions. As we sat in his spacious air conditioned office on the eighteenth floor at the bank's headquarters in Lagos, he put it this way: "We have millions of people who have no food, no water, no education, no health care, but there is one thing common to them, religion. A politician does this as a political calculation but to the people it is not politics. People are just fed up, and Sharia fills the vacuum." The irony is that Kyari's statement could be equally true for Christians and animists simply by substituting "opposing Sharia" for "Sharia."

———

THE CURRENT crisis in northern Nigeria dates to the arrival of Islam on the heels of the Arab occupation of North Africa in the seventh century. The introduction of the camel opened major trade routes linking the tropical forests of the West African coast to Egypt and Tripoli. The ivory, salt, slaves, horses, and gold necessary to support the currencies of the Middle East and Europe crisscrossed the Sahara in giant caravans. Kano was particularly celebrated for its leatherwork and embroidery of cloth. In West Africa, the Arabs found trading partners in the great empires of Ghana, Songhai, and Mali whose kings were fabulously wealthy. The king of Mali, Mansa Musa, reached Cairo in 1324 on his hajj pilgrimage to Mecca with five hundred porters carrying staffs of gold. In what is today Nigeria, powerful trading centers grew around the Hausa city-states of Kano, Katsina, and Zaria, and at Borno among the Kanuri people of the northeast.

While Islam reached Kanem-Borno near Lake Chad in the eleventh century, its initial entrance into Kano and the other emirates in the northwest—the focal point of the current unrest—was strictly through the corridors of power. Traditional rulers placed a high value on the literacy and good administration skills of the Muslims, much as their medieval European counterparts valued their clerics. Islam's first royal convert in Kano was a man whose hot temper as a boy had earned him the name Yaji or "chili pepper." Ali Yaji b Tsamia, the Sarki of king of Kano, converted in the fourteenth century on the advice of some visiting Muslim preachers. His was largely a palace religion, with the great mass of people, even those living inside the city walls, twelve miles of thick embankments 30 to 50 feet high, left untouched by the teachings of the Koran.

The Hausas worshipped many gods, and over time the Koran became the subject of some unexpected rituals, such as the *Dirki*, when the holy book served as a fetish for cattle sacrifices. And however much they appreciated the Muslims' talents, over time the emirs became increasingly suspicious of their constant demands for the establishment of a pure Islam. The emirs had problems with their own people as well. Costly military campaigns increased the tax burden and stirred unrest among the Hausa peasantry. As in modern Nigeria, bribery, corruption, and illegal taxes were commonplace.

By the mid-eighteenth century, prophecies spoke of a great reformer, the Mujaddid, who would cleanse the land of oppression and anti-Islamic behavior. He turned out to be Shehu Usman dan Fodio, a student of the great Muslim scholar of the day, Mallam Jibril of Agades. Dan Fodio was a member of the Fulani, the light-skinned, cattle-rearing nomads who spread from the Senegal River valley across West Africa. He was a renowned preacher whose sermons attracted large crowds in Hausa areas such as Gobir and Zamfara. The King of Gobir, in the far northwest of what today is Nigeria, hired dan Fodio as a tutor to his children.

The Fulani had already led Islamic rebellions against what they considered corrupt kings elsewhere in West Africa. For dan Fodio the immediate spark was the rise to the Gobir throne of a former pupil, Yunfa, who cracked down on Islamic practices such as the wearing of the veil. Espousing Islam as an ideology and deriding the corruption of the Hausa kings, dan Fodio forged an alliance between the disgruntled Hausa peasantry and the Fulani to launch a jihad in 1802. Although dan Fodio took the title of Amir al Mu'minin ("Commander of the Faithful"), he was the intellectual leader of the *jihad* who left the fighting to his brother Abdullahi and his son Muhammadu Bello.

Within a decade their light cavalry had overwhelmed the more ponderous Hausa armies and established an Islamic Caliphate, based in Sokoto, that stretched some five hundred miles and brought a regional system of administration and taxes, a police force, and Sharia. The empire reigned for one hundred years, and by the end it had pushed across the dry, hot savanna to the edge of the great rain forests of the coastal region. Horses and camels could not long survive there, and the Yoruba generals of Ibadan put up a fierce resistance. The seemingly irresistible tide of Islam petered out.

The Fulani formed an aristocracy over the Hausa, placing their own emirs in the palaces of Kano and Katsina and the other emirates. Their covenant with the masses was based less on social justice than on orderly government. The Islamic faithful were divided in two. The Fulani and Hausa elite, including the *ulama*, or learned men, enjoyed a progressive life of scholarship and piety. Dan Fodio's daughter, Nana Asmau, was an intellectual and writer who formed what today would be called a nongovernmental organization to teach women. Below the cream of the new society were the *talakawa*, the free commoners, who consisted of the Hausa-speaking peasantry, small artisans and traders. The underclass consisted of slaves, mainly from the middle belt, a hilly region to the south where hundreds of tiny pagan ethnic groups lived.

Aspirant Fulani commanders were handed the green flag of Islam and told to ride out and conquer the unbelievers, which they did with remarkable effect. But many jihadists were motivated less by religion than by the spoils of war, and they also embarked on slave-raiding expeditions against the middle belt ethnic groups. Slaves formed the basis of the tribute the emirs had to pay to Sokoto. Slaves farmed, slaves built cities such as Zaria, and slaves gave birth to Fulani children. The mother of Ahmadu Bello, dan Fodio's great-great-grandson, who was the premier of the Northern Region and the most powerful man at the time of independence, was said to have been a slave.

Eventually ossification took hold in the Caliphate, like the Hausa city-states before it. Dan Fodio's extended family monopolized the leadership. There was a revival of once-banned Hausa titles, and debilitating scourges of patronage and bureaucracy spread. By the mid-nineteenth century, young revolutionaries, taking a page from dan Fodio's book, had begun criticizing the Caliphate for backsliding on Islam. But although it was undermined by dissension and squabbling with emirate rulers, the Sokoto Caliphate faced an even bigger danger from the British. By 1903, Lord Frederick Lugard's West African

Frontier Force had occupied Kano and Sokoto, killing the Caliph in the process. (The British appointed a new one, though with the less impressive title of sultan.) The British invasion was not without its supporters. "The emirs never had support; the feudalists ruled by force," Lawal Danbazau, an old northern radical campaigner once told me. "When the colonialists came to Kano, the people jubilated. There was a song the women used to sing: 'Nasara ka dade ba ka zoba, ko ba hau dokin hawainiya ne?'" The translation is: "White man, you took so long to come, is your horse a chameleon?"

The caliphate had grown weak and decrepit, and the defeat by Lugard's forces destroyed whatever legitimacy it had left. At the same time, however, British colonialism benefited the emirs. The policy of indirect rule both masked their subordination to an alien power and effectively handed them control of areas in the middle belt that they had never been able to conquer. Lacking all pretense that their power emanated from the people they ruled, the emirs grew even more autocratic. To become sultan, a successful candidate required the approval of the British governor, and today the Sokoto State government confirms him on the recommendation of powerful palace officials, the so-called kingmakers. In the case of the emirs of Kano, Katsina, and other former city-states, the final word on the issue often comes from the central government in Abuja. "The emirs actually have nothing," Ibrahim Zakzaky, one of Nigeria's leading Islamic fundamentalists, once told me. "They are just there to romanticize what used to happen." Zakzaky was referring to the pomp and pageantry of the emir's office that I had first seen in 1992 when I attended a Durbar in Kano.

The Durbar is held twice a year, on the Prophet Mohammed's birthday and at the end of Islam's month of fasting, Ramadan. It is a celebration of the day the Prophet is said to have offered his son as a sacrifice, and Allah decided that a ram would do. It is the time of the Sallah, meaning the mounting of horses, when, after prayers, district and village chiefs converge on the emir's palace in a daylong procession accompanied by musicians and *kirari* singers.

The Durbar is also a legacy of British colonialism. The word itself comes from the Persian word *darbar*, "courtroom" or "hall of audience." A special *darbar* marked the proclamation of Queen Victoria as empress of India in 1876. After the British occupation of northern Nigeria in 1903, Durbars were organized to remind their subjects and the old emirs of their subordination to the Crown. A grand Durbar ushered in Nigeria's independence from Britain in 1960.

The Durbar I witnessed was a spectacular affair. Tiny outlines of tendons and muscles flashed like electric impulses every few seconds along the brawny legs of horses draped with chain-mail. Platoons of ceremonial foot soldiers fired nineteenth-century Dane guns, the booming explosions reaching a crescendo as the emir of Kano, encircled by his mounted *Dogorai* bodyguards in royal scarlet-and-green uniforms, rode in. A rowdy fist-pumping crowd had been waiting patiently under a withering sun at the margins of the Sahara desert. After seeking solace at the appointed spot in the shade beside his palace, the emir settled impassively on his steed and enjoyed the breezy attentions of servants wielding giant fans of ostrich feathers.

Next, in rode lesser potentates and Islamic rulers from across northern Nigeria ahead of huge entourages of family, local dignitaries, musicians, and praise singers, coming to pay their respects. Thirty thousand commoners pushed and shoved their way onto the dusty parade grounds, many attracting a few good licks from the whips of overzealous policemen. Horns up to five feet long blared, and the voices of two masters of ceremonies screaming simultaneously exploded from the loudspeakers. Senior government officials and foreign dignitaries and diplomats in their khaki suits and sundresses sat high above the procession in a shaded viewing gallery.

Then the crowd suddenly fell silent. A dozen riders with swords and 7-foot lances formed a line 100 yards away. There was a moment's hesitation before they sprang into a full gallop. Their charge sent up clouds of dust as the horses strained toward their target: the emir. The heaving throng of spectators rushed forward from all sides, narrowing the running field to a human corridor just 50 feet wide. At the last moment, the riders jerked on the reigns, leaned back and saluted by raising their lances, now pointed away from the emir in a show of respect. Their minute of glory finished, the horsemen sauntered off under the trees to scrutinize the next group's performance. For the next several hours, wave after wave of warriors lunged toward the exalted ruler.

With the light fading and fatigue setting in, riding skills and police control deteriorated markedly. After several brushes with the rows of onlookers, one rider plowed into a tightly packed human wall. Miraculously, injuries were slight. With the last run pulling up at dusk, the revelers started walking back to their homes in old Kano. Within minutes, the prayer mats emerged from inside small mud block homes and whole neighborhoods were on their knees praying, facing east toward Mecca.

If, as Zakzaky had suggested, the emirs' strength has declined, that of their faith has not. Until Obasanjo took office, Islam was the religion of power in Nigeria. Of the nine different government leaders since independence, only three have been Christian. "When the military come, having no popular base, they depend like the British on the emirs," said Abdullahi Mahadi, a history professor and the current vice chancellor at Ahmadu Bello University (ABU) in Zaria, about eighty miles south of Kano. "So they keep on reinforcing each other. The military undertakes not only to give them fat salaries, they build very beautiful palaces for them and hand them big contracts."

When I met Professor Mahadi he was heading up ABU's research and historical documentation center, which is situated in Kaduna, some eighty miles south of Zaria. (Professor Mahadi's office at the research center was in the old house of Ahmadu Bello, the saradauna of

Sokoto who was assassinated in the January Boys coup of 1966.) In many ways the highway from Kaduna, a major political axis, to Zaria, the intellectual heart, and on to Kano, the economic engine, represents northern Nigeria's spinal column. I went to see Mahadi to discuss the wide gulf in perceptions of "the north" held by southern Nigerians and by the vast majority of northerners themselves.

Southern leaders and the Lagos press view the north as a monolithic entity that enjoys all the benefits of Nigeria's vast oil riches while leaving the rest of the country to rot. Whether in Lagos, Port Harcourt, or the middle belt, "the north" is generally blamed for squandering the nation's wealth and leading the country to ruin. The common wisdom is that although most civil servants and middle-ranking officials in state-run companies are southerners, principally Igbo or Yoruba, the man at the top is always an alhaji, that is, one who has made the hajj to Mecca. Typical is the view of Bola Ige, a prominent Yoruba leader, a former state governor, and the new minister of power and steel in Obasanjo's administration. Ige grew up in Kaduna and learned to speak Hausa at an early age. When I asked him who actually controlled Nigeria, he said bluntly, "There are not more than two hundred Fulani families and they are connected with the conservative emirates and the military. They are the only group that has no territory because they are immigrants. They are all over the place; they have no home."

But the all-powerful northern monolith is a myth. Nearly forty years after independence, poverty is as great or greater in northern Nigeria as it is elsewhere. Investment in the economy is virtually nonexistent, infrastructure is decaying, and the fuel shortages that recurred throughout the 1990s were even worse in the north than in the south. A shortsighted elite has tried to keep it that way.

"Look at education," said Professor Mahadi.

The very little segment of the society that has been able to get education work very closely with the southerners, in government, in boardrooms of companies, in banking, in virtually all the institutions. Any benefit from the federal government falls to a handful of people in the north. Together with the southerners they reap a lot of benefits. They are the same people, who when they feel they are losing out on sharing the so-called national cake, say "no domination." When things are going fine, they don't care.

Yet the relationship between the military and the northern elite has been a troubled one. In 1966 military officers murdered the most influential northern politicians, and the Buhari coup of 1983 threw out the north's chosen president, Shehu Shagari. Nor was the north spared when Abacha's intoxication with power and money led him to strike out at any opponents, real or imaginary.

Abacha's first northern heavyweight target was Yar'Adua, a multimillionaire Katsina prince and leader of the 1975 Murtala Mohammed coup. (Had Babangida not disqualified him in the 1992 primaries, Yar'Adua would have been the favorite to win the 1993 president election. Yar'Adua's political machine would play a decisive role in propelling Obasanjo to victory in the 1999 elections.) Abacha had much to fear in Yar'Adua: a massive financial endowment, unrivaled political astuteness, and impeccable military connections. Urbane, self-confident, and of blue-blooded heritage, Yar'Adua was the opposite of the introverted Abacha, whose family had immigrated to Kano from Borno. Abacha also had a personal grudge against Yar'Adua. The family of Abacha's wife Maryam initially felt that Abacha was not good enough for her and so agreed instead to a marriage to Yar'Adua's uncle. They later divorced, and Maryam joined her childhood sweetheart, Abacha. Family tensions remained high, and there were whispers about the paternity of the couple's first child, Ibrahim, who died in a still-unexplained plane crash in Kano in January 1996.

Thus Yar'Adua was a threat in all senses, and when he publicly called on Abacha to relinquish power to an elected government that he, Yar'Adua, would surely dominate, Yar'Adua had to disappear. In 1995 he joined Obasanjo and Abacha's former principal staff officer, Brigadier Lawal Gwadabe, before a military tribunal on charges of joining other officers, human rights activists, and journalists in plotting a coup d'état. After an international outcry, the original death sentences were commuted to lengthy prison terms, long enough to ensure that the primary suspects would spend the rest of their natural lives in jail. In 1996 Abacha's agents went one step further. They moved Yar'Adua from Port Harcourt to the Abakaliki Prison outside Enugu. He was taken to the governor's State House for an encounter with Major Hamza al-Mustapha, Abacha's top security aide, who ran a paramilitary dirty-tricks outfit known as the Strike Force. Yar'Adua's hands were cuffed behind his head and he was injected with an unknown substance by Lieutenant Colonel Ibrahim Yakassi, a gynecologist by training. By December 1997 Yar'Adua was dead, at the age of fifty-four.

Ibrahim Dasuki, the sultan of Sokoto, was next to fall in Abacha's sights, and the blow against him demonstrated more clearly than ever before the frailties of the once powerful traditional authorities of northern Nigeria. Dasuki's son, Sambo, was declared a wanted man and forced into exile; the sultan himself was deposed, replaced by Mohammed Maccido, and jailed in April 1996 on Abacha's orders. He served more than two years in detention in Jalingo, a town in the remote state of Taraba.

Initially Dasuki's dismissal was warmly approved by the public because of the popular belief that he had won the office of sultan eight years before thanks to business connections with Babangida and Abacha. Dasuki, an Oxford-trained businessman, was cofounder of the defunct Bank of Commerce and Credit International (BCCI). His relationship with Abacha was complex. Like many senior military officers, including Babangida, Abacha was a business partner of the sultan's nephew, Aliyu. After Aliyu died in a British hospital in 1993 without revealing the numbers of their joint foreign bank accounts, Abacha held the Dasuki family, with Ibrahim as its head, responsible for the debt and wanted the money from the account. At one point Abacha presented Dasuki with a one-page financial claim, on which most of the items were tallied in kilograms (suggesting gold reserves in a foreign bank). Abacha was also irked when Aliyu's widow Jamila married Aliyu Mohammed, who was considered one of Babangida's boys. "Abacha didn't like it at all because he thought Babangida, Aliyu Mohammed, and Dasuki were ganging up on him," said one of Aliyu Dasuki's friends.

When I met Ibrahim Dasuki at his Kaduna home in August 1998, one month after his release by Abacha's successor, Abubakar, it was clear that even at seventy-six he still attracted considerable attention. Dozens of people were milling outside in the driveway, and inside the waiting room were fifteen VIPs stretched out on sofas and chairs awaiting their turn. Probably because I had been escorted to the meeting by Dasuki's burly son, Ahmad, now the administrator of Aliyu's business empire, I moved to the head of the line.

Dasuki was sitting by the window chatting with his aides in Hausa. He gestured me over to the chair next to him. Despite the importance of the office he had once held, his reputed wealth, and his long service in government as an administrator and ambassador, Dasuki came across as remarkably humble, almost shy. Before we began he wanted to have an idea about what I wished to ask. I told him I would like to know how the most powerful Islamic figure in Nigeria, the successor to the great Usman dan Fodio, could be removed and detained on the whim of a military dictator.

"Ah," he said gravely. "The idea was not to insult the sultan himself. The main thing was to terrorize everybody. They wanted to show that they could remove the highest person in the land." The sultan knew he was in trouble with Abacha as early as 1995. While he was passing through London, the British Foreign Office requested a meeting to discuss the deteriorating situation in Nigeria under Abacha. "They told me about unpleasant things, about corruption from top to bottom, about Abacha not caring for the ordinary man, about his not listening to any advice." Upon returning to Nigeria, Dasuki sent a written report to Abacha about the encounter. The dictator had apparently been appalled that Dasuki had not argued his case to the British. "How could I defend him? How could I deny that the ordinary man is suffering? How could I deny that there is corruption?"

A year later the military governor of Sokoto State called the sultan for a meeting and handed him a letter complaining that he had been traveling without authorization. It was an absurd accusation because he was under no restrictions. In the next minute the governor handed Dasuki another letter informing him that he had been deposed as sultan. "I looked at the letter and then I said, 'Only Allah knows what tomorrow brings,'" he said, quoting from the Koran (31:34). Dasuki had said the same thing to his friend Abiola when Babangida annulled the 1993 presidential elections. "I called Abiola to Sokoto to discuss the issue and I told him that 'this is the will of Allah.' It was the will of Allah that Abiola should suffer, and he suffered." The state police commissioner escorted him out a back door and took him to the airport. An aircraft flew him to Yola, the capital of Taraba State, and he was driven to Jalingo. There he was held in the administrator's house under a security detachment sent directly from the head of state's office in Abuja. The guards were changed every month.

Dasuki's invocation of God's will is echoed often by northern Nigerians, especially the rich and powerful when attempting to justify their privileged position in an ocean of poverty. "The people of the north are guided by Koranic injunctions, whereby you should be patient, and you know whatever comes to you is from Allah," Dasuki explained. "What you get and what you don't get is from Allah."

Not all in northern Nigeria agree with that philosophy. There are other, less patient Muslims who regard the succession of Muslim military rulers and their allies among the emirs as un-Islamic. Although they are still a far cry from dan Fodio's jihad, these groups have gained steady ground in the slums of Kano, Zaria, and Kaduna, especially among the unemployed youth who are known as the *yan daba*, or "sons of evil" in Hausa.

———

MY INTRODUCTION to Islamic radicalism in Nigeria came in October 1991, just eight days after my arrival in Nigeria. Late in the afternoon I was sitting in my room at the BBC office in Lagos when my foreign editor called from London to say that news wires were reporting major clashes between Christians and Muslims in Kano. How quickly could I get there?

The next morning at the airport departure lounge I was relieved to see Tunde Obadina, the Nigerian correspondent for *Reuters*, whom I had met earlier in the week while doing my rounds of initial contacts in Lagos. Although I hardly knew him, Tunde was obviously a level-headed sort, and if I stuck with him, I would be relatively safe.

Religious clashes were no mild affairs, especially in Kano, the second biggest urban center in Nigeria after Lagos. They conjured up the frightening images of the pogroms against the Igbos in the 1960s on the eve of the civil war and the Maitatsine riots of the early 1980s in which hundreds died. The previous April, religious and ethnic riots in another northern state, Bauchi, left upwards of a thousand people dead. There were two million people in Kano. I had no idea what to expect or how bad it might be.

I got a hint soon. Several planes from Kano landed and disgorged panic-stricken passengers fleeing the fighting. In the early 1990s, much more than in later years, chronic overbooking on domestic flights meant that passengers literally fought their way onto planes, planting themselves in the nearest seat and refusing all entreaties to budge. The fact that our flight to Kano was nearly empty spoke volumes about the drama unfolding there.

Two hours later as our aircraft made its final approach to the runway, the handful of nervous passengers scooted across the aisle to gaze out the windows at what looked from the air to be a battle zone. Thick black plumes of smoke rose from half a dozen points that appeared as if they marked direct hits by an aerial bombing raid.

At the front parking lot of the Kano airport, the normally eager taxi drivers stood by their vehicles shaking their heads to our request for a lift into town. The violence was widespread, they said, and they were waiting here until everything cooled down. After a few minutes of pleading, however, we found one taxi driver willing to ferry us into the city for about $50, five times the normal price.

As we drove in, women and children loaded down with parcels marched along the road leading out of town like refugees from a war. We negotiated our way slowly along a wide avenue dodging metal shards and bits of concrete. At a military roadblock a pair of riot policemen strongly advised us against advancing. We foolishly ignored their warning. Around a short curve we came upon a gang of youths carrying sticks and metal pipes and preparing to set fire to a building housing the offices of Kabo Airways, a private airline owned by a prominent Muslim businessman, Alhaji Dankabo. Tunde yelled at the driver to retreat. But the panicky driver never made it. Youths with axes, clubs, and pipes, their faces twisted into masks of outrage, surrounded our car and banged on the hood and roof. "What are you doing here?" one shouted. "Don't you know we are at war?"

The shouting continued, but because I was a foreigner and Tunde and the driver were dressed in Western clothes, the young men must have realized that we were not Muslims. They did nothing to stop us from going back the way we had come. Our driver said he knew another way into town. He was as good as his word, and forty-five minutes later we walked through the lobby of the Central Hotel. From talking to the hotel staff and various taxi drivers, it was clear that the fighting was between Kano's traditional adversaries, Muslim Hausa youths and Christian Igbo traders living in sabon gari (the "strangers' quarters").

The riots were sparked by the attempted arrival of a Christian fundamentalist preacher, the Reverend Reinhard Bonnke of Christ for All Nations, who was planning to bring his Good News Revival to Kano. The Muslims did not stand for it. Eight thousand militants marched through the city chanting "Allah akbar" ("God is great"), and a substantial breakaway group of extremists set upon sabon gari. Reverend Bonnke, a German, apparently never got further than the airport. When he learned of the trouble, he flew back to Lagos.

Tunde and I decided to head for the police headquarters. We found a driver at the hotel who suited our needs perfectly. First of all he was a Muslim, so if we were stopped by any of the militants and asked to recite the Koran, we were in good hands. He was also a Yoruba, so any Igbo fighters we encountered would let us pass.

At the police station hundreds of civilians carrying suitcases, food, and children gathered outside the main gate. One elderly man bleeding profusely from his head was stumbling around shouting, "They have killed my first son." His cry sent a wave of hysteria through the crowd.

We walked into the barracks looking for a police spokesman. The officers were racing around the building, not surprisingly, in a state of confusion. Eventually we found the office of the commanding officer, who was remarkably attentive to our questions, given the scope of the crisis. His men had been completely overwhelmed the first day, but by this morning he thought they had the situation under control. The problem was that the Igbo youths had regrouped and were launching revenge attacks. But because the military authorities had just issued orders to shoot on sight, he was confident that his forces could reestablish their authority. As he was talking, a walkie-talkie on his desk crackled into life with a desperate call from an officer in the field.

"They have overwhelmed us. ...can you give us assistance?... can you give us assistance?"

Although we were only a few blocks from sabon gari, burning barricades and crowds of marauding youths made the streets impassable. We decided instead to make our way to the Nassarawa Hospital on the edge of the city. The driveway was another scene of frightening chaos. Taxis commandeered by the police arrived every few minutes with a new load of casualties suffering from horrific stab and gunshot wounds. Inside, the floors and steps were covered in blood. One nurse stood at the door staring blankly into the distance. "There are so many people that we are treating them in the halls and on the floor," she said.

The state governor had imposed a dusk-to-dawn curfew, and Tunde and I reached the Central Hotel just in time. I ran upstairs and booked a call to my newspaper. To my surprise, I was speaking to the night news editor within a few minutes. He was eager for the story, and I sat down to write, calm in the knowledge that there was plenty of time to make the first edition with my first major story from Nigeria. An hour later, I called down to the operator to file the copy. The phone rang and rang, but the operator did not pick up. I flung open the door in an anxiety attack and found Tunde standing there. He too had been trying to ring downstairs with no luck. We found the hotel manager at the reception desk, and he had bad news. The telephone operator had ridden off on his bicycle to see if his family was all right, and he had taken the key to the switchboard room with him. Even the manager could not get in. Until the operator returned, there would be no outside calls. One hour, then two hours passed with no sign of the operator. Finally, at 9:00 P.M., my phone rang. It was Tunde to say that the operator was back. The call to London came straight through.

By the next morning Kano had returned to a semblance of normality. Joint army and police units patrolled the streets, and the emir of Kano, the then defense minister Lieutenant General Sani Abacha, and Kano's state governor, Colonel Idris Garba, issued radio appeals to halt the violence. Residents of the city were busy sweeping the streets and sifting through the wreckage of their homes, shops, churches, mosques, and sometimes their lives.

We pulled into the compound of the state-owned daily newspaper, *Triumph*, to seek out the Hausa perspective. At first the guard at the gate did not want to allow us in, but he relented when we convinced him we were journalists. The paper's editor, Nuuman Habib, was sitting behind his desk with the look of a person who had not slept in days.

Blame for the crisis, he said, fell squarely on the shoulders of the Christians and Babangida's military regime. The Muslims were already angry about the government's refusal to permit the visits to Kano of foreign clerics, such as Louis Farrakhan of the Nation of Islam and the South African Ahmed Deedat. Both men were popular among Kano's Muslims, who watched their preaching on videos that circulated widely in the underground of Islamic radicalism. The announcement that Reverend Bonnke had been granted a permit to stage an open-air revival at the racecourse pushed them over the edge. The Christians raised the temperature by driving around in cars and trucks and using loudspeakers to promote the meeting in Muslim neighborhoods. "They went around in areas which had been prohibited by convention," he said. "Young Muslim men stood along the streets and shouted back, 'We do not want it, it is a lie.'"

We drove to the headquarters of the Social Democratic Party (SDP), one of two legal political parties at the time. Kabiru Isa Dambatta, the SDP spokesman, was a tall, good-natured Hausa man who did not seem to take the riots that seriously. "Some bad eggs took a minor issue and carried it to the highest issue. A good Muslim should always be in peace, not in pieces," he said with a smile of satisfaction at his wordplay.

At sabon gari rows of shops had been burned to the ground. The foundations of several buildings had buckled from the heat of the fires. We walked along the streets speaking to Igbo merchants who had lost everything to the rioters or to the looters who came in their wake. "We are refugees in our own country," screamed a businessman named Pajeane, whose house had been set alight by Hausa rioters. Another bystander, Hyginus Ofoebu, said he had seen six people stabbed to death.

Suddenly, a muscle-bound young man about 6 foot 5 inches tall jumped off the back of a motorbike and strode over to introduce himself. Ndubusi Ikena was a twenty-year-old Igbo youth leader who admitted to participating in the killing and the torching of mosques. His aggressive bearing left little doubt that he had. "They have been treating us like slaves for years," he said of the Hausas. "When they started attacking us, we carried out revenge."

In response to the calls for peace, Ikena said, the warring gangs had approached each other on the street we were standing on, Galadima Road. Above their heads they held sticks and metal bars, as well as green leaves as symbols of peace. Then, as they came together, they downed their weapons and began embracing each other. "We did it because they begged us to stop fighting," he said. "But it is not finished."

"THAT RIOT helped us enter the people," said Abubakar Mujahid, a bespectacled forty-year-old sounding like an Islamic Lenin. "We sent representatives to see what we could do. We spoke with the people's voice. We took up any issue on which the people felt they were being oppressed, even if it did not concern us," he said with a wry smile.

Mujahid was sitting on the floor of his drab prefabricated house, whose quality of workmanship is best described by the popular nickname for the entire neighborhood: Low Cost. He was talking about the role of Islam in Nigeria and why he broke with the most famous radical preacher, Zakzaky. Mujahid was not exactly underground at the moment, but he was a difficult man to find. Muslim militants have often been targets of government security sweeps. Mujahid had spent the best part of the past two years in detention.

Mujahid had the air of a bookworm, and he spent his free time reading about world history and agriculture. Almost no one had ever heard of him outside the intellectual circles of Zaria and Kano, and even there he was known only among those in touch with the radical Islamic movements. As a rule Mujahid did not speak with journalists, though not because he was particularly hostile to them. He just did not think they were very relevant to the task at hand. I was able to track him down after a circuitous route of contacts that started at Ahmadu Bello University, included a stop at a mosque, and ended up at the local Polytechnic, where an associate agreed, somewhat reluctantly at first, to lead me to Low Cost.

A former lieutenant of Zakzaky, Mujahid now led his own faction called Ja'amutu Tajidmul Islami, the "Movement for Islamic Revival." If and when the time came for another revolutionary Mahdi, both Zakzaky and Mujahid had an eye on the job. As the champions of two wings of the radical Islamic movement, known collectively as the Muslim Brothers, they represented what was potentially a formidable grassroots force. The movement has proved capable of bringing out a half-million people into the streets of Kano, something no Nigerian politician or military strongman could ever dream of doing. So far, though, poor organization and factionalism, traditionally the Achilles heel of Nigerian society, has kept the movement in check.

Braced against the wall in his sitting room, Mujahid gave me a short history of the movement. Radical Islam of the modern era was nurtured in the late 1970s during Obasanjo's first, military administration. After bitter debate and walkouts, the Constitutional Assembly decided to reject Muslim demands for the inclusion in the new constitution of a federal Sharia court of appeal to handle cases of personal law, such as adultery. Christian opponents saw the proposal as part of an attempt to impose Islam on Nigerian society, although the

Muslims argued that the court was voluntary and had been available in the Northern Region during the first civilian government of Tafawa Balewa. Under a compromise, three judges schooled in Islamic law would handle cases sent by the state Sharia courts.

The conclusion was hardly satisfactory to Muslim intellectuals, especially young university students in Kano and at the Ahmadu Bello University in Zaria, who were fired by the Iranian revolution. Zakzaky, then an economics student at Ahmadu Bello, organized a pro-Sharia demonstration in Zaria and was promptly arrested for unlawful assembly. Mujahid met Zakzaky through Aliyu Ibrahim Al-Tukri, also known as Tukur Tukur, a classmate at his high school, Barewa College. Together with thirty other bright young students, they formed the nucleus of Zakzaky's movement. "What attracted me was the revolutionary spirit. At the time we heard about Afghanistan in flames, Iran. We never expected Islam to rise, and here was Islam rising. But we really didn't know what Islam was, so many of us dropped out of school and studied at the Islamic schools in town."

Mujahid is from a relatively well-off family of teachers. His father was a principal who rose to a director's position in the ministry of education, and he made sure his son attended the best schools. Most of the teachers at his primary school in Kaduna were Europeans. "At one point, I didn't know how to speak my language, Hausa, because all of the teachers were white." His father wanted Mujahid to become an engineer. But feeling cut off from the society around him, he opted instead for Islamic revolution. Mujahid and his comrades in the core group began by wandering the slums preaching about justice and government corruption. "We pointed out that all the leaders who do not rule with the book of Allah should be fought against," said Mujahid. "Because then almost everybody was frustrated with the government, we had a lot of sympathy, especially among the youth."

The 1991 riots in Kano over the Bonnke affair convinced the Zakzaky movement that it had to create a paramilitary force to confront the police.

Mujahid was put in charge of the group that was designated *horas,* "guards" in Arabic. He insisted that they had carried no weapons. "I designed it along the lines of the Revolutionary Guards in Iran, and I had also read about the Hitler youth movement," he said. "If the police came to break up one of these processions, the mission of the *horas* was to confront them and allow the women and children to withdraw."

They produced two newsletters, to which Mujahid contributed articles on history. Ironically, they printed their tracts denouncing the government on the copy machines at military barracks in Kaduna and Zaria. Mujahid said the printers produced their newsletters surreptitiously in return for direct payment.

Nigerian Muslims are overwhelmingly Sunni, and over time a number of Zakzaky's key advisers grew disenchanted with what they saw as his embrace of the Shia school of Islam practiced by the majority in Iran. The Iranian government, Mujahid and others said, covered most of Zakzaky's expenses, including his annual trips to Mecca in the hajj. The dissidents also criticized what they claimed were his dictatorial tendencies and his suggestions that students should leave school to devote themselves full-time to the movement. Zakzaky has always denied that he urged students to drop out, but I heard the same charge from Professor Mahadi. "He virtually ruined their lives because many of the undergraduates left their studies to embrace his Islamic movement," he said. "Many of these young men thought they could get a proper Islamic education with him. But Zakzaky is not really learned in the Islamic sciences. He is more interested in the power that Islam can give him than the intricacies of Islamic law, science, and traditions."

When Mujahid, Tukur Tukur, and others began preaching against Shiism, scuffles broke out with Zakzaky's supporters. In 1994 Mujahid alleged that a gang of *horas,* which had grown under his tutelage to a force of five hundred youths, beat up one of Mujahid's friends at Jaji, the site of the military training college just north of Kaduna. In July Mujahid formally split with Zakzaky and set up the Ja'amutu Tajidmul

Islami. His faction came to dominate in Kano; Zakzaky was strongest in Kaduna.

By December 1994 Kano was once again on the boil, and militants claiming to support Mujahid's faction were guilty of the provocation. They accused the wife of an Igbo trader named Gideon Akaluka of desecrating the Koran by allegedly using pages from the holy book as toilet paper for her baby. The police detained Akaluka for his own protection. But a gang of militants broke into the jail, killed Akaluka, and led a great procession around Kano with his severed head on a pole.

Mujahid said he had had nothing to do with the lynching, but at the time his movement's newspaper, *Al-Tajdid*, declared that Akaluka was "properly punished for blaspheming the Koran." Six months later a fight between a Hausa and an Igbo in sabon gari sparked a new riot. "It was a communal ethnic conflict," Mujahid said. "It had nothing to do with Islam." But again his movement took advantage of the unrest to criticize the government and call for an Islamic state.

Several of Mujahid's Kano-based followers were allegedly picked up and shot by the police. More clashes ensued. The police accused the Ja'amutu Tajidmul Islami of launching a campaign to drive all Igbos out of Kano. In July 1995 Mujahid was detained indefinitely. That same day he read in the papers the news of Obasanjo's arrest for allegedly plotting to overthrow Abacha. For a while they were held in the same prison in Jos. Despite obvious ideological differences, Mujahid remembers Obasanjo, a Christian, as a good man. "He didn't know the plight of the people, that prisoners stayed in subhuman conditions for years without ever going to court. He called the state attorney general, Christian leaders, and Islamic leaders, and some of the prisoners were released because of his efforts."

A few weeks after Mujahid's arrest I was in Kano to gauge the strength of his breakaway faction, though at the time I did not know he was its leader. I visited the home of Suleimanu Kumo, a prominent lawyer who had been in the forefront of the Sharia debate in 1978 and was on good terms with the young radicals. A giant portrait of Ayatollah Khomeini in his sitting room betrayed his sympathy for the Iranian Revolution, but he was hardly an extremist. When the state government established a committee called the Kano Forum to try to ease the ethnic and religious tensions in the city, Kumo was enlisted to open a dialogue with the Tajid, that is, members of the Ja'amutu Tajidmul Islami. The shootings of their members and the detention of Mujahid forced the movement underground. They came to Kumo's house under the cover of darkness.

"They are far more educated than I thought," he said. "Some are engineers, others medical students. They are men, seventeen, eighteen, up to twenty-eight years old, who have nothing to lose, who have life rather more than death to fear. They are very highly strung. They want to be self-reliant, to avoid the corrupting influence of the military government. They don't want to lick the government's boots." Ever since the Sharia debate, Kumo said, there has been "a simmering feeling that Muslims are being relegated to the background and that Islam is being stampeded out of existence." Such perceptions would be laughed at in southern Nigeria, where it is commonly suspected that the central government wants to create an Islamic state. Every head of state since Obasanjo handed over power to Shehu Shagari in 1979 has been a northern Muslim, except President Obasanjo himself. Abiola believed he was stopped from assuming the presidency because, among other things, he was a second-class, southern Muslim.

Kumo drove me to the office of Maitama Sule, a longtime power broker in Kano who is a personal friend of the emir and who was close to Abacha. His office, crowded with pictures of himself with various heads of state and world leaders, testified to an obvious feeling of self-importance. Sule was clearly worried about the rise of militant Islam and its implications for the northern elite that he so proudly represents. "If we do not nip this thing in the bud now, we may end up with a revolution which is just not religious, but may be political, social, and economic," he said gravely. "Symptoms of revolt loom large on the horizon today." With his typically flamboyant rhetorical style, he described the Muslim Brothers as "a group of disgruntled elements who are out to vent their anger and who are joined by undesirable waste products of humanity."

For Kumo, nipping the potential for trouble in the bud meant talking with the militants and listening to their concerns. Abacha favored the rather more direct approach of extrajudicial execution and indefinite detention. A year after Mujahid's arrest, the police came for Zakzaky with a warrant to search his house for weapons. They did not find any, but like Mujahid, he too was held. Mujahid remained behind bars until six months before Abacha's death in June 1998. Six months later, Zakzaky emerged from detention.

Whether his time in jail cooled his passion or he has simply mellowed with age, Mujahid sounded positively moderate as he described the future plans of his movement. "General enlightenment is our most important goal," he said. But it was difficult to know what "enlightenment" means to a man who is an admirer of the Taliban in Afghanistan and who feels that the reformist Iranian president, Mohammad Khatami, is, as he put it, "getting loose." (He used the same expression to describe the behavior of women he saw in Teheran during a 1990 visit he made with Zakzaky.) But Mujahid insisted that a modern Islamic state could be flexible and could coexist with other religions, whose followers he was confident would come to see "the beauty of Islam." Western education was a necessary tool. "It's like a knife," he said. "A knife can be used to cut things or it can be used by a thief to steal." Technology too can be useful. "It's a matter of introducing Islamic values. Look at TV. You can use it to produce uplifting programs for the people." As he described it, the Ja'amutu Tajidmul Islami was less interested in sparking an Islamic revolution than in promoting education and economic development. The movement ran a small primary school in Kano, a pharmacy, and a wholesale food shop for its followers. Its eventual goal was to start farms to produce cheap food and to offer credit on a small scale, of course lending without interest according to the dictates of Islam.

Mujahid is not the only resident of Zaria with grand plans. In Zaria, ideas and conversation are the stock in trade, and one can find conservatives, liberals, Marxists, and Islamic scholars and preachers in abundance. Partly that is owing to the university, which, however downtrodden, remains one of three important institutions of higher learning in Nigeria, along with the universities at Ife and Ibadan. To the north Kano is the city of commerce and to the south Kaduna is home to the bulk of northern politicians, the so-called Kaduna Mafia.

Despite the role of the Zaria Emirate as a feudal overlord, a radical streak runs through the city. Almost every conversation ends with a ringing condemnation of the politicians, the generals, and the emirs who claim to speak for the north and for Islam. They have left the path of Islam, which, above all, should champion justice for the common man. Whatever their differences on other issues, almost all agree that if in Nigeria justice is fleeting, in the north it has rarely put in even a brief appearance.

"The strategy of those in power is feudalistic," said Sabo Bako, a specialist on religious and ethnic conflict in northern Nigeria at Ahmadu Bello University. As we chatted in the shade at the university's Staff Club, Bako swiveled in his seat and gestured toward the rundown patio and a leaf-strewn swimming pool that had not seen a drop of water in years. In its heyday fifteen years ago, the club was a meeting point for Nigerian and numerous foreign scholars carrying out research in Zaria. Now only a handful come, and the few who come now are attracted by the club's subsidized prices. With a meager monthly salary, the professors cannot be too choosy. Once a prestigious university, Ahmadu Bello has fallen on hard times. The libraries are decades out of date, lecturers must engage in petty trade to feed their families, and at the campus bookstore a thirty-minute search for any recent publications on Nigerian history will turn up one or two volumes.

The neglect of the universities is just part of a bigger plan to maintain control, Bako said with a sigh. "The only way you can remain in power is by keeping people down. You must not allow people to know what you are doing and how much money you have. So don't give them education, don't give them fertilizer, don't establish industries for them." He paused for a moment and then snapped, "a revolution is imminent here, and the northern elite will be the first target."

IBRAHIM ZAKZAKY, many believed, would lead that revolution one day, though I had my doubts. When I first met Zakzaky in 1993, he was living in the heart of old Zaria in rented quarters in a back street to the side of the emir's palace. He was harassed constantly by the police and maintained the bearing of an angry young revolutionary. Since I had last seen him, his landlord had tired of the police searches and thrown him out. The authorities bulldozed a second house he was building, and he was taken away for two more years in detention. In December 1998 Zakzaky walked out of jail and returned to a hero's welcome after a Kaduna court dismissed charges of sedition. There was little sign that he felt cowed by the prison experience. "They wanted to crush the Islamic movement, and they did all they could but to no avail," he declared.

Fiery and charismatic, Zakzaky immediately caught the eye of the public, and all too often the police. He surrounded himself with gangs of young men who acted both as bodyguards and as a ready-made crowd of supporters through which he dramatically walked like a boxer heading for the ring on fight night. Zakzaky was born of radical roots. His great-great-grandfather, Imam Hussein, had migrated from Mali at the turn of the nineteenth century to join Usman dan Fodio's jihad and served as religious adviser to Mallam Musa, the Fulani commander who routed the emir of Zaria.

I caught up with Zakzaky again in February 1999 in his newly refurbished home, which he had purchased while in prison. It was a large, freshly painted compound with a row of flowers along the front wall and a sophisticated internal telephone/intercom system. Compared to Mujahid's place at Low Cost, Zakzaky's house was positively bourgeois. As I approached the gate, ubiquitous young men searched me nervously for weapons before relaxing and letting me through with a smile. In the waiting room another young man, who said he wanted to be a journalist, crouched down on the carpet next to me and told me in a conspiratorial voice that Zakzaky is the new leader Nigeria needs.

For a short while no one was able to let Zakzaky know that I was waiting because a power cut had rendered the intercom useless. Eventually he wandered out into the waiting room. He was immaculately dressed in a flowing white robe and sandals. I noted the gray in his beard and mentioned that he had aged since the last time we met. "Have you looked at yourself lately?" he retorted swiftly with a giggle. We settled down on the carpet and snacked on Coke and biscuits under the watch of an immense portrait of Ayatollah Khomeini.

Despite that talisman of Islamic revolution, what was striking about the 1999 version of Zakzaky was how unrevolutionary he appeared. He laughed a lot for a man billed as a cutthroat extremist, and his political views had mellowed. He insisted he had not so much "changed" as "developed."

Zakzaky was hopeful that the civilian government would mark a big improvement over military dictatorship because "people will talk and make revelations about the misappropriation of funds and things like that." He was happy too that the press had stopped referring to his movement as "fanatics, fundamentalists, troublemakers." He was still having difficulties, however, with the police, who had refused to let him return to his favorite platform, Friday prayers at the ABU mosque. "They're frustrated," he said with another giggle. "They thought they had finished with us." Since his release he had been spending most of his time receiving visitors from around the country, but he vowed that the movement would continue. "The people are awakening."

When I tried to probe him about Mujahid's Ja'amutu Tajidmul Islami breakaway faction, at first he said he did not know who they were. But when I told him I knew Mujahid and Tukur Tukur, he dismissed them as irrelevant, though in the next breath he accused them of making an attempt on his life. They were used, he claimed, by the government security agencies to split the movement. Zakzaky denied Mujahid's charge that he was a Shia but admitted to embracing both Sunni and Shia teachings. His Islam was eclectic.

Zakzaky walked into his study, where there was a desktop computer complete with a collection of CD-ROMs, produced in Iran, of the Koran and various Islamic writings. During the jihad dan Fodio used to travel around with camels laden down with his library. "All the books that dan Fodio used to have I can carry in my pocket," Zakzaky announced proudly. "This CD carries one thousand volumes. Since my grandfather did not have this technology, should I study the way my grandfather did?"

But though Zakzaky appeared to be the paragon of a moderate Islamic scholar, the appearance was deceiving. As he started to talk of his future plans, there was none of Mujahid's concern with enlightenment, cooperative farms, and low-interest credit schemes. "It is fine to change the individual, but what can you do with those corrupt people who have guns and authority?" he asked in a clear reference to Nigeria's rulers, civilian or military. The emirs were of no use because "they will support whoever is in power. Yesterday they dealt with Abacha, today with Abubakar, and tomorrow they will deal with Obasanjo." The trouble with Nigeria is evident from the driving habits of its people, he said. "You will be driving calmly on the highway to

Kaduna and some vehicle will race up behind you and force you off the road. No matter how law-abiding you are, somebody who is crazy will come and jam you."

In a similar vein, he claimed that when his supporters staged peaceful demonstrations, the police cracked down on them and accused them of causing trouble. "This is the sort of society we are living in," he said with a slightly ominous grin. Then came the only threat I heard that day: "It is time we should think of some action, not just talk." I asked what he had in mind, but he waved off the question. "The possible actions are many, but if you don't do anything, nothing will come out of talk. If you have no confidence that you can make any change from within, you can try it from without."

Another delegation of visitors was waiting for him, so we walked together out to the driveway inside the compound, and there, sitting in the shade, were thirty tiny boys not yet in their teens. He sat and greeted them in Hausa, and they responded in a high-pitched chorus. As I passed through the open metal gate, I wondered what he could be telling them. I was certain that it was not "only Allah knows what tomorrow brings."

The long-festering Sharia debate that had originally given birth to the Zakzaky phenomenon resurfaced in October 1999, when the newly elected governor, Ahmed Sani, announced that the previously obscure northern state of Zamfara would adopt Islamic law on January 27. Sharia, he said, was necessary to prod Nigeria's Muslims to return to clean living in a decadent society.

The decision deepened Nigeria's religious rift and constitutional crisis, for Zamfara appeared to have effectively adopted a religious legal system separate from the legal system of the rest of the secular federation. Other northern states soon followed Zamfara's lead. In January Niger State declared Sharia and the Kano State legislature sent a Sharia bill to the governor for his signature. Several others, including Yobe, Borno, and Sokoto, were actively considering similar measures. Critics, mainly Christians, immediately cried foul and described the actions as secessionist. The southern press pilloried the Zamfara governor for leading his state back into the dark ages. The Christian Association of Nigeria vowed to go to court to challenge the measure. Condemnations of the Sharia spread quickly from leading Christians to the southern houses of assembly in Enugu, Cross River, and Lagos States. The Cross River assembly threatened to declare a "Christian state" if Zamfara were allowed to go ahead with the legal change.

Supporters of the Islamic law argued that the federal constitution, by guaranteeing freedom of religion, enshrined the right of all Muslims to live under Sharia. It would only affect Muslims, and the 10 percent minority of non-Muslims in the state could go about their normal lives. In a dispute involving members of the two communities, they said, the non-Muslims would be able to choose whether to settle the matter in a Sharia or secular court.

Besides, in northern Nigeria Sharia principles had long been applied to issues of civil law, such as marriage, divorce, and adultery. They operated during the time of the Sokoto Caliphate and in a more limited way under Lugard's regime of indirect rule. After independence, leaders of the northern Nigerian region had established a penal code that differed from that of the south, which was based almost exclusively on English law. All along, about 80 percent of the northern penal code has been based on Sharia. But the change introduced by Governor Sani's edict expanded Sharia into all criminal cases. This raised unsettling questions about the application of Sharia sentences for crimes such as theft—potentially amputation—which the Nigerian constitution's stipulation against cruel and unusual punishment would appear to bar.

Governor Sani's announcement came amid a stirring of northern resentment over a perceived pro-southern and pro-Christian bias in the Obasanjo administration. Governor Sani's Sharia declaration forced Obasanjo on to sensitive territory. Many of the northern powerbrokers who had promoted his candidacy were now convinced they had made a mistake. They feared that he was, after all, pandering to his Yoruba kinsmen in his choice of ministers, advisers, and alleged perpetrators of human rights abuses and corrupt practices. He was too close to the rabidly anti-Islamic Pentecostal churches and had shown bad taste in inviting Reinhard Bonnke to a church thanksgiving service held for him a day after the inauguration.

President Obasanjo, unwilling to provoke a northern backlash, remained largely silent on the issue, although during a speech at Harvard University he suggested that Zamfara's action was illegal. Spokespersons for his government, keen to play down the controversy, later said Obasanjo was voicing a personal opinion.

Ironically, sharp criticism of Governor Sani's imposition of Sharia came from Ibrahim Zakzaky himself. His argument, simply put, was that Sharia could not operate properly in a secular nation-state; Sharia can only truly be the law of the land in an Islamic state. "Islamic law is meant to be applied by an Islamic government in an Islamic environment," he told one interviewer. "If you introduce Islamic laws under an un-Islamic environment, under a system of government which is not Islamic, then it is bound to be an instrument of oppression."[5]

But others I talked to disagreed. Dr. Kumo, the Kano-based lawyer, believed that if properly implemented, a return to Sharia could clean up the chaotic judicial system in northern Nigeria. Since independence that system has decayed to the point of collapse. Justice is meted out by inept and often corrupt "area courts" presided over by judges of highly questionable moral character. The level of abuse, according to Dr. Kumo, is unimaginable. "They are the worst courts. Ninety percent of the area judges, if you were to apply the Sharia rules that witnesses must be upstanding citizens, would not even be competent to testify."

Bilikisu Yusuf, a prominent Muslim journalist who works with Transparency International to promote good government and accountability in Muslim communities, welcomed Sharia. When we met in her office in Kaduna as I was preparing to visit Zamfara, she said that any good Muslim had to support Sharia. "Living in a state of Sharia is living in a state guided by social justice," she said. But proponents of Sharia, she warned, must respect its central tenet of equality before the law. If the northern elite were simply using Sharia to promote their political prospects and were not prepared to face equal treatment before the law, they would be sorry. "I hope they know what they are promising because it is a system that cuts across all segments of society. If they are not sincere they should not toy with people's expectations."

And playing with people's hopes that Sharia would somehow bring a more just society was exactly what Governor Sani and his supporters were trying to do, according to Dr. Bala Usman, a professor of history at Ahamdu Bello University. Unless Zamfara and the rest of northern Nigeria worked to promote development, invested in schools, and provided people with the basic necessities of life, such as drinking water and health clinics, Sharia had little practical meaning. "People have been imbued with the notion that Sharia is the answer to their frustration with life. These politicians want to use Sharia as a cover because the upper class in the north has come to the end of the line."

Nevertheless, by any measure Governor Sani's move was a clever one. On the one hand, he, and the northern political elite he represented, had stolen the thunder of radicals such as Mujahid and Zakzaky and presented himself as the champion of Islam. On the other, he had put the Obasanjo government in a no-win situation. Should the authorities in Abuja be seen to challenge the measure in the courts, northern Muslims would claim what they believe is their inalienable right to practice Islamic law. Should Zamfara's gambit succeed, Governor Sani would be seen as the man capable of slaying the dragon of central government headed by a born-again Christian Yoruba.

APPROACHING Zamfara by road from the east, the first thing one sees at the state border is a sign welcoming travelers to Zamfara, "the home of farming." Someone has recently added, "and Sharia." Fifty yards into the Sharia state, it was clear that so far the Islamic taboo on corruption was taking its time sinking in. A policeman manning an impromptu checkpoint stopped my car and requested a dash. "Anything for me?" he asked. When I said there was not, he wondered about a soft drink. Only water, I said. After expressing disbelief, he settled for a cigarette. Yusuf, a Hausa man who was driving me from Kaduna, chuckled and said with a grunt, "Sharia? This is still Nigeria."

But by the time we were cruising along the windblown, dusty streets of Gusau it was apparent that significant changes were under way. The state Ministry of Information had plastered posters throughout the town that read "God's Law is Supreme." Green-and-yellow taxis with the image of a woman with a covered head painted on their doors or with the inscription *"mata kawai"* ("women only") ambled by.

As we pulled into Government House, dozens of bearded men in flowing robes were gathered over by the mosque for their morning prayers. I had set up an interview with Governor Sani through his press aide, Bashir Sanda, and I was stopping by to confirm the appointment. Sanda suggested that I return at 3:00 P.M., so Yusuf and I went to find Ibrahim Dosara, a local fixer for foreign journalists, who worked at the state Ministry of Education.

As a Muslim, Dosara was naturally sympathetic to Sharia, but he kept an open mind about its actual implementation. "There is pure Sharia and then there is Sharia the reality in Zamfara," he said. "They might not be the same thing." Dosara, who was born in a nearby village of the same name, was the first of his father's seventeen children to earn a university education. He was more worried about making ends meet than about religion. He was currently earning about 15,000 naira, or $150, a month, which was an excellent salary in Zamfara. He augmented that by doing some freelance work as a radio journalist and acting as a guide and translator for visiting correspondents. But he was feeding thirteen people: two wives, six children, and other relatives.

Dosara gave me a quick outline of the governor's Sharia program, as he understood it. There were two phases. The first, from October to January 27, the day Sharia was to become operational, included bans on alcohol, corruption, the local cinema, and "fornication," the commonly used term for adultery. "There should be nothing that goes against our religion," he said. After January 27 the second phase would kick in. After the twenty-seventh Muslims could no longer be deceitful (except in a life-threatening situation), distrust their neighbors, or gossip. I asked if gossiping and distrust wouldn't be difficult to eliminate. Dosara smiled knowingly.

There was no doubt, he said, that Sharia was immensely popular. When Governor Sani announced the measure, thousands of people converged on Gusau from all over northern Nigeria to celebrate.

A lightly populated state of some two million people, mainly subsistence farmers, Zamfara is literally a world apart from the hustle and bustle of Lagos and Kano. Many of its people still have posters of Abacha in their offices and homes because of his decision to carve Zamfara out of Sokoto State in 1996. It is an area of extreme poverty, and most of its people survive by farming potatoes, millet, guinea corn, rice, cowpeas, and beans. The only significant cash crops are cotton and groundnuts. The most recent tally of the indicators of the quality of life in the region, in the UN Development Program's Human Development Report of 1993, portray the situation in the old Sokoto State, but they probably reflect the current reality of Zamfara. According to that report, life expectancy is forty-nine years, compared to sixty-one in Lagos, and less than one in five people has access to clean water. Fewer than three out of one hundred people can read and write. As in most of the north, although the masses live in poverty, a tiny elite has enriched itself, often through illegal means such as kickbacks on contracts and diversion of moneys sent by the central government in Abuja to pay the state's bills.

In Gusau itself it was difficult to find a Muslim who spoke against Governor Sani's Sharia program, a fact that I found somewhat chilling. The closest I came was a pharmacist named Abdullahi Abubakar. He worried that some government officials charged with implementing the new laws, members of the all-powerful Ministry of Religious Affairs, were insincere. Several officials had told me that the ministry, the only one of its kind in Nigeria, was already skimming off funds meant to feed the poor. "What they say with their mouth, they do not believe in their heart," Abubakar said.

Dosara helped me check into the Gusau hotel, and while we were eating lunch, the waiter came over to say that a man wanted to see me. A security man, the waiter added, meaning that he worked for the State Security Service (SSS). Only once before in all my time in Nigeria had I been approached directly by someone who identified himself as an agent of the SSS. A stocky man in his late forties approached the table and began asking me routine questions, such as what I was doing in Zamfara, whom I worked for, and how long I planned to stay. I was somewhat unsettled by the man's inquiries, but Dosara took it all in his stride and offered him a soft drink, which he readily accepted. We shook hands and departed, and Dosara told me not to worry. The man was in charge of monitoring the movement of all foreigners in the state to make sure no one came to cause trouble over the Sharia issue. The SSS man reported directly to headquarters in Abuja and had nothing to do with the state government itself. "Feel free in Zamfara," Dosara repeatedly said.

We drove back to the governor's office at 3:00 P.M., and Sanda, the press aide, was nowhere to be found. Inexplicably, he was said to have gone home for the day. Several good-natured Nigerian correspondents were sitting in his office trying to contact him by telephone, and they said not to worry. Sanda apparently did this all the time, and with or without him the governor would see me. As the time passed, I began to get nervous because I knew the governor was scheduled to leave town the next day on a rural visit. Finally one of the journalists kindly went to tell the chief of protocol that I was around. Within minutes I was ushered into Governor Sani's office.

A 27-inch television was blaring out Sky TV's live coverage via satellite of a British House of Commons debate as the governor finished a meeting. After a few minutes he stood up at his desk, lifted off the receivers of five telephones so we would not be disturbed, and asked me to sit down next to him. His newly grown beard—he had urged all men to grow beards in Islamic tradition—made him look older than his forty years. Soft-spoken and self-assured, Governor Sani came across immediately as a charming man. He started his explanation of why he decided to champion Sharia by saying that in recent years parents had withdrawn their daughters from public schools because they feared that mixing with boys led to teenage pregnancy. Mixed schools, he said, were "immoral," and since his decision to segregate the student enrollment had skyrocketed.

When he first decided on Sharia, he had no inkling that it might become a national issue. It was purely a local affair, he said. "I don't want it to be a problem for the nation." He had been discussing his plans for Sharia with Christians in the state, and he felt sure that once everyone understood his program, the religious tension would ease. "We have forty-five churches in the state capital, and some are right next to the mosques and there has been no problem," he said. "We are preaching that Muslims must be allowed to remain with Islam and the Christians with their religion."

At least half a dozen times Governor Sani repeated the refrain that Sharia would only affect Muslims and would in no way prejudice Christians' way of life. In a dispute between a Christian and a Muslim, then of course the Christian could decide whether to take the case to a Sharia court or a regular tribunal. Christians would only be affected by the prohibitions on the sale of alcohol and prostitution. It was hard for me to take these bans as signs of Islamic oppression because prostitution, though widely practiced in Nigeria, was technically illegal throughout the country. And in my home state of Kentucky a large number of counties are "dry," and the sale of alcohol is illegal.

All the concern about amputations and beheadings, he continued, was exaggerated. "During the thirty-three years of the prophet Mohammed, there were only five hands removed," he said, speaking of the time of the Medina. "So it is not going to be rampant, and in fact, it may never happen during my time in government. First, because it only affects someone who has stolen out of greed. If you are in need, and the government has not given you the necessary social welfare, if you steal you have a lesser punishment than amputation." Theoretically, this is true, as Dr. Kumo, an expert in Sharia, had explained to me. Imposing a sentence of amputation is technically difficult under Sharia, as is conviction on the charge of adultery. In the latter case, for example, four upstanding males must have actually witnessed the "fornication" before guilt is proven.

Because the Nigerian police are under the authority of the inspector general in Abuja, Governor Sani said he was setting up what he called the Joint Aid Monitoring Group, in effect Muslim vigilantes, to ensure that Sharia was respected. The group was made up of volunteers from the various Islamic sects operating in the state. "They are so pure and they believe in the reward they are going to get from the God Almighty. They are the ones who are going around and watching to see that things are being implemented by the government, by the people."

Then came his first, troubling contradiction. Ten minutes before, he had laid great stress on the promise that Christians were not liable under Sharia. Now he was saying they could be. Can Sharia be applied to non-Muslims? I asked. "In terms of crimes against the state," he responded.

"What constitutes a crime against the state?"

"Theft."

"So if I stole a television set from a shop?"

"Yes, that is a crime against the state," the governor clarified. "If we realize that the thieves in our state are Christians, we may have to change our stand. This Islamic law may have to be applicable to everybody in terms of crimes against the state. They may want to take advantage of the fact that the Muslims are no longer stealing, and now if the Christians steal, we take them to magistrate's court and send them to jail. Because the Muslims will not allow it. Society will definitely pressure us to change our stand."

The next issue was corruption, and his plan to deal with it appeared severely flawed. In Zamfara and in Nigeria in general, for government officials to take cash commissions before private companies have completed their contracts to build, say, a road or a school is a time-honored tradition. Under Governor Sani's new regime, such practices were banned, he said defiantly. If, however, a company paid an official the bribe after finishing the contract, that was acceptable. "I warned in the presence of the public that I am going to remove any commissioner as soon as I learn that he is taking money from the contractor before the contract has been implemented. After the execution of the contract, I don't care what happens between him and the contractor. If the contract was for 5 million naira and the contractor went around to give the commissioner 200,000 naira [$2,000], I don't care."

I asked the governor about his own apparently rather sudden conversion to strict Islam. He said it had occurred in 1993 while he was still employed at the Central Bank of Nigeria under Babangida's regime. During worship at a mosque in Saudi Arabia, "the Imam was talking and praying and everybody around me starting crying. Suddenly I started crying too but not because I was hearing what he was saying but because I was not able to hear what he was saying." It was then he realized that he was not a good Muslim, he said. Sani resigned his post at the Central Bank and took a less demanding position as the commissioner for finance in the Sokoto state government. That left him time to attend Islamic classes.

It was at this point that Governor Sani told an untruth. In early December he had explained his substantial personal wealth in an interview with three foreign journalists by admitting that he had received payoffs from soldiers for delivering large sums of cash from the Central Bank. The cash was needed to finance the operations of Nigerian troops participating in the West African peacekeeping force, ECOMOG, in Liberia. "When I was at the Central Bank, in the foreign exchange [department], I would take $800,000 to the [presidential] villa for the ECOMOG operations and sometimes the officer would dash me $10,000 or $5,000," he had said.[6] "If it was now, I would never take that money," he had added. When one of the journalists asked whether he was prepared to give back the properties that he had bought with the bribes, he explained that he would not because "I allow relatives and other people to stay in my houses."

But to me, Governor Sani now denied that he had ever had anything to do with ECOMOG and said he was involved merely in the issuance of traveler's checks. "My own office was only limited to the selling of traveler's checks. That was the only thing we were doing. ...The area where there was a lot of money was the funds office, the investments office, where they transferred a lot of money for ECOMOG and things like that. I was not part of it. I was not in that office."

Even by his own account, however, Governor Sani was a wealthy man. In his original statement declaring Sharia in October, he had publicly declared his assets. They included nine houses, seven farms, one rice-threshing factory, one unspecified "enterprise," two tractors, seven cars, and shares in two private companies. Earlier he had said he was earning the equivalent of $3,000 per month at the Central Bank and later $150 per month in Sokoto. I asked how he had managed to acquire such assets with such modest earnings. His answer indicated how lucrative it can be in Nigeria to be simultaneously a public servant and a businessman:

You know we have family businesses, and I am from a royal family. In Sokoto I bought one house valued at 1.5 million naira, and now it is valued at about 15 million. I bought a 2-square-kilometer farm at 800,000 naira, and now it is worth more than 6 million. My brother is in Abuja at the electoral commission, and we bought the complete rice factory through a connection. He was able to buy it for 1 million naira, but the value now is 30 million. I have a tractor which I bought at 230,000 from a former commissioner, and that tractor now is valued at 2 to 3 million naira. All these things are the type of assistance that I consider I normally get from God Almighty.

His political career, it seemed, had come about in much the same way. After his time in Sokoto Sani became a director general for lands and housing, traditionally a prime source of patronage, under Colonel Jibril Bala Yakubu, the Zamfara military administrator during Abacha's rule. (Yakubu, along with Abacha's Chief of Army Staff Lt.-Gen. Ishaya Bamaiyi and his chief security officer Major Hamza al-Mustapha, is currently on trial for the attempted murder of the *Guardian* newspaper publisher Alex Ibru.) Sani said he became involved in politics when Yakubu urged him to run for governor of Zamfara. "The military administrator called me into his office and asked if I was going to contest or not. Abuja had called him and said I should be involved in politics, and I was so popular in Zamfara, everyone was pressuring me." He ran for office under the banner of the All People's Party, nicknamed the Abacha People's Party. Significantly, he is one of the few state governors who has not instituted a probe into the financial dealings of his military predecessor.

Since his Sharia declaration, Governor Sani has shored up his popularity by distributing free food to civil servants and the needy during Ramadan, the Islamic month of fasting. He has also offered to pay prostitutes a lump sum of up to $250 dollars if they will quit their profession and use the money to start another line of employment. "The government has to ensure that every needy person during this month can afford the basic necessities of life," he declared.

This is one reason why "all Muslims want to be governed by Sharia," he said. "Everybody must follow our lead," he added, contradicting his earlier statement that Sharia should remain a local issue. He felt sure that once his program was understood, all over Nigeria states with significant Muslim populations, even Lagos, would accept Sharia. "It must be a national issue," he said. His worst opponents were not the Christians but the Islamic radicals. "Extremists in the Muslim group like Zakzaky say there must be a revolution in Nigeria before there is Sharia. There should be no churches; there should be no Christians. They are fighting us. But Allah told us that Islam is peace."

At that point the chief of protocol entered the room and announced that the governor was needed to speak to some people outside. Together we walked to the parking lot, where a crowd of several hundred men and boys in a variety of white-and-green uniforms stood in a relaxed military formation. These were members of the Joint Aid Monitoring Group from a local government area outside Gusau. They had come to pay their respects. The governor took a microphone and shouted, "Allah akbar," and the gathering roared back, "Allah akbar!" These were the morality police who were to ensure that everyone lived good clean Muslim lives. They ranged in age from eight to sixty years old.

In the evening Dosara took me to one of the last drinking establishments in Gusau, the Gusau Sports Club, which had been built in the 1940s by the British. The other places where one could find a drink were the military barracks and the officers' mess, and there was little chance that the governor's writ would be respected there. One popular story was that when the governor sent a messenger to the officers' mess with a written order informing them of the ban on drinking, the poor man was forced to swallow the piece of paper.

When we entered the reception area at the sports club, it was clear that the attendants' nerves were on edge. The appearance of Dosara, a Hausa, prompted one Igbo man to shout "Who are you?" I explained that I was a writer in town and that Dosara was just showing me around. After a few minutes we convinced them that we were not informants for the morality police, and the Igbo gave me a short tour of the bar, the outdoor patio—where a table of Hausa men were drinking beer—the Ping-Pong table, the darts room, and the tennis courts. The club manager, a good-natured man in his sixties, wandered over and explained that they feared the bar could be shut down at any moment. Whenever a car pulled into the parking lot, he said, "We think it might be the vigilantes coming to shut us down."

Yusuf and I dropped Dosara off at his home in the Abdulsalami Abubakar housing estate, and by 9:00 P.M. we were back at the Gusau Hotel. As I picked up my key, I noticed the SSS man standing in the lobby with a portly gentleman who was speaking into a walkie-talkie. While I walked to my room I noticed the SSS man running out to the car park, but I did not think anything of it. The next morning Yusuf and Dosara told me that the man had questioned Yusuf about where we had gone and who we had seen that day. Yusuf had responded that he had no idea because he sat in the car while I was conducting my interviews and that because he was from Kaduna, he really could not enlighten the man about our visits. The agent ordered Yusuf to take him to Dosara's house, where the SSS man put the same questions to Dosara. But Dosara called his bluff. Dosara knew the local chief of the SSS and insisted that they go straight to SSS headquarters. After a short while the SSS man retreated. "As soon as he accepted that soft drink we gave him at lunch, I knew what he really wanted," Dosara said. "He just wanted money."

To understand how the monitoring group would work, Dosara took me to see Bala Umar Chafe, who wore a number of official hats. He was simultaneously the secretary of the Committee on the Joint Aid Monitoring Group, director of administration and finance in the

Ministry for Religious Affairs, and a member of the state anticorruption commission. A young man in his thirties, Chafe was conspicuous by his lack of a beard. He explained that the monitoring groups were deployed throughout the state's fourteen local government areas to keep watch for un-Islamic behavior. They received their orders from the Ministry of Religious Affairs.

The teams mainly limited themselves to cajoling offenders onto the straight-and-narrow path, but they did have the power to detain people and take them to the police. "We normally have informants who help us catch people committing the crime so we sit and discuss with them on different ways of living," he said with a smile. "In fact, it is rare that they would take anyone to the police. Because in most cases, when these joint aid groups talk to you, certainly whatever you are doing you must just stop it." The monitoring groups could expect to work long hours. "Usually, they will not go home until 1:00 A.M. or 2:00 A.M., going around the town checking all those places where immoral activities used to take place." Already they had scored some success. "There is one place called the University where they used to gamble and have harlots. Now that place has become an Islamic school."

I said that some of the group members I had seen with the governor were mere children, and I asked what their role was. "Someone you train very young will rise up with such spirit in him. Having the kids around is just an encouragement to the older people, but the small children do not circulate because in Islam, you must assume the age of maturity to do this."

And how, I asked, was it going to be determined if someone had flouted the ban on gossiping, deceit, and distrust. "Such things are very difficult to monitor because you don't know what is in a person's heart," he admitted gravely. "You only judge someone by what you have seen with your eyes. That is why in Islam, it is very hard to establish the crime of fornication. God has done that in order to ensure the dignity and honor of mankind will be protected."

Despite the promises that Sharia would apply only to Muslims, Christians in Gusau were worried. At the Pentecostal Eternal Life Bible Church, a ramshackle structure consisting of a tin roof and wooden benches, the forty-one-year-old pastor, Sunday Akolo Ochi, saw Sharia as a conspiracy to undermine the Obasanjo government.

"The Muslims are not happy that a Christian is in power," he said. "They are very upset that the president is probing past governments, because most of the corruption was carried out by the Muslims."

The problem the governor faces, he argued, is that he has no program to develop the state. The weakness of Islam, Pastor Ochi said, echoing a typical Christian view, is that it is not interested in economic development. He asked whether it was right to spend money meant for the state on religious matters. He wondered whether the governor really believed that segregating boys and girls in schools would stop teenage pregnancy. "Zamfara is so underdeveloped and the governor has no project for the people. So this Sharia is like a mask, because they have nothing else to offer," he asserted.

Women were supposed to ride either in the backs of buses or in segregated taxis. "So if a young man and his girlfriend want to travel to Kaduna, they have to ride separately? It's ridiculous. The members of our church are now praying seriously against this Sharia because if this continues, the rest of Nigeria will just cut off Zamfara and let it go back to the dark ages."

Pastor Ochi's harsh views mirrored his origins. He was a member of the Igala people from Benue State in the middle belt, and it is there that the conflict between Nigeria's Christians and Muslims is potentially its most combustible. Three weeks after I met him, Kaduna was in flames.

7

Children of Ham

———

Because the Nigerian State is so fragile we will be faced with these bush fires for some time to come.

FATHER MATHEW KUKAH

THE MIDDLE BELT, home to more than half of Nigeria's estimated three hundred ethnic groups, is its most complex and at
times most politically explosive region. It is not a formal region or
state; rather, as its name suggests, it stretches like a wide girdle across
the hilly central plateau that separates the strongly Islamic cultures of
the Hausa, Fulani, and Kanuri peoples in the north from the mainly
Christian Igbos in the southeast and the southwestern Yorubas, who
have embraced both religions.

The middle belt is generally considered the birthplace of sub-
Saharan Africa's greatest ancient artworks. Two millennia ago the region was home to thriving iron-working cultures, such as the Nok,
which produced famous terra-cotta sculptures of human figures.
These peoples are believed to have emigrated from what is now the

Nigeria-Cameroon border area, the source of the Bantu language group that came to dominate much of east, central, and southern Africa.

In precolonial days the middle belt provided a vast reservoir of slaves for the Sokoto Caliphate. Following the jihad of Usman dan Fodio, the emirs made annual pilgrimages to the sultan with hundreds and sometimes thousands of slaves in tow. The result was a massive though largely undocumented internal migration and mixing of ethnic groups. The slaves' experience with Islam made them ripe candidates for conversion to Christianity. After the arrival of the British the middle-belt peoples embraced their new faith and its offer of education as a way to raise themselves from their perceived second-class status and to declare their independence from the Islamic emirates. For the same reason, many middle-belters enlisted in the Nigerian armed forces as a means of rapid social advancement.

Since independence the middle belt has been the scene of frequent flare-ups. The Nigerian and international media describe the frequent clashes as religious riots, but in fact they stem from minority ethnic groups' attempts to wrench themselves free from what they see as domination by the Hausa-Fulani establishment. Other eruptions involve disputes between neighboring ethnic groups over land and access to political office. The people of a given area often claim they are the "indigenes" and that their enemies are the "strangers" or the "settlers" seeking to upset the mythical natural order of things.

These controversies have crackled across the middle belt for as long as Nigeria has existed, and they have claimed huge numbers of lives. But they intensified in the 1990s as economic, political, and educational opportunities waned with the collapse of the national economy. Invariably the struggles in the middle belt at the end of the twentieth century are argued on the basis of events that occurred hundreds of years before.

My first exposure to the explosive politics of the middle belt occurred in February 1992, when I stumbled upon a virtual civil war between the Tivs, the biggest ethnic group in the middle belt, and Jukuns, one of the region's smallest. I had just accompanied a friend and colleague, Kabiru Yusuf, to attend a wedding in the northern city of Jos. The following morning we headed south for Taraba State. With its mild climate and clean, crisp air, its university and national museum, Jos is commonly regarded as Nigeria's most attractive city. It grew up around the tin mines of the plateau, and for a while during the colonial period Jos hosted the second biggest population of whites in Nigeria, after Lagos. The former British prime minister John Major once worked in Jos as a bank manager before a car accident sent him back to London.

When Kabiru turned to look out the back window of the car at the fading sight of the city, he said ruefully, "We're going from the best to the worst." Our route was the highway heading south toward the Benue River, and our destination was the remote state of Taraba, arguably the poorest in Nigeria.

Kabiru was working as the editor in the Lagos office of the weekly magazine *Citizen*. Despite his blue-blooded lineage as a descendent of a royal family from the far northern city of Katsina, at heart Kabiru is a reporter, and he was frustrated sitting behind a desk supervising other people's copy. Years before in Zimbabwe, where he spent a year as a correspondent for the BBC's Hausa-language service, we had teamed up to do a story on the impact of the civil war in Mozambique on the communities straddling the two countries' common border.

We decided to renew the partnership to investigate what was occurring in Taraba. Little had been reported about the Tiv-Jukun fighting in the press in Lagos, some five hundred miles away, except for occasional one-paragraph stories. Most observers put the number killed at five thousand. At the time, the international press was filled with screaming headlines about the clan fighting in Mogadishu, but for a while the Somali death toll paled in comparison to that of the Tiv-Jukun war. The then sultan of Sokoto, Ibrahim Dasuki, was describing the conflict as "this threat to our survival as a nation."

Winding down from the highlands of Plateau State toward the flat-
lands near the northern bank of the Benue River, the road deteriorated
to the point where it was little more than a dirt track. The cool, clean
air of Jos was a distant memory, having given way to a heat that by the
early afternoon baked the landscape to a crisp. The Peugeot 505 that I
had recently acquired for my reporting trips around Nigeria had no air
conditioner. It was imported from the used-car markets of Holland,
and the radiator was too small to cope simultaneously with an air conditioner and the West African climate. It was not, as they say, "built for
Nigerian roads."

In the early afternoon we rumbled into a small collection of
wooden stalls that served as the rather shabby market at a makeshift
river port. Before the rains come in April, the Benue retreats from its
wide banks into a bright blue, shallow stream that weaves around is-
lands of white-hot sand. The river appeared shallow enough to walk
across, though it was not. We stood for a moment on a ridge above the
river and gazed at a massive ferry resting on a sandbar on the far side,
wondering how we were going to cross. Then a pickup sped by and disappeared straight down the riverbank. The drop was at least twenty
feet. Only then did it dawn on us that we would have to emulate the
truck if we were to reach the other side.

Turning back to Jos was out of the question, but going forward
seemed a perilous course, even more so when the means of crossing
came into a view. A pair of young men stood on a wooden barge about
75 feet long and a mere 10 feet wide. It rammed into shore with a distinct thud. The young men gave every indication that they were prepared to take the pickup, my 505, and another car across at the same
time. I forlornly asked Kabiru if there was any other way, and he shook
his head with a laugh. "If the car falls in, your newspaper will pay for
a new one," he said. I was less confident.

Such moments require a leap of faith. As gingerly as I could, I
drove over the edge and slid the car down the slope and, without losing

momentum, straight onto the raft. We positioned the car at the far end of the vessel and watched as the pickup and the third vehicle successfully imitated our maneuver. They were followed by a motorcycle and about fifty men and women hauling bags of food, goats, and several ill-disciplined pigs. The boatmen cranked up their 60-horsepower Suzuki engine, shoved the front end off the shore, and pointed the raft, now with a distinctly uncomfortable leftward tilt, toward the far side of the Benue and the port town of Ibi.

For hundreds of years Ibi has been a port of call for travelers up and down the Benue River, which flows from neighboring Cameroon into central Nigeria, joining the Niger River at Lokoja and continuing on to the Atlantic Ocean. In 1854, when the boats of the Royal Niger Expedition sailed up from the Niger delta to Ibi, the mission's leaders, Dr. W. B. Baikie and Samuel Crowther, asked someone to point out the boundary between the two ethnic groups in the area, the Tivs and the Jukuns. The man, a Jukun, is said to have intertwined his ten fingers to indicate that the two peoples lived as one. Indeed, fifty years later Lord Lugard's West African Frontier Force had to suppress a rebellion by the Tivs, who had come to the aid of the Jukuns in a dispute with local Hausa traders.

Over the years, however, the relationship soured, initially as a result of Britain's policy of indirect rule. Unlike the Tivs, a loosely organized farming people who live in isolated homesteads, the Jukuns were ruled by a king, the Aku Uka, who is regarded as the near-divine representative of God and custodian of the people's welfare. His authority is absolute, because disobeying the Aku Uka is tantamount to defying the Almighty. The British, determined to rule through local sovereigns, elevated the Aku Uka to the supreme political figure over Jukuns and Tivs alike.

The initial troubles between the two occurred on the eve of independence during the elections to the federal House of Representatives in 1959. The Tivs formed an electoral alliance with the Hausas to elect a Tiv man. It was not a popular move among the Jukuns. After independence the Jukuns and the Tivs fought a number of skirmishes, usually just before elections, when the two sides attempted to use brute force instead of a fair vote to determine who would reign in the area. In October 1991, on the eve of a new national census, the western part of Taraba State erupted into a full-scale war. Had the Jukun man questioned by Baikie and Crowther been alive, he would have smashed his two fists together.

Our makeshift barge reached the asphalt landing at Ibi with surprisingly little trouble, and with great exhilaration we set out to find our modern equivalent of the Niger Expedition's informant.

There were no outward signs around the port or the nearby open-air market that anything was amiss in Ibi, a town of one-story white-washed buildings and some five thousand people. In the 90-degree heat of the early afternoon, business activity had slowed to a minimum, with most residents preferring to remain indoors until the cooler evening hours. Yet even given the heat and time of day, Ibi seemed far too quiet for an average Nigerian market town. Kabiru stopped a passerby and asked the whereabouts of the local government. Within half an hour we were ushered into a dark lounge to meet Tanko Mohammed, a barrister who was the local government secretary, and a Tiv politician, Francis Iaregh.

They asked us to sit down and offered us warm soft drinks. When Kabiru briefed them on our mission to reach Wukari by the end of the day, they looked at one another aghast. It was suicide, they suggested. Gunmen were hiding in the bushes along the road waiting to ambush passing vehicles. All the villages were burned down and deserted. Even the soldiers were too frightened to patrol the road, they said. What was worse, the Mobile Police were in cahoots with the Jukun fighters. "The Tivs played a large role in the federal forces in the war against Biafra, and the Mobile Police are mostly Igbos," Mohammed said. "So it is much easier for the Jukuns to buy the Mobiles."

This was most unwelcome news. The Mobile Police—nicknamed Kill and Go—were notoriously ruthless. Their reputation for extortion and extrajudiciary executions across the country was so extreme that Babangida had recently withdrawn them from nighttime patrols of the roads.

Kabiru and I glanced at each other, both of us weighing the dangers of proceeding against those of returning to the wooden barge and driving back up to Jos. We opted for pressing ahead to Wukari. We thanked them for their hospitality and resumed our journey.

At the outskirts of town a roadblock was manned by a group of drowsy police. A young man came to lift the barrier and looked at us quizzically, as if to ask whether we wanted to reconsider. He waved us through, and I decided to see how quickly the 505 could scoot.

Within minutes the first village, or what was left of it, came up on the left. Half of the fifty or so houses had been burned to the ground, and someone had clearly made a good attempt to do the same to the other half. Their roofs had collapsed, and their doors and windows were blackened where fire had licked their edges. The area was littered with pots and pans, clothes, and plastic bags—the telltale signs of the panic of human flight. I told Kabiru it reminded me of scenes from the civil wars in Mozambique and Angola.

"Stop the car," Kabiru said suddenly, his voice tinged with anxiety. I looked at him as if he were crazy. "Stop the car and move over. I am taking the wheel. If we get stopped, you are the journalist and I am your driver."

As we continued down the road, village after village was in a similar state. Occasionally we passed a scorched truck or car that had been waylaid by the highwaymen. Sometimes, when the kill was fresh enough, the bitter smell of blistered rubber filled the air. For the next twenty-five miles, until we reached Wukari, we peered into the waves of heat rising from the pavement on the lookout for any threatening figures. But there was not one living soul, not even a stray dog.

Wukari itself was remarkably calm, given the destruction we had seen on the way in. Roadside merchants were manning their stalls, selling everything from cigarettes to soft drinks to candles to biscuits. Trays of raw meat were laid out next to small grills as the cooks prepared sticks of *suya*, the West African version of a shish kebab that is flavored lightly with chili powder. Inevitably there were rows and rows of gray yams, the giant roots that are a staple food and for which the region is famous, stacked like logs. The only sign that something was amiss were trucks filled with heavily armed regular police and the Kill and Go units patrolling menacingly every few minutes.

We found a run-down motel on a side road and walked into the reception desk to check in for the night. Out of the shadows a young English couple approached me. They asked if I knew what was going on here. They had ridden into town that day and noticed that all along the road the villages were in ruins. I asked them what they meant. They'd ridden in on their bicycles, they replied. They had started in Gambia and were heading to Cameroon, but in all their travels they had seen nothing like this. At one point some policemen had stopped them and accused them of being spies. "They simply didn't believe that we had ridden our bikes from the Gambia," the young man said. Kabiru could hardly contain his laughter. I explained that they had landed in a small war and that it might be better if they took the road out toward Katsina-Ala and into Benue State in the morning. They thanked me and returned to their room. "Can you imagine riding bicycles through this?" Kabiru asked, giggling and muttering something rather uncomplimentary about crazy Europeans.

In the morning we set out for the palace of the Aku Uka to ask for an interview. Initially his private secretary, a scowling unfriendly sort, was dismissive of our request. One had to book an appointment well in advance. Kabiru insisted that we had to leave the following day and that his magazine and my newspaper really wanted to hear the Jukuns' side of the story. We had been led to believe that the Jukuns were largely at fault, and we needed to obtain a balanced picture. Kabiru has a knack for getting his way.

We were soon ushered into a dank, dark room, where a dozen elderly men sat on cushions on the floor. Against the far wall was an extraordinary sight. A robed figure, the Jukuns' representative from God, sat on a small throne between two mortars. The private secretary said the weapons had been captured recently from the Tiv forces.

Kabiru conducted the interview in Hausa, and the divine emissary spoke in such a low voice that I could hardly hear him. Luckily we had brought a tape recorder. His first point, that "before the advent of the colonial masters, the Tivs were under us," revealed a hard line the Jukuns took in the conflict.

The historical evidence, although fragmentary, suggests otherwise. The Tivs are believed to have migrated from modern-day Congo, through Cameroon, and to have settled in the greater Benue region by the sixteenth century. At that time the Jukuns, who had come from somewhere near the Lake Chad basin, were settled in the Gongola River valley, well north of the Benue in what is today Plateau State. The Jukuns established a powerful military state called Kwararafa based on a well-trained cavalry. Well into the seventeenth century Kwararafa's horsemen, armed with long spears, pillaged far and wide, threatening Borno to the northeast and the Hausa city-states of Kano, Katsina, and Zaria to the west. By the early eighteenth century, however, Kwararafa had mysteriously disappeared. The remaining Jukuns set out in search of a new home, and after crossing the Benue River they settled in Wukari. During colonial rule the British established the Wukari division, over which the Aku Uka was sovereign, and a separate domain for the Tiv in what is now Benue State. As far as Aku Uka was concerned, any Tiv not willing to submit to his rule should return to Benue. Those who "confirmed that they are our children," as he put it, were welcomed. "We received them wholeheartedly and ate together and drank together."

In the Jukun view, the recent trouble started because Tivs refused to recognize the Aku Uka's authority over parceling out land and appointing local ward chairmen and chiefs. "In their little minds, they want to regard Benue and Taraba as one estate to be under their sovereignty."

The Aku Uka continued along this line for another hour. The Tiv were guilty of "colonizing" Jukun land, of refusing to respect his will, and of perpetrating atrocities against his people. He cited the razing of a village called Kente in which seventy-five people were killed and a December 31 raid on Wukari itself in which two people died, although one suspected that the violence might have been more closely linked to the New Year's Eve revelry. "We think the Tivs are fighting against God," the Aku Uka said, as someone who would know. "They have fought on different fronts, but they did not succeed, so they must be against God."

The interview was over, and as we stepped out into the blinding light, the private secretary called us into his office. He shut the door. The Aku Uka, he announced, wanted to present us with a gift. From under his desk he pulled out a stack of naira a foot high. "This is for your expenses while in Wukari," he said. Kabiru started to laugh but caught himself. We both expressed gratitude but said that we could not possibly accept it. His countenance turned sour. "But this is from the Aku Uka himself, you must accept it," he said with the slightest hint of a threat.

Two things were at work here. Traditional leaders throughout the country are expected to provide funds for their visitors. When subjects come to pay homage to their sovereigns, they count on receiving something on the side. And unfortunately, paying journalists has become a tradition in Nigeria. It is the brown-envelope syndrome. Journalists covering a politician's press conference, for example, often receive a little brown envelope. The more important the person, the greater the amount in the little brown envelope, and of course the more extensive the coverage is expected to be. Reporters accredited to the presidency can anticipate annual bonuses courtesy of the head of state. If one politely refuses the gift, there are usually no hard feelings. But something in the private secretary's body language and his insistence that we accept made it feel like a bribe. Our respective newspapers were looking after our expenses, we said, so there was no need for the kind contribution. "You cannot refuse," he said sternly. "You cannot!" It was a delicate moment. Kabiru and I suspected that it would not be healthy to remain in Wukari for another night if we insulted the Jukuns' emissary from god.

Luckily, at that very moment our salvation knocked at the door. A tottering old man stepped in and addressed the secretary. He was from Kente, the Jukun village that had been destroyed. His people were living as refugees on the outskirts of Wukari, and they were starving. We turned to the private secretary and said we would be happy if the money went to the people of Kente. The old man's eyes lit up, and after initially hesitating, the private secretary handed him the money.

The next morning we decided to visit the scene of the most recent attack, a Hausa settlement called Bantaji about thirty miles east. The panorama was similar to the stretch from Ibi, but this time there were several checkpoints manned by the regular police and the Kill and Go. We knew we had reached Bantaji when we were forced to pull into one village by a group of young men waving sticks and metal pipes in the air and dancing in the middle of the road.

The smoldering ruins of shops and huts sent wisps of smoke overhead as Kill and Go police trampled through the rubble. We approached one tall man in his early twenties, Rabin Bantaji, who was staring into space. We asked who had done this. He nodded at the police. "The same ones who are here now," he said, spitting on the ground in disgust. We moved to the side of one building so we could talk in private. "They shot my father in our home," he said. "The rest of my family ran away into the bush and I have not seen them since."

Rabin was nervous and said we had better speak to his uncle, Galadima Adamu Bantaji, who was a member of the chief's council. We walked along the uneven dirt road into the heart of the settlement and found Adamu Bantaji sitting in front of his destroyed home. A few yards away a crowd of men and women were standing guard over seven young men who were stripped to their underwear and lying face down in the dust, their arms bound together with wire. I thought for a moment that the captives were dead until one of them groaned. Several of their faces were bruised, and they were bleeding. A group of Nigerian police sat uneasily between the men and the villagers who were taunting them. Every few minutes someone ran up to kick one of them. The police said they were waiting for reinforcements to take the men back to Wukari.

Adamu Bantaji said that the men, all Jukuns, had arrived in a truck several hours earlier, firing homemade shotguns in the air. They apparently thought the village was deserted and were returning to loot whatever was left, which from appearances was not much. When they climbed down from the vehicle, local residents emerged from the shattered buildings and overpowered them.

The initial raid, which had occurred five days before our arrival, was surprising because the village was populated by Hausas, who for the most part had stayed out of the Tiv-Jukun war. But Adamu Bantaji said his people became a target after they allowed Tiv farmers to sell their produce at its market after they were forced to quit doing business at a nearby Jukun settlement called Gindin Dorowa. The Tivs were regarded as excellent farmers, and the Hausas, being natural traders, welcomed them in the hope that the market would have an improved produce selection.

This was not the first violence in the town. A gang of Jukun fighters had first attacked Bantaji in early February, but they were beaten back after killing two people and wounding seven. In response, residents of Bantaji erected an illegal roadblock that angered the police. (Only the police have the right to mount roadblocks.) The police warned them several times to remove the barrier. Nine days later on a Wednesday, Bantaji's market day, a joint force of Jukuns and Mobile Police armed with automatic weapons arrived in four trucks.

The assailants set fire to the market, shot up the place, looted some of the nearby shops, and drove off. "Most of the killing was done by the police because they were in the front," Adamu Bantaji said in clear earshot of the policemen waiting beside the captives. "We have buried thirty-one people, but we are still finding bodies," he shouted. His three wives and five children disappeared in the raid, and he had not been able to locate them. "Most of the people fled into the bush, some with wounds to go and die there."

When we returned to Wukari, we drove over to the police station in search of the officer in charge to seek his comment on the allegations of police collusion in the Bantaji raid. Near-bedlam reigned inside the compound as dozens of officers were running about gathering their weapons and climbing aboard trucks and an armored personnel carrier. We found the senior officer inside the building, barking orders at his men. He clearly had no interest in speaking with reporters and curtly informed us that all press inquiries had to be handled at headquarters in Lagos. He was extremely busy, he said. Five policemen had been kidnaped. One had escaped, and the four others were missing. We later learned that their corpses were found in shallow graves.

We wanted to depart from Taraba State by dusk, so we climbed back into the 505 and headed for the border with Benue State. Unfortunately, the road was filled with debris, and we sustained a puncture right in front of a ransacked village. The tire was changed in great haste.

Our next destination was the palace of the Tiv traditional leader, the Tor Tiv, who resides in the city of Gboko, about eighty miles west of Wukari. The institution of the Tor Tiv is a relatively recent creation. Despite sharing a common language and culture, the fiercely independent Tivs had never been under a central authority. They defeated all attempts by the Sokoto Caliphate to conquer them, and they were among the last groups in Nigeria to be pacified by the British. In an effort to bring, from their point of view, some order to the Tivs, the British created a Tiv council and the post of the Tor Tiv in 1947.

The current Tor Tiv, who served more as a spiritual leader than a chief, was Alfred Akawe Torkula, an educated former civil servant and businessman. Walking through the palace waiting room, we passed a dozen or so elderly men who were seeking an audience. Kabiru, experienced in these matters, knew that the trick to seeing any traditional leader quickly was to get past the waiting room and find the private secretary.

Initially the secretary, a cheery young man, seemed the exact opposite of his dour counterpart in Wukari. But after consulting with his boss, he returned with the same answer. The Tor Tiv was far too busy to meet with us without an appointment. Once again, Kabiru explained that we had come for the Tor Tiv's response to some serious accusations that the Aku Uka had made during our interview in Wukari. The news that we had seen the Aku Uka caught his attention. "Wait a minute," he said, and he rushed off.

The secretary returned and ushered us into the Tor Tiv's modern office. Except for his traditional attire—His Royal Highness is fond of wearing a leopard-skin cap—everything about him suggested a modern, businesslike approach to his duties.

As soon as we started to outline the Aku Uka's assertions that the Tivs were disrespectful land-grabbers, the Tor Tiv dismissed them with the wave of his hand, saying, "wrong" and "Obviously that is falsehood." He provided a persuasive counterhistory to that of the Aku Uka, precise in its details of the rise and fall of Kwararafa and the migration of the Tivs to the region well before the Jukuns ever set foot below the Benue River.

"Whether he agrees or not, the Tiv people occupied the countryside over a period of three or four hundred years," he declared. "They believe that they are the indigenes and that the Tiv communities there are settlers, strangers. I am saying that is wrong."

Then the Tor Tiv launched into an attack on Jukun discrimination toward the Tivs living in their midst, asserting that as fishermen the Jukuns relied on the Tivs to keep their local economy afloat. "Ninety-five percent of the economy of that place is generated by the Tiv community because they are the people who farm, they produce the foodstuff, and they are the people who feed Wukari and the Aku Uka himself. It is the tax paid by them that sustains Wukari, including the Aku Uka's palace. But they are regarded as second-class citizens," he said angrily. "There is no Tiv man who is allowed to be even a cleaner or night guard in Wukari."

We asked whether it was true that Tivs in Wukari do not recognize the Aku Uka as their ruler. His Royal Highness smiled knowingly.

"Well, agreed. Any Tiv man—whether in London, or in New York, Washington, or Moscow, anywhere in the world—refers to the Tor Tiv as his spiritual leader. But that does not mean that he does not recognize the Aku Uka as his immediate ruler."

As the interview drew to a close, the Tor Tiv smiled. "I suppose I should not even try to offer you a contribution to your expenses," he said. No, that was quite all right, but we thanked him for the offer. "I didn't think so."

The Tiv-Jukun war eventually calmed down after Babangida deployed the army to maintain the peace, though tensions between the communities continue to this day. In 1998 another ethnic conflict involving the Jukuns exploded in the Taraba State town of Takum. This time the fighting involved the local Jukun community, known as the Chambas, and a small ethnic group called the Kutebs. Jukun youths armed with rifles and machetes and allegedly with the support of the police ransacked Kuteb communities in the farmlands surrounding Takum.

A story in the national newspaper, *The Guardian*, painted a picture tragically similar to the one we had witnessed outside Wukari:

Most government buildings were destroyed. Health facilities and services are almost non-existent following havoc wreaked on its activities. People who escaped from the crisis take refuge in neighboring villages and towns at the mercy of friends and total strangers, while those who could not go to any town or village are taking refuge under trees and mountain tops in the bushes without enough food or access to medical facilities.

The report, entitled "Ethnic Cleansing in Takum, Taraba," said that it was common to see Jukun youths "displaying human heads and other human parts openly as they chant victory songs round the town."[1]

———

SIX YEARS after my first visit to the middle belt, I made my way to Kafanchan, one of the most explosive focal points in modern Nigeria. Rather than a feud among rival minorities over land, the conflict here pitted the non-Muslim ethnic groups against what they regard as their overlords, the predominantly Islamic Hausa-Fulani.

Despite its position as a key railway junction, like Minna, Kafanchan has enjoyed none of the economic largesse from the rich and powerful that so quickly transformed Babangida's hometown. The growth industry in Kafanchan, run-down and generally underdeveloped, appeared to be religion. There were churches—Pentecostal, the Ecumenical Church of West Africa (ECWA), Catholic—and of course mosques everywhere. Since the colonial occupation of the area at the turn of the century, Kafanchan and the surrounding area have witnessed a variety of uprisings dating back to tax revolts against the British in 1922 and 1946. Riots between Islamic and Christian students erupted at the Kagoro Teachers College in 1987, and in 1992, just three months after my visit to Wukari, clashes between the Katafs and Hausa traders in the Zango Kataf market sparked full-scale fighting between Christians and Muslims throughout the state of Kaduna, fighting that claimed hundreds of lives.

Another source of tension has been the long-standing demands by the largely Christian minorities to be ruled by their own chiefs instead of the Muslim emir. Underlying the simmering tension is a grinding poverty that fuels a common sense of discrimination and economic oppression. Some of the resentment of the emirate stems from the time of Usman dan Fodio's Islamic jihad and the internal slave trade, the collective memory of which remains fresh. "I remember as a kid, if I was eating too quickly, my grandmother used to say, 'Why are you eating as if you are running from Hausas?'" Father Mathew Kukah, the secretary of the Nigeria's Catholic Bishops Conference, told me one afternoon at his office in Lagos. "The Hausas used to come on their horses, so when our people were in the villages, if they saw dust rising in the distance, they would run. My grandmother used to say there was a cave where they always hid."

Kafanchan is a relative backwater, and yet it has produced individuals of extraordinary accomplishments. They include Father Kukah, who is also an author and a well-known commentator on national issues; the late former secretary to the federal government, Aliyu Mohammed; and Biyi Bandele Thomas, one of Nigeria's most exciting playwrights, whose works are regularly performed by the Royal Shakespeare Company in Britain. I was also anxious to visit the site of the discovery of the first Nok terra-cotta sculptures, which had had such a powerful impact on the development of art in West Africa and beyond.

I reached the Roman Catholic cathedral, where I was to link up with Father Kukah and renew an acquaintance with the newly installed bishop of Kafanchan, Joseph Bagobiri, whom I had met in 1995 when he was a parish priest in the northern city of Kano. Father

Kukah arrived in the early afternoon and immediately took me on a whirlwind tour of his home area. He could only stay in Kafanchan for the day, so he was hoping to introduce me to a few key people and help me set up some interviews. Gregarious yet serious, intellectual but down-to-earth, small and compact but bursting with enough energy for two men, Father Kukah is somewhat of a phenomenon in Kafanchan. He travels the world and is on good terms with the present and past heads of state; he is the local boy who made good, a symbol that it is possible for someone from this forgotten part of Nigeria to make a mark.

Father Kukah decided to join the priesthood partly because of a pickup truck. As a boy of twelve living with his grandmother, he was fascinated by the local priest, "one, because he was white and two, because he had a truck." The priest used to slow down when he drove by the Ikulu village where Mathew grew up so that he and his friends could climb on board for a ride. One day while Mathew was in grade school, he came home with the news that he was going to sit for the examination to enter the seminary so that he could become a priest. His grandmother wanted to know what a priest was. He explained that the white man with the pickup was a priest. She asked whether, if he became a priest, he would also become white. He said no. Then she asked if by becoming a priest he would drive a truck. He said yes. She snapped her fingers and said, "do it."

The problem was that he had just two weeks in which to pay the examination entrance fee of 3 shillings, which at the time, he said, "was a helluva a lot of money." His grandmother sold baskets for cash, and Mathew remembers waking up in the middle of the night to find her weaving. "One basket would be something like four pence, so she needed quite a good number to get the three shillings. Day and night she was weaving those baskets." She eventually earned the three shillings.

We headed east through Kagoro, past the railway yard and out to Zango Kataf, the site of the bloody 1992 clashes. At the entrance to the hamlet, several soldiers cradling automatic weapons stood guard at a checkpoint. It had been six years since the troubles, but the security forces were not relaxing.

The tension was symbolized by the name. *Zango* is a Hausa word meaning market, and *Kataf* is what the Hausas called the local ethnic group, although the people call themselves Atyab. The way the locals see it, Zango Kataf should have been called *Zangon Kataf,* with the extra *n* denoting that the market belongs to the Kataf people. But because the Katafs were not Muslim, they were not deemed fit to own a Zango. Furthermore, the Hausas insisted that because they had established the market, it belonged to them.

Zango Kataf itself was quiet. Trade was brisk at the mainly Hausa-owned shops that lined the narrow dirt streets. The only signs of the mayhem that rocked the town in May 1992 were a few burnt-out buildings that were never repaired. The immediate cause of the 1992 dispute had been the decision by the Zango Kataf local government, which for the first time was headed by a Kataf man, to transfer the market to a new site. The Katafs favored the move because it would provide them with more space, whereas the Hausa traders opposed the decision because they feared it was aimed at curtailing their business. Father Kukah explained that Zango Kataf dates to the mid-eighteenth century, when it was established by Hausa and Fulani traders as a rest stop on the route to Lokoja, the large settlement at the meeting point of the Benue and Niger Rivers. From the mid-nineteenth century to the arrival of the British, Zango Kataf functioned as a base for slave raiding into the neighboring villages. The emir of Zaria ruled Zango Kataf until the 1950s, and all the important officials were Hausa or Fulanis.

As usual, Father Kukah was in a hurry. He had to return to Jos and then drive a couple of hours to Abuja to appear in a television debate, and he was due in Lagos the next day. He wanted to find a local historian, Simon Yohanna, who would be my guide through the rest of my stay. So it was back to Kafanchan for a stop at the Kagoro Teacher's

College, where Simon worked as the registrar. As soon as we entered the gate, the guard told us that all staff members were attending a farewell meeting for a college official.

We stood outside the large meeting hall, where one hundred people were in the middle of lunch and listening to speeches of gratitude, and asked a young man to find Simon. As soon as Father Kukah was spotted, several college officials dragged him in. He protested that he was in a hurry, but they would have nothing of it. In he went, and I with him. Chairs were placed at the front of the room, and plates of chicken and rice were thrust in our laps. The master of ceremonies announced that Father Kukah had arrived and had agreed to say some words. Father Kukah stood up, grabbed the microphone, and immediately started telling jokes like a late-night talk show host. It was nice to be back, he said to a warm round of applause, and then he explained that he was here to show me around. "My friend is a writer who used to be a journalist," he shouted with a mischievous smile. "You know, the only difference between a writer and journalist is that a writer takes much longer to write."

After a few precious bites at the grilled chicken we ducked back out of the room with Simon in tow. Simon graciously agreed to Father Kukah's request that he show me around for the next couple of days. We agreed to meet in the morning.

———

SIMON AND I decided to start at the beginning, and there was no better place to do that than in the village of Nok, about twenty miles outside of Kafanchan. Today the village of Nok is a small maze of earthen homes that rest in front of a hillside lattice of rocky alcoves and caves. Although people have certainly inhabited Nigeria's northern savannas, central plateau region, and coastal tropical forests for thousands of years, some of the earliest archaeological evidence of human habitation comes from the iron-working peoples who lived in the middle belt some 2,500 years ago. Terra-cotta figures believed to have been produced around 450 B.C. were first discovered in 1936 in Nok. The sculptures range from 4 inches to 4 feet in height, and the human faces portrayed are large and stylized.[2] Many experts believe that Nok gave birth to another major sculptural style that produced terra-cotta and cast-bronze work sometime around the sixth century A.D. in the southern Nigerian city of Ife, the spiritual home of the Yoruba people. The Nok and Ife traditions are the only two known in Africa that attempted to produce human forms in terra-cotta sculpture in near-life-size proportions.[3]

In the history of Africa, Nok is second only to Egypt in terms of culture and civilization, claimed Chief Ibrahim Nok, the village head, as we sat on his verandah. "We were melting stones into iron even before the British people," he said. The migration of the Noks' forebears began in Egypt at the time of the Pharaohs. The people of Nok, he declared, are the children of Ham.

Ham was a son of Noah who survived "that big rain that submerged all the nations at that time," Ibrahim Nok said, describing the great flood for which Noah built the ark. The story goes that after becoming involved in a dispute with the Pharaohs, Ham decided to set off from Egypt with his clan on a trek that took them through Algeria, Sudan, Chad, and Cameroon and finally into Nigeria's central plateau. The village of Nok was their final resting place.

"They found shelter here, because to the east you have the mountains, and on the other side you have the marshlands. If you tried to cross you would sink because it is like quicksand. Enemies cannot cross," he said. "There are so many living caves, and if one can get into one then you will see how God works. They are natural caves, and as soon as there was any trouble, the people would retreat into them."

In one of the caves, which has been closed to the public, there is a medicinal tree, which Ibrahim Nok said is so slippery "even a monkey cannot climb it." It is called the Life Tree, and people from all around Nigeria, especially Yoruba pilgrims, used to come to pray and tear off the bark for medicinal purposes. Because the practice of stripping the bark was threatening the health of the tree, the chief eventually ordered that no one be allowed to visit it.

Ibrahim Nok proposed that I take a tour of the village's sights, with a visit to some of the rock formations, the caves, and the site of the traditional court system. Because he had a bad leg, he deputized as my guide his assistant, Haruna Agwey, a tall, wiry, ancient man able to cover a yard or more with each stride. A group of elders who decided to join us struggled to keep up.

We set out on a short walk through the center of the village until we reached a clearing. This, the lower court, handled mainly theft and adultery and was still used from time to time. Two roughly rectangular stone pillars, one about 8 foot tall and the other about 6 foot tall, were planted in the ground. Around the back under a giant tree were large round boulders where the elders sit. The accused would stand on a stone about 10 feet in front of the rectangular pillars and swear an oath to tell the truth as the trial opened.

If the case required an appeal or involved two adult males, then it went to the appeals court, which took place twenty yards away inside a small clearing surrounded by huge, 20-foot-tall boulders. At the base of the outcrop are a dozen small flat stones on which the jury of elders sat. The accused stood on a larger flat surface a few yards away. Generally, anyone found guilty was asked to pay a fine of five goats and ten jugs of *burukutu*, the local favorite beer brewed from sorghum. If he refused, he could face death. Below one of the large rocks is a clearing where, Agwey assured me, many bodies are buried. For less serious offenses, if the accused failed to pay the fine, it was believed that his family would quickly die off. No one had been executed lately, Agwey said with a chuckle.

Agwey led on to the site where the first terra-cotta was discovered near a small stream that runs through the heart of the village. He pointed down to the earth below a rather nondescript bush. "That's where the sculpture was found by our miners," he said. He was not sure exactly when the discovery was made, but he said that he had been told it was about the time of his birth seventy-one years earlier.

Forward we marched through a well-tended field of manioc, then we turned right and climbed up a massive flat, slanting rock overlooking the entire village. There we met a gristly old man who looked as though he was starving. Agwey introduced him as Nyet Yak, the village's chief priest. He was carrying a wooden staff and wearing a University of Wisconsin Whitewater T-shirt. He had been the chief priest since he was fifteen, but no one could really say how old he was.

I asked Nyet Yak what the priest's chief attributes are meant to be. "Dependability, perseverance, and especially someone who is not long-winded," he said with a straight face. "Oh, yes, and someone who has the ability keep secrets, especially from the women." Everyone laughed knowingly. The rock is the meeting place for the entire village in times of crisis. Whatever is discussed here is to be kept secret from the outside world.

We continued on through a series of boulders that led into a naturally formed chamber about 10 foot high and 10 foot wide. This was the Supreme Court. Again, if found guilty, the accused was fined a certain number of goats and a certain quantity of *burukutu*. Once the fine was imposed and paid, the goats were slaughtered and the beer was drunk, and there was dancing and general merriment all around. Women were only allowed in when they came to grind grain on the flat rock at the entrance. They were never permitted to witness a court case. Agwey said that there is a belief that once you tell a woman something, there is no longer any secrecy.

We returned to Ibrahim Nok's house, and he told me that because of Nok's obvious historical interest, for the past thirty years there had been plans to set up an archaeological institute and a tourist center, but so far little had come of them. A neglected museum at the back of the village stood empty because thieves had been stealing the terra-cotta sculptures housed there. All the figures had been sent to the museum in Jos. These days the villagers eke out a living in small-scale agriculture, farming crops such as ginger, soy beans, cowpeas, yams, cocoyam, and cassava. Ginger is so plentiful that Simon negotiated a car trunk load for the equivalent of $3.

But Ibrahim Nok did not want to talk about the village's meager economy. He was more interested in history. "Every spot," he said proudly, "has a history of its own. When you were coming into the village, you cross a small spring that we call Kwemnet where we used to produce iron from stones." It is nearly impossible to reach the place, however, because the village intentionally refuses to clear it of brush so that no one can damage the ancient furnaces.

A few yards beyond the stream, at the very entrance to the town, stands a large wooden statue carved in the manner of terra-cotta sculpture. That, said Ibrahim Nok, is where the commander of the first British occupation troops pitched his tent. A community development center halfway up the hill to Nok's house was built in 1957 to mark the spot where the British army was encamped. "The people here built it on their own, and it was among the first community development works carried out in the whole of southern Kaduna," he said. "It was built for a reason: so that the young generation coming up would not forget that spot."

Unfortunately, the new generations are forgetting. The traditional courts are hardly ever used, and the village youths almost never take part unless one of them is directly involved in a dispute that does not require a hearing in the Nigerian court system, such as petty theft or adultery. Originally the people of Nok were sun worshippers like the Egyptians, but Christianity and Islam have displaced the old ways. "The elderly people are dying away, and these new religions are taking over everybody," Ibrahim Nok said.

As his first name suggests, Chief Nok is a Muslim, but the faith was not imposed on him. "I became a Muslim while I was still a small boy. I decided to do so on my own. My parents believed in the traditional religion, but they encouraged me to do what I wanted. Later on my father became a Christian and so did his wives. In our family we had both Christians and Muslims."

In other areas around Kafanchan, rivalry between Islam and Christianity is fierce, I said. Did Nok have such religious problems? "Not at all," he replied with a wave of his hand. "We have no such problems here. Once you accept the scriptures, then you must accept anybody who believes in God. I always invite all the Christian leaders for talks, and if they have problems they come to me." The apparent absence of religious tension in Nok—similar to the experience among the Yoruba people—tends to confirm the theory that in Nigeria religious rivalry is a facade disguising the real competition, among ethnic groups.

After bidding farewell to Ibrahim Nok, I asked Simon if he could introduce me to someone who could provide a historical perspective on the region's ethnic relations. The most knowledgeable person he knew was Yaned Afuwaj, a retired teacher and former president of the Southern Kaduna People's Union. We drove to his home in the settlement of the Kagoro people east of Kafanchan below the imposing Kagoro hills. Probably because the Islamic emirate never subdued it, Kagoro has been the traditional meeting place for the neighboring communities for generations.

It was an oppressively hot afternoon, and Afuwaj was resting as we entered his sitting room. When we apologized for disturbing him, he laughed and said, "It's all right. Since my retirement, I don't have anything to do but sleep."

Afuwaj proceeded to sketch a detailed historical outline of the Kafanchan region, beginning with the arrival of the first Fulani herders in the area well before the Islamic jihad of 1804. The story began with an act of treachery, with the Fulanis as the victims. Soon after the Fulanis settled on Kataf land, the local chief of the Kajuru people decided to marry a Fulani woman named Ndema. The chief was happy to host the Fulanis because they regularly presented him with gifts of cattle, and he always invited them to attend local festivities. At a certain point, however, the chief decided he wanted to conquer the Fulanis to bring them directly under his control.

The chief made a silly mistake, one that anyone at Nok could have warned him about. He told his Fulani wife of his plans. She could not warn her people of the impending raid by sending a message, so she made up the excuse that she was suffering from stomach pains. Only the Fulani doctor could cure her, and it was no use sending for medicine. It had to be taken on the spot. Her husband agreed to allow her to travel back to the Fulani encampment for treatment. Although he dispatched a couple of escorts, when they reached the Fulanis, she alone went into a hut for the treatment. Out of the escorts' earshot, she told her people of the chief's plans to attack.

When she and her escorts returned to her husband, she said she had been cured. The following day the chief sent a war party to capture the Fulanis, only to find that they had abandoned their settlement. The fighters tracked them to a place that today is known as Waterfall near Kafanchan. A pitched battle ensued, but the forces of the Kajuru chief were defeated. The Fulanis again moved, and they settled near the Daroro hills among the Ninzam people, who were still subject to the same Kajuru chief. A second attack resulted in another defeat. He never tried again. The Fulanis called their settlement Jema'a, and they lived in relative peace.

When news of Usman dan Fodio's Islamic jihad reached Jema'a, the community sent a representative to Zaria to request permission to join in. Fulanis who wanted to participate in the jihad were presented with the green flag of Islam and sent out to conquer peoples in the name of the Prophet. They returned to their settlement and launched a successful military campaign against nearly all the communities in the area except the Kagoro. The surrounding Kagoro hills provided a defensive line that the Fulanis of Jema'a were never able to break. But perhaps there was another reason, Afuwaj suggested. "One of their *Mallams* [Islamic teachers] predicted that whoever defeated Kagoro would not live up to one year. Because of that, I think they abandoned the struggle against Kagoro."

The standoff continued until the arrival of Lord Lugard's West African Frontier Force in 1903. The British announced that they had come in peace and did not want to fight. Nevertheless, if they saw anyone armed with a bow and arrow, they would shoot him. Because of the superior firepower of the British, the Kagoro people retreated to the near impregnable caves in the Kagoro hills.

At a certain point a group of people led by a leper named Tagama Bitiyong decided to parley with the British. The delegation went unarmed, and after a short discussion it brought the British to meet the Kagoro chief Kolai Ayin. "The peculiarity of the chief was that he didn't wear clothes. Even if you came as a stranger to the house you would not be permitted to enter the house with clothes on. But when these people appeared with guns, they were allowed to come in, an admission that the British were considered superior. The British said they wanted to install the chief as a leader under their authority. But Ayin considered this to be a disgrace. It meant that he would have to wear clothes." The British commander responded that if the chief did not want to be named the official leader, he could recommend someone else. He chose a man named Kaka Bishut who in 1905 became what the Kagoro regarded as "the first British chief." Up to this day, the Kagoro people have two chiefs, one recognized by the government and one revered by the people.

In 1927 Scottish missionaries made their first appearance in the person of Reverend Thomas Archibald. At first few converted, and those who did were made the subjects of insulting popular songs. Gradually, though, the missionaries made headway because of their ability to treat minor injuries with their first aid kits. Over the years the Kagoro people grew to respect the missionaries and to fear the British administrators, whom they regarded as authoritarian and always pro-Fulani.

The attractions of Christianity to the non-Muslim communities were that it helped them maintain their independence from the Fulani emirate and that it was not too demanding on their social life. "If you are a Christian, you can backslide, but you still have your independence. It doesn't make too many demands on your culture," Afuwaj said.

By the time Afuwaj's family moved from Palendaje to Kagoro in 1939, many local people had converted to Christianity, and children were attending missionary schools. Neither the Fulanis nor, ironically, the British were very pleased about the inroads of missionary education, Afuwaj said. "The British supported the Fulanis and they did not want any other group to be educated because one day they might use that education to drive them from power."

Afuwaj became a grade school teacher in 1949 and later assumed the position of headmaster. But disillusionment set in after the government took over the schools from the missionaries in the 1970s. Although he had initially supported the move, he later came to see it as a disaster. "Before 1972, the schools were well equipped. There were moral teachings; everything needed to make a nation a good nation. We were taught how to behave towards each other. Now the schools are so bad I don't even want to go to them. The objective of taking over the schools was to suppress the general progress of the community."

From Afuwaj's point of view, the government's neglect of education reflects something deeper in the culture of the Hausa and Fulani people, who he believes wield true power in Nigeria. "In Hausa culture, no child, no matter how intelligent, can attend school unless he is the son of an emir or of the emir's extended family. An ordinary man with no connections will find it difficult to go to school. They want the administration of the country to be controlled by their children. That was unlike the missionaries' schools, where you could sit next to the son of a chief and you could do better than him, no problem."

This perception—that the Hausa and Fulani people control Nigeria —runs deep among the non-Muslim peoples of the middle belt. It fuels their collective belief that they are second-class citizens and that the authorities in Abuja will do anything to make sure that the middle belt remains downtrodden. Afuwaj continued:

> The government has been run by the Hausas. All the big contractors are Hausas. Nobody from one of our tribes has ever won a contract for even 1 million naira. But the Hausas will get 100 million naira, 200 million naira. The government wants the economy to remain strictly controlled. That is why they depend only on oil. A wise administration would tap into all the necessary sources of income, but not the Nigerian government. So there is no more timber, no more palm oil, no more cotton. The economy is no good. We have no class of rich people, and the only individuals people can look up to are a few retired generals. I am afraid the future for us is bleak.

Despite Afuwaj's downbeat assessment, he admitted that there was a greater sense of optimism in the region because of the government's decision in 1996 to recognize four traditional chiefs. The move, in response to an age-old demand of the non-Muslims to assert their independence from the Jema'a emirate, has given non-Muslims an increased sense that their destiny is finally in their own hands. Father Kukah had told me that he thought the fixation on recognition of traditional titles—he called them "fig leaves to cover their nakedness"—missed the point. "I told one guy that I found this whole question of traditional leaders like two bald men fighting over a comb. The future for our people lies in whether we can channel our resources into education."

When I traveled to the Zonkwa home of Nuhu Bature, the Agwam

Baju, the paramount chief of the Baju people, he conceded that the traditional leaders faced a difficult task. He thought that the new chiefs were only third-class chiefs in the government's classification, whereas the emir was considered a first-class chief. "The new chiefs are really low down on the ladder," the Agwam Baju said. "We are not like the emirs, who can just ring up a government official and say come. We simply don't have that facility." Nevertheless, he described the government's recognition of the new chiefs as a small victory and said, "The demand for the chiefdoms became a rallying point for our own identity."

Bala Ade Dauke Gora, the Agwatyap I, or chief of the Kataf people, made much the same point. It was a sign of his own feeling of vulnerability that as we sat in his temporary offices a few minutes' drive from Zango Kataf, he was very nervous about allowing me to tape record our conversation. The government, he said, may not appreciate some of his comments.

Many people credit the government's new attitude to the chiefs to the events of May 1992, when Zango Kataf exploded in a violent confrontation. One of those intimately involved in the crisis was James Kude, a retired army major known as Atomic. When I reached his home a few miles outside Zango Kataf, a burly, powerful man in his fifties was standing in the driveway waiting for me. We settled down on a log in front of his house.

I asked him if he would mind explaining how he got his nickname. "Oh, that one," he said somewhat embarrassed. "Do you really want to know?" I assured him I did. He was a soccer player during his days at the Kagoro Teacher's College, and one day he struck the ball so hard that when it hit the goal, a puff of dust came off of it. Another shot slammed into the face of the goalie and knocked out three front teeth. Then he tackled one of his lecturers, who was playing for the other team. The man was hurt so badly he did not return to work for six months. So Kude's friends decided to nickname him Atomic.

Then the talk turned to the Zango Kataf riots. The first clashes actually took place February 1992, but the police were able to control the violence. On May 15 a Kataf farmer discovered that someone had uprooted his yams. When he went to investigate, a sniper shot him. A group of Kataf youths were passing by, saw what happened, and trumpeted a bugle to signal that the Katafs were at war again with the Hausas. "Every Kataf man got his bow and arrows. The ex-servicemen who were in possession of any arms got them out."

The Katafs laid siege to the town. Atomic, then an education counselor, first heard of the trouble while in a security meeting with community leaders at the local government headquarters in Zonkwa, about ten miles away. The police interrupted the meeting to announce that trouble had started in Zango Kataf. Atomic; Bala Gora, the future Agwatyap; and several others decided to drive over to investigate. Before leaving, Atomic told the other community leaders to warn their people of the violence "because the Hausa man, after finishing with the Kataf tribe, he will jump into the next tribe since the main idea has been to wipe us all out." When they reached the scene, Zango Kataf was in flames. The fighting continued for eighteen hours and left dozens of casualties.

When the seriously wounded among the Hausas were taken north to Kaduna, the fighting erupted anew. "They started using the loudspeakers from their mosques announcing that the non-Muslims had finished all the Muslims in Zango Kataf," Atomic said. "All true Muslims were urged to come out for the jihad." The riots continued for two days, claiming the lives of several hundred people and causing heavy damage to churches and mosques. The army intervened to quell the violence.

Atomic and eight others, including retired Major General Zamani Lekwot, who was in Kaduna at the time, and Bala Gora, were arrested and condemned to death by a military-appointed tribunal. When the sentence was read out to the court, Atomic, living up to his name, was caught by the television cameras attempting to leap over a table to throttle the judges. Atomic was sent to Port Harcourt prison, where he met Ken Saro-Wiwa. "We were fighting the same struggle," he said. On August 27, 1993, the day of his departure from office, Babangida commuted the sentences to five years. Eventually, in 1995, Atomic and the others were released, after forty months in detention. No one from the Hausa community was ever arrested.

Even with the violence, however, Atomic felt that the Zango Kataf riots marked a turning point for the minorities in the Kafanchan region because non-Muslims were able to assert themselves. "We got what we wanted. Victory was ours." He saw the appointment of Bala Gora as the Agwatyap and the recognition of the other chiefs as the next step in that process.

> We will have to look for means of developing ourselves. We don't have
> to lean on anybody now; we don't have to work for the government or
> any organization. We have to form our own organizations and societies
> so that we create ways of getting money for whatever we want to do.
> We have to work hard because depending solely on the government as
> in the past made everybody a lazy man. We have to be very realistic
> and cut our cloth according to our size.

That evening, as I sat in my room going over the notes of the day, Bishop Bagobiri knocked at my door to say he wanted to introduce me to someone. In the reception lounge was Isa Muhammadu Jr., the twenty-eight-year-old son of the emir of Jema'a, who had died at the age of ninety-five the previous day. Muhammadu and Bagobiri were regular squash partners, and the young man was visiting the bishop to seek his support in calming local nerves over his imminent appointment as the new emir. Muhammadu was worried that several local ethnic groups living in and around Kafanchan wanted to use his father's death as an opportunity to establish their own chief and withdraw recognition of the emir. "I feel for this young man," said Bishop Bagobiri, "but the problem is the local people are tired of the emirate system. Times have changed, and they want their own leaders now."

To bolster their case, non-Muslim community leaders sent a memo to Kaduna state governor Colonel Farouk Ahmed warning of trouble if the government tried to install the new emir without guaranteeing them their own chief. "We cannot be held responsible for any break-down in law and order in the area," the letter reportedly said.[4] After several months of negotiations, the controversy appeared to have been smoothed over. The Hausa community agreed that the local groups could have their own chief, and in turn the new emir could be in-stalled. Representatives of the two sides met on May 7, 1999, to confirm the deal.

To the apparent dissatisfaction of both the Hausa community and the local non-Muslim groups, two weeks later, just days before Obasanjo's inauguration, preparations were begun for the ceremony to install the new emir. By the time the governor, Colonel Ahmed, reached the outskirts of town from Kaduna, Kafanchan was engulfed in a riot. The governor was forced by the scale of the violence to turn back to Kaduna. Dozens of people were injured, several were reported killed, and hundreds of shops, homes—including the emir's palace—and mosques were damaged by a series of raging fires. Within days a heavy deployment of police brought the return of a fragile peace to Kafanchan. The city was still bitterly divided by the issues of installing the new emir and naming a chief for the local communities.

8

The Spirit of Odùduwà

*My father said that a sheep that makes a friend with a dog
surely produces a waste product.*

GANIYU ADAMS

D R. FREDERICK FASEHUN sat at his desk at the Best Hope
Hospital and giggled as he flipped through snapshots of naked
men lying in rows on a dank prison floor. "That's me, and over there is
Falae," he said in reference to Olu Falae, the former finance minister
and failed presidential candidate. "These are the conditions we were
kept in, but don't ask how I got these pictures because I won't say. You
never know if we might go back for another stay." Suddenly a young
man burst into the room and began prostrating half jokingly in front
of Dr. Fasehun, as Yoruba commoners traditionally do in the presence
of an *oga*. "Oh, come on," he said with a wide-eyed smile, "you are
embarrassing me."

A distinguished looking sixty-two-year-old general practitioner
with a quick wit and a melodic voice, Dr. Fasehun hardly looked the

part of a serious security threat to the state. Most mornings he roamed through the dreary hospital halls in his white surgical coat looking after patients from the surrounding area of Mushin, one of Lagos's poorest neighborhoods. By the afternoon, he could be found at the well-appointed Century Hotel he owns in Isolo.

Yet Abacha regarded Dr. Fasehun as a dangerous extremist bent on the secession of the Yoruba people, who at some twenty-five million strong dominate the western part of the country. Dr. Fasehun's offense was to establish the Oodua People's Congress (OPC), a five-year-old Yoruba movement with a reputation for bruising street battles with the police. For his trouble, he spent nineteen months in a jail cell and only walked free eighteen days after Abacha's demise.

After several fruitless attempts at trying to get through to him by telephone, I drove to Mushin in the hope of learning about what press reports and hearsay led me to believe was the most militant grassroots Yoruba movement since independence. After a brief exchange in the office, we arranged to meet in the afternoon at the hotel. He walked me to my car, and while we were chatting under the baking morning sun I quickly inquired about a curious aspect of the OPC, one that had heightened its notoriety among friend and foe alike. OPC members, youths in particular, were reportedly using juju (magic) to protect themselves from police gunfire. They were especially known for waving white handkerchiefs in the air to halt police bullets. I had heard of others doing such a thing. The Egbesu boys among the Ijaws in the Niger delta were doing something similar. Years ago, I said, I had met a traditional healer in the southern African nation of Mozambique who after "vaccinating" his soldiers against bullets captured half a province from what at the time was one of the most feared rebel movements in Africa.

"I'm an orthodox doctor, so I don't practice it myself," he said with a laugh. "But yes, I have seen it work. I was standing in a demonstration, and the police were shooting at this young girl. The bullets just fell to the ground, and the girl picked them up and with her outstretched hand offered them back to the police. I saw it with my own eyes!"

When I arrived later that day at the hotel, Dr. Fasehun was with a dozen young people, mainly men, lounging on sofas in the dark and relatively cool lobby. After a round of introductions, we moved off to a corner of the room with Kayode Ogundamasi, the twenty-nine-year-old OPC secretary general, who goes by the name of Sankara, after the late revolutionary leader in Burkina Faso, Thomas Sankara. As Dr. Fasehun offered a brief history of the movement, Sankara occasionally passed him notes as if to highlight the salient points to stress.

The OPC was born in the ashes of the June 12 election annulment and the incarceration of Chief Abiola. The Yoruba people were just fed up, Fasehun said. The only reason Babangida had canceled the elections, he argued, was that the northern Hausa-Fulani Muslims who wielded the real power simply refused to accept a Yoruba as president. Nor was this the first time the Yorubas had been denied the presidency. The Yorubas' most famous son, the late Chief Obafemi Awolowo, was also denied the fulfillment of his burning presidential ambition. "Chief Awolowo was the best politician ever in this country and was not allowed to attain the presidency for the simple reason that he was a Yoruba man," Dr. Fasehun continued. "The Hausa-Fulani did not like him. They thought he was too primordial in his sentiments," meaning too much of a Yoruba tribalist.

By mid–1994 Abiola was in jail, and it had become apparent that the peaceful protests of the main opposition umbrellas, the Campaign for Democracy and the National Democratic Coalition (NADECO), as well as the traditional Yoruba movement, Afenifere, were having little impact on the Abacha dictatorship. In July of that year Campaign for Democracy president Dr. Ransome-Kuti, a close friend of Dr. Fasehun, was jailed in connection with the alleged coup plot involving Obasanjo, another Yoruba man. A significant number of Yoruba human rights activists, intellectuals, and businessmen began to question seriously whether it was worth staying in Nigeria. With a large population that included highly educated professionals, and living primarily in an area that contained fertile land and much of what remained of Nigeria's manufacturing capacity, the Yorubas felt perhaps it was time to think of going it alone.

Dr. Fasehun and activists from the Campaign for Democracy set up the OPC specifically dedicated to promoting the Yoruba cause. The congress took its name, Oodua People's Congress, from Odùduwà, who according to legend was sent down from the heavens by his father, the supreme God Olódùmarè, with some soil, a cockerel, and a palm nut to establish the earth around the town of Ile Ife, the university town that Yorubas regard as their spiritual home. Increasingly at demonstrations, protesters held up banners advocating an "Odudua Republic".

When the police arrested Dr. Fasehun in December 1996, the OPC went underground but continued to thrive. "The OPC had spread its tentacles all over the place," Fasehun said proudly. "Wherever we were having our activities the police would come and start shooting tear gas canisters and sometimes live bullets. They killed many people."

Five years later it was impossible to verify the OPC's claims of a membership of several million organized in four hundred cells in 150 local governments of the nine states with significant Yoruba populations. But its numerous demonstrations and running battles with the police over the preceding several years suggested a wide following. It was particularly vibrant among jobless university graduates and the vast reservoir of unemployed youth in Lagos, Ibadan, and other Yoruba towns.

Like the old guard Yoruba movements, Afenifere and the political party the Alliance for Democracy, the OPC demanded "restructuring." By that it meant that Nigeria should abandon its centralized state and return to the powerful regional governments of the early independence days. The regions should run their own schools, their own economies, and most controversially, their own police forces and armies. "If you like there can be central command, but let us have regional armies," said Dr. Fasehun. "What you have here now is an occupation force. When you see ten policemen on the street, nine of them come from the north. They don't understand us. They don't speak our language, they don't eat our food, they know nothing about our traditions or our history."

A considerable strain of pure ethnic chauvinism infects the OPC. "The Yorubas have merited being at the helm of affairs since 1960 but they have been persistently kept away. The Yorubas have been responsible for the unity of this nation." Dr. Fasehun also echoed the common belief perception of the Hausa-Fulani as greedy and incompetent. "These people come here and steal the money, stash it in an underground vault, and grin. They don't have the intelligence to manage such funds," he said without batting an eyelid.

There is a sense among the vast majority of Yorubas that they have always represented the progressive spearhead in Nigerian society, first against colonialism and then in opposition to military rule. Soyinka once told me that he believed it had something to do with traditional Yoruba religion. "There is something very democratic about the Yoruba Pantheon," he said. "The Yoruba allocates to every deity some kind of flaw. It brings them down to mortal level, makes them accountable, makes them undergo penance."

But Yoruba flaws were rarely mentioned in a conversation with Dr. Fasehun. The Yorubas, he maintained, are "the best nation in Africa." Even more conservative figures invariably unleashed a mantra on the Yorubas' accomplishments: their early pro-independence stance, their adoption of free education in the Western Region, and the establishment of once world-class universities at Ibadan and Ife, the first television station, and the first skyscraper in Africa. Critics of the Yorubas, however, argued that their achievements reflected their quick adoption of the European way of life.

That wasn't the only criticism of the Yorubas. When it came time to defend Chief Abiola's democratic mandate, again the Yorubas were in the forefront of the struggle that saw strikes and riots rock Lagos.

But would they have taken such a forthright stance, their critics asked, if Abiola had been a northerner or an easterner? After all, when the military overthrew Shagari in 1983, Yorubas were among the first to celebrate. Abiola actively supported the army putschists. When the Yorubas said *pro-democracy,* the critics argued perhaps somewhat harshly, they really meant pro-Yoruba.

Nevertheless, there was little doubt that as a people the Yorubas had paid a heavy price for their defiance of the recent dictatorships. Hundreds had been shot dead in pro-democracy demonstrations, and Abacha's henchmen murdered Abiola's wife Kudirat and the elderly Yoruba campaigner Pa Alfred Rewane. Security agents attempted to blow up a plane carrying Abacha's second in command, Oladipo Diya, the highest-ranking Yoruba general, and when that failed he was lured into a sting operation involving a coup plot and jailed. "Those who were hounded into exile, very many of them were Yoruba. Those who were incarcerated for no reason, Yoruba. Those who had been assassinated, Yoruba," Dr. Fasehun said touching his fingers as if ticking off a list of injustices. "The Yorubas had always been running on one political leg, and it's very uncomfortable. You can only hop and after some time you get tired."

But however true their claims that they had been the targets of a northern conspiracy to maintain a grip on Nigeria, historically the Yorubas had been at times their own worst enemy. "The bane of the Yoruba people is that you can hardly get them to speak with one voice," the veteran human rights campaigner Chief Gani Fawehinmi, himself a Yoruba, once told me. "They are very gregarious; they hate being led through the nose." Internal divisions have often opened the door to external manipulation.

Such divisiveness dates at least to the demise of the old Oyo empire at the beginning of the nineteenth century. By the early nineteenth century Oyo was facing pressure from the Fulanis in the north and from the Dahomey kingdom to the west (in modern-day Benin).

Dahomey's powerful slave-trading king, Gezo, fielded imposing armies led by thousands of female warriors. The power of the king of Oyo, the Alafin, collapsed when his army commander, Afonja, rebelled and captured the town of Ilorin with the support of the Fulanis pushing south on their Islamic jihad. Afonja's revolt convinced Yoruba provincial kings to the south that they too could rebel. For the rest of the century Yoruba land was beset by nearly continuous civil conflict that degenerated into slave-raiding wars. For a good part of the nineteenth century Yorubas sold Yorubas into bondage. If they had united, they probably could have defeated the Fulanis and retaken Ilorin, but they opted to fight each other instead.[1] The wars only came to an end when the British governor of the Lagos Protectorate, Sir Gilbert Carter, used a combination of diplomacy and military muscle to force a pan-Yoruba peace treaty. The legacy of those wars has continued until today in the fighting between the Ife and Modakeke clans around the city of Ife. The Modakeke are the descendants of refugees from the Oyo wars who were given refuge by the people of Ife. A running dispute over the land erupted in the late 1990s in a series of bloody clashes that have defied easy solution.

In the early independence years, infighting between Chief Awolowo and Chief S. L. Akintola, his deputy in the Yoruba party, Action Group, precipitated the declaration of a state of emergency in the Western Region and helped set the stage for the 1966 coup. When Chief Awolowo ran in the 1979 presidential elections against the northerner Shagari, Chief Abiola used his newspapers, Concord Group, to undermine Awolowo's campaign. In the 1999 election both contestants for the presidency were Yoruba, but the majority of Yoruba politicians and voters opted for the loser while the dominant power brokers in the north rallied around the eventual winner, Obasanjo. So whatever questions there might be about the northerners' business acumen, on the political front they have consistently run circles around the Yorubas.

The OPC too was wracked by divisions. General Abubakar's transition to civilian rule had provoked a deep schism, one that saw Dr. Fasehun under attack, not for his allegedly extremist views but for being too tame. A more radical faction claimed that he had sold out the movement's ideals by associating with discredited mainstream politicians. Trouble erupted in late 1998 when he began meeting with the presidential candidates Falae and Obasanjo. The OPC had rejected Abubakar's program, arguing, as did a number of human rights activists and minority groups, that Nigeria first needed a meeting of all its nationalities in a "sovereign national conference." Such a gathering would determine whether Nigeria should be a unitary state, a federation, or a more loosely run confederation in which all ethnic groups would enjoy a wide degree of political and cultural autonomy. But when the mainstream Alliance for Democracy opted to contest the elections, Dr. Fasehun supported Falae, its presidential candidate. "The OPC as a movement would have nothing to do with the transition, but I am very close to Falae," Dr. Fasehun explained. "There is no way I wouldn't sympathize with him and support him."

The breaking point occurred after a local newspaper published a story entitled "Obasanjo Woos Oodua Leader."[2] There Dr. Fasehun used a Yoruba saying to explain why he was prepared to meet with Obasanjo: "Omo eni o ku buru titi ka fi f'ekun je" ("A child cannot be so notorious that the parents would throw him to the den of leopards"). Fasehun reportedly added, "The Yorubas must learn to play a safe politics such that if there is any of their own they would not support, they should for God's sake let the sleeping dog lie, and should not do anything to injure the interest of their brother."

Dr. Fasehun's erstwhile deputy, Ganiyu Adams, and his supporters on the National Coordinating Council were furious. Dr. Fasehun was called to a meeting to explain himself. There he said that he had met with Obasanjo but only in his personal capacity. It was not a satisfactory answer. Because of such meetings and because of his public description of the OPC as a "sociocultural organization" rather than a

Yoruba political movement, the Adams faction decided to remove Dr. Fasehun as national coordinator. Dr. Fasehun's faction countered by expelling the Adams group for "hooliganism, antiparty activities and unnecessary terrorism unleashed on innocent citizens."[3]

From there the story becomes murky. Following Obasanjo's victory in the February 27 elections, OPC youths engaged in several days of battles with the police in the Isolo and Mushin. According to the Adams camp, Ganiyu was holding a press conference on March 1 when he learned that the police were arresting OPC members. He sent a delegation to the police station. When the OPC activists approached, the officer in charge ordered his men to fire on them. But because the youths were protected by juju, the Adams faction maintained, the bullets ricocheted and hit the officer in the abdomen. Another bullet struck a drum of gasoline that the police were hoarding to sell at black market prices to Okada motorcycle taxis. Other witnesses said the OPC militants attacked the station with petrol bombs and explosives fashioned by filling eggshells with sulfuric acid.

During the battle with the police, the station exploded in flames, and the OPC members rushed in and opened the cell doors to free the prisoners. The police proceeded to surround Dr. Fasehun's Century Hotel, roughed up the hotel manager and several guests, and broke a front window in their search for him. Dr. Fasehun was briefly detained until he denounced the violence as the work of area boys. Over the next several days eleven people died in the clashes. Since then Dr. Fasehun has referred to Adams as a "misguided youth" and a "hooligan" of little importance, and Adams has labeled Dr. Fasehun a traitor to the true Yoruba cause. To complicate matters, Dr. Fasehun's supporters saw in the dispute the mischievous hand of the maverick lawyer Gani Fawehinmi. "We are not bothered," said Dr. Fasehun. "It's just a minor faction of the organization. [Gani] tried to control OPC, but he knows that he cannot control where I am."

Sankara leaned forward and broke in. "We will not allow anybody to give the picture that the average Yoruba man is a senseless murderer who does not think but just goes into the streets. If you look at the people they killed, who are they? They are Yoruba police officers, Yoruba public. We students and graduates want revolutionary change, but that does not necessarily mean go and slap the other man."

Sankara is a former president of the National Association of Nigerian Students. Like Dr. Fasehun, he seemed to be a reasonable, composed man, nothing like the hothead I had expected to meet. So I asked him about whether he believed in the power of juju against the weapons of war. "I am a Christian," he said, "but I think it is part of the culture that works. There is a strength of belief which you cannot deny. It may be a matter of choice but it exists."

I told them a story related to me by Dr. Ransome-Kuti, who was elected treasurer of the OPC at a convention held in May in Ibadan. He was very skeptical, if not dismissive, of the powers of juju, in which his late brother the Afro-beat musician Fela had been a great believer. When some Yoruba students tried to convince him that juju could stop bullets, Dr. Ransome-Kuti arranged an experiment to put it to the test. They bought a goat, tied some charms around its neck, and shot it. What happened? I asked Dr. Ransome-Kuti. He smiled and said, "It died."

But Dr. Fasehun said that he had seen people protected with charms who were struck with machetes but suffered no wounds. "You may have no belief in it but that does not rule out its existence." One day, he said, an OPC colleague came to his office to convince him, as a medical doctor, of the power of juju. Her particular talent was to drink acid with no ill effect. At first she poured the acid on her hands with no damage. As she was preparing to have a drink, the bottle spilled on his desk and started to eat through the wood. "My brother brought a rag and the acid burnt right through. You could see it smoking. The woman put the acid in a small cup and drank it, and she is still alive. Then I tried it and I am still very much alive four months later and," Dr. Fasehun said patting his stomach, "I am still eating."

UNLIKE his adversary, Dr. Fasehun, Ganiyu Adams was a man of little means who maintained a low public profile. He often traveled around Lagos not in cars but on the back of the ubiquitous motorbike taxis known as Okadas, so named after a Nigerian commercial airline. Okadas can carry up to four passengers, sometimes an entire family, and they dart noisily in and out of the long lines of sluggish cars and trucks caught in go-slows like metallic insects buzzing through a herd of cattle. I took a hint from Fasehun's supporters on where I might find Adams and went looking for the home of Gani Fawehinmi in Ikeja. My driver was a bit unsure of the exact road, so we stopped an Okada driver and asked directions. He immediately pointed out the correct route, confirming the popular Lagos saying: Okada always knows the way!

Gani, as he is popularly known in Nigeria, is a national phenomenon. Surely the most active lawyer in the country, probably anywhere, he has filed some six hundred court cases against the state and hundreds of others on behalf of the poor and students. "Since I cannot carry the gun and go straight to Aso Rock to shoot my way in, the only instrument I use is the machinery of justice," he explained. "When I sue I call attention to the absurdities of this society." Nigerian society kept him quite busy.

By his own count the number of times he had been arrested tallied roughly with the years he had been practicing law, thirty-five. Imprisonment was such an ordinary occurrence that he kept a packed overnight bag at the ready. Constantly appearing in the national press and being interviewed on foreign broadcasts such as those of the BBC and the Voice of America, Gani was king of the sound bite, always brash and sometimes outrageous, a virtual one-man wrecking crew on the national political scene. The walls of his spacious sitting room were adorned with at least two hundred framed newspaper cuttings with headlines such as "Gani Spits Fire," "Fiery Gani Stirs Lagos," and "Gani Erupts Again."

On the cover of a biographical pamphlet that his office had printed there was a short note that described the booklet as a mere preface to a ten-volume set, totaling 4,364 pages, marking his sixtieth birthday on April 22, 1998. Inside, it opened with the following introduction: "We present to you Chief Gani Fawehinmi, a lawyer, an author, a publisher, a philanthropist, a human rights crusader, a social critic, the scourge of irresponsible governments, a thermometer with which the blood pressure of dictators is gauged, the veritable conscience of the nation and the champion of the interests and causes of the masses."

Even his old nemesis, Babangida, whom he has sued and publicly lambasted too many times to remember, told me that he rated him "the most credible civil rights activist. Gani is a general. But the moment you win that war, the best thing is to take him away from that war theater, because he cannot win the peace. He makes all the noise, all the fight. But to get him to win the peace, it's hard. His first reaction to everything is no and he stands by that no."

When we met, Gani had just come through a bout of malaria, and although initially he was subdued, it did not take long to get the juices flowing. Not surprisingly, he was preparing a new suit against the government to have the new constitution thrown out as, well, unconstitutional. "I am going to challenge the constitutionality of the entire constitution," he announced with a satisfied air. He would base his case on the 1979 constitution, which said, "The Federal Republic of Nigeria shall not be governed, nor shall any person or group of persons take control of the Government of Nigeria or any part thereof, except in accordance with the provisions of the Constitution." Since the new constitution was approved solely by the Abubakar government, which was a successor administration to regimes that took power by force, the document was in his view illegal. He might have had a point in law, but even he knew there was little chance he would succeed. It was the principle, he said.

Gani was clearly impressed with the OPC, which was why, Sankara and Dr. Fasehun told me, he was meddling in the congress's internal affairs. Gani maintained that he was not directly involved in the dispute between Dr. Fasehun and Ganiyu Adams but that he was interested because the congress was part of the opposition alliance he chaired, the Joint Action Committee (JACON). Yet he handed me a pamphlet published by his office entitled *The OPC Crisis: The Truth,* which robustly set out the charges against Dr. Fasehun. On the back was a picture of the young man described as the OPC leader, Ganiyu Adams. "Fasehun betrayed their trust," Gani said. "He mellowed and supported Obasanjo. That's why there is trouble. The OPC people also accused him of taking funds from abroad."

The secret of the OPC's strength, Gani said, was the movement's penetration of every nook and cranny of Yoruba land. "They are well organized down to the ward level. Within three days they can command half a million people to attend a rally." Which is why Abacha feared them, I suggested. "Precisely! He sent the police against them, but they are like the Lord's Resistance Army [in Uganda]; they are always coming. They rely so much on native medicine. There are stories that an OPC man would throw an egg at a police station and the station would catch fire."

The Yorubas had never seen an organization like this, he said, except perhaps in 1968, when farmers around Ibadan took up arms to protest high taxation. That movement was called Agbekoya, which Gani translated to mean "we reject suffering and social injustice." There were thousands of them, he said, and like the OPC "they organized themselves in military fashion with native medicine." Far from manipulating the OPC, Gani claimed to have acted as a moderating influence on the radicals by arguing that the Yorubas should remain within Nigeria, albeit a Nigeria in which the regions, not the central government, dominated. "They want self-determination. Their battle cry is the Yorubas must secede."

Gani was under no illusion, however, that Obasanjo would meet the demands for a sovereign national congress to redesign Nigeria. When I asked him his opinion of Obasanjo, his voice, and probably his notoriously volatile blood pressure, soared. "He's the stooge of the northern oligarchy and doesn't have the courage to bulldoze his way and damn the consequences! You need a dangerously courageous person to attack the military in the country. We need an Atatürk, a de Gaulle, or a [Ehud] Barak." Interestingly, Gani, a man who has made a career out of denouncing military rulers, cited three former soldiers as the kind of leader Nigeria required.

Gani was confident that Nigeria would remain as one country for the foreseeable future and that the Yorubas would not secede. "I have had a feeling for so many years that this country will not break up, though it may be rocked to the very foundations." In his view, it all depended, ironically, on Obasanjo's survival. Yorubas were now resigned to his presidency. "They feel that since he is head of state, there is nothing they can do. But if anything should happen to him in Aso Rock, it will have a very, very devastating effect on the continued existence of this country."

Gani agreed to put me in touch with Adams, and a week later I received a call from his legal chambers to appear there in two days' time. On the phone, the secretary said the purpose was a meeting with "the chief," a reference to Gani. But I knew she was speaking for the benefit of anyone who might have been eavesdropping on the line so that they would not know that Ganiyu Adams would be there.

———

AS I SAT DOWN in Gani's spacious office in June 1999 just a week after Obasanjo's inauguration, it was clear that Adams was the archetypal angry young man. He possessed neither Dr. Fasehun's grace nor Gani's bubbly sense of humor. Tall, wiry, and stern-faced, Adams radiated unbridled intensity and, initially at least, suspicion. His English was typical of the Lagos streets, with a rough pronunciation that flowed in streams of staccato bitterness.

Dr. Fasehun and Gani were the fruit of those earlier, more idealistic days in the 1950s and 1960s when Nigeria strode onto the world stage with prestigious universities, a thriving economy, and dreams of a limitless future. Dr. Ransome-Kuti remembers that when he returned from his medical studies in Britain, "we thought that in ten years' time Nigeria would have surpassed the United Kingdom." Obasanjo once predicted that Nigeria would become a superpower by the turn of the millennium.

Adams was the child of the nightmare Nigeria had become, born in the midst of civil war, nurtured in a society of lost opportunity and decaying morality, and enraged by the chaos his forefathers had bequeathed him. "Our leaders are cheating us. They have sold their birthright out of selfishness," he said, spitting his words. "We have many betrayers in the Yoruba race, people who call themselves the leaders but are selfish."

The son of a truck driver who lived with his family on the road, Adams wanted to attend university, but he dropped out of school for lack of funds and took up an apprenticeship as a cabinetmaker instead. He strongly resents those who benefited from the educational opportunities that Nigeria once offered its people and who now ridicule the younger generation that does not enjoy them. "This Fasehun who is calling me illiterate went through free education. If I had a chance of free education, you know what I could have been now? I could be a Ph.D. in political science, but I came from a very poor family."

It would be easy, as some of his elders have done, to dismiss Adams and his ilk as area boys, as thugs who from time to time strike out at all forms of authority in a blind rage and who find spiritual refuge in crude ethnic chauvinism. But forget for a moment that he is a Yoruba, and Adams could be speaking for the rebellious Ijaw youths of the Niger delta or the Islamic militants of the north. However divided by geography, ethnicity, and culture, Nigeria's lost generation is united by a powerful lack of the one thing that can steer a society forward, no matter how troubled it might be: hope. "Nigeria's problem will not be solved peacefully," Adams insisted chillingly. "When the child is coming from his mother's womb, he will come with blood. You can't give birth to a child without blood. If there is no bloodshed, this country cannot have justice."

Yoruba land is in the early stages of a revolution, he said. "People are more enlightened every day. The problem of June 12 and Abiola has opened many people's eyes. When you are being cheated gradually, you will get to the stage where you won't fear the gun because the hungry man is an angry man."

"Yeah, Bob Marley," I said, and for the first time Adams laughed, if only briefly.

"The Yoruba hates cheating, and we believe in justice and we are highly principled. We see in the history of Nigeria only the Yoruba fought for this nation. At the end of the day, they try to push the Yoruba aside. Abiola died not just because he was a Yoruba, he died for the whole country."

It was sometimes difficult to understand why the Yoruba poor were so fascinated with Abiola, a man who made hundreds of millions of dollars in shady business deals with the military hierarchy. Part of the attraction, clearly, was his Yoruba ethnicity. At the time of the elections there was also the popular feeling that because he was so rich, he need not steal while in office. But what also attracted have-nots like Adams was that Abiola could have gained his release from detention under Abacha simply by declaring that he was no longer interested in assuming the presidency. He refused. Even after Abacha's death several high-level international figures, such as UN Secretary-General

Kofi Annan and Commonwealth Secretary-General Emeka Anyaoku, met with Abiola in the hope of convincing him to renounce his election mandate in return for his release.[4] Adams said that Abiola's jailers offered to "settle" Abiola with money. "He said no, the people had given him the mandate. Abiola is the messiah of the masses because he died for the struggle."

A month after Abiola's election victory was annulled, Adams joined the Mushin branch of the Campaign for Democracy and worked as a public relations officer. At the time, a colleague asked him how many Hausas, people from the middle belt, and Igbos were demanding that Abiola be installed as president. The answer was very few. "Ninety-five percent of the people fighting for the freedom of this country were Yorubas," he said. "The remaining tribes were frustrating our freedom. So we asked ourselves, why can't the Yoruba form their organization?"

It was at this time that he remembered one of his father's old sayings about how different ethnic groups cannot mix. "Yoruba is not a corrupt tribe. It's only the people around us. My father said that a sheep that makes a friend with a dog surely produces a waste product."

I asked him what he considered the best attributes of the Yoruba people, and at once he said, "They believe in justice and fair play." The Yorubas, he claimed, "hate cheating, and we believe in justice and we are highly principled." And the worst attribute? "The Yoruba man is weak in the mind; he does not quickly understand what is going on. We fear fighting a war, and that is why the Hausa-Fulani are so brave because they don't care about death. When a thousand die, they say 'Allah akbar' and they fight on." A few minutes later, however, he was praising the military prowess of his people. "Yoruba know how to plan war! Yoruba is power. We don't quickly respond to an action, but when we respond we respond."

Adams said the Yorubas faced the same problem that confronted the Ijaws in the oil-rich Niger delta. "The Ijaw people have been marginalized," he said. "Look at the place where they are drilling oil.

Nothing was done there. They have no water, they have no roads, they have no electricity." The OPC and the Ijaw Youth Council, both of which he described as secessionist organizations, met regularly to discuss what they considered to be their common exploitation by the Hausa-Fulanis. "This is what we saw that makes us crazy every day, that makes us ready to give our lives."

But Adams rejected claims that his supporters provoked violence with the authorities. "We are not thugs. Do I look like a thug?" I did not answer. "I don't do anything bad. I don't kill people. I don't believe the police are chasing me, but if that is their plan, that's their fucking problem because I am not the one that is selling out [a reference to Dr. Fasehun]."

"How will you struggle?" I asked. "Through violence?"

"We are mobilizing," he said.

"For what?"

"We are mobilizing and we are planning every day. We change our strategies and we change our system every day. The struggle in South Africa started in 1897, and they only released Mandela in 1992."

"Will it take that long here?"

"No, no, no it can't take that long. We expect our victory this year or next year. You know the Yoruba are very powerful. We even have a word that can stop bullets. Just by saying one word."

"Really?" I asked. "And what is that word?"

"I will tell you later," he said, but he never did. Some of the old traditional healers were now working with the OPC to develop new, mightier juju for the struggle. "There is power in Yoruba land!" he shouted. "We have never used one percent of it!"

Despite their differences, Adams shared with Fasehun an ambiguous position regarding Obasanjo's administration. On the one hand, he described Obasanjo as a pawn of the retired northern generals, as incapable of making the necessary changes to give Nigeria a new direction. "As soon as the government makes a mistake, the people will take advantage and strike," he warned. But on the other hand, he felt that if

Obasanjo were to die while in power, Nigeria would collapse into three independent nations, led by the Hausa-Fulani, the Yorubas, and the Igbos. "That is the end of Nigeria. Take it or leave it." And Adams was certain that the Yoruba people would be the determining factor. "In the history of this country, any government that the general masses of the Yoruba do not endorse will collapse at the end of the day. You won't make any headway without the Yoruba if you want to end injustice, if you want to go out of this fucking joke of a country."

We agreed to meet again, and as I got up to leave I had no idea that in just a few months this young man would emerge as one of the most famous people in Nigeria.

———

THE GROWING anger of the Yorubas spilled over into unprecedented clashes with Hausas in mid-July. The scene of the initial trouble was the southwestern town of Shagamu, a traditional center of the kola nut trade. It lies thirty-six miles north of Lagos, and Hausas have lived and traded there for generations. The trouble began with the murder of a Hausa woman after she was caught allegedly watching traditional Yoruba religious rites known as *Oro*. (There is a strong taboo against women witnessing the ceremonies involved in *Oro*.) The subsequent violence claimed the lives of up to sixty people, including at least one Yoruba who was mistaken for a Hausa because of the way he was dressed. Dozens of homes, shops, mosques, and market stalls were burned to the ground both in Yoruba neighborhoods and in the mainly Hausa quarter known as Sabo. The arrival in Kano of Hausa victims of the Shagamu clashes provoked a wave of retaliation on July 22 against Yoruba residents. Up to seventy people were killed, dozens were wounded, and hundreds were driven from their homes.[5] The violence was carried out largely by *yan daba*—"the sons of evil"—that is, street youths. Ironically, some analysts said the gradual disappearance of the

245

biting fuel shortages had created an increased sense of frustration among the unemployed youths (*yan daba* were heavily involved in the black market gasoline trade).[6] During his tour of the battle areas in a plea for calm, Obasanjo said the violence had been "highly instigated" by unnamed opponents of the new civilian administration.

Adams and his wing of the OPC had grabbed the initiative firmly with both hands. The Best Hope Hospital was ransacked and Lagos was rocked by waves of ethnic riots. Inevitably, the police blamed Adams's supporters, although as was usually the case they had merely taken advantage of the explosion of mainly local disputes. "A state of madness in society" was the way Lagos police spokesman Fabulous Enyaosu described the turmoil. Obasanjo, acting more like a military strongman than a civilian president, ordered police to shoot rioters on sight and told a national television audience that "when people decide to behave like animals they must be treated like animals."

Dr. Fasehun's boys got in on the act too. They rioted at the Lagos port in Apapa in support of Yoruba workers who had been sacked from their jobs. In an interview with the BBC Dr. Fasehun attributed the clash to the fact that Yoruba workers were in a minority at the port and that they had been sacked by "nonindigenes," meaning non-Yorubas. "We think our fatherland was being taken over from us ... and if there is any group of people trying to exercise their rights in Yoruba land, the OPC has to solidarize with such a group," he said. The meaning of his statement was clear: In Yoruba land, Yorubas should enjoy greater rights than any other ethnic groups even though all are Nigerians.

In November Yorubas and Ijaws fought pitched battles in the Lagos slum of Ajegunle. The fighting cost some forty lives and linked, at least indirectly, to the army massacre in Odi. Several days later Yorubas and Hausas set upon each other in the outlying suburb of Ketu in a dispute over control of the Mile 12 market. The death toll was believed to be at least one hundred. The violence at Ketu prompted the establishment of a northern counterpart to the OPC, the Arewa People's Congress (APC), headed by a former military intelligence officer. The deepening of Nigeria's seething ethnic hatred was written on the walls of Ajegunle homes. On one someone had scribbled, "Here lives an Igbo man"; on another was simply "Hausa House."

The following month in downtown Lagos a group of OPC gunmen were involved in a shoot-out in the early morning hours with bodyguards escorting state governor Bola Tinubu. The OPC later admitted involvement in the battle but said it was an accident. They said they believed the bodyguards were armed robbers.

In the first few days of January the Adams faction entered the slum of Mushin in an operation designed to flush out gangsters on Akala Street, a notorious den of armed criminals. The OPC said it went on the offensive after a gang of bank robbers had shot dead a young woman who happened to be an OPC member. At least fifty people were killed in the mayhem, and burned corpses littered the road. Yet the action won widespread praise from local residents, who told Governor Tinubu that before the OPC's arrival life had been unbearable and the local police were doing nothing about it. They accused the police of involvement with the criminal syndicate, and they dubbed the special anticrime unit, the Rapid Response Squad (RRS), "Robbers Reign Supreme."

By now Ganiyu Adams had become a household name in Nigeria, and a vast majority of Yorubas regarded him as a latter-day Robin Hood. His picture adorned newspapers and the weekly magazines. Northerners in places as far away as Kano and Zamfara were talking about Ganiyu Adams, the Yoruba terrorist. For those who believed that the Yorubas were all talk and no action, Adams was their worst nightmare.

The Lagos police declared Adams a wanted man and offered a reward of 100,000 naira ($1,000) for information leading to his arrest. After the police blamed the OPC for the abduction and murder of a police superintendent in the Bariga neighborhood of Lagos, the security forces responded in typically brutal fashion. They went on a rampage, emptying houses of suspected OPC members and setting their belongings on fire, beating their relatives, and arresting hundreds of young men. Obasanjo wrote a rather absurd letter to Governor Tinubu urging him to crack down on the OPC and threatening to impose a state of emergency in Lagos. But the governor had no means of cracking down because he had no authority over the police; that responsibility lies with the president and his inspector general of police in Abuja. And with every act of police repression, Adams's popularity soared. Yoruba land was on the boil, and any accident could provoke a riot. Ethnic clashes broke out in the city of Ibadan when a salt truck driven by a Hausa man crashed into a commuter bus full of Yorubas.

I returned to Lagos in early January 2000 and immediately set about attempting to renew my acquaintance with Adams, though given the arrest warrant and the price on his head, I knew it would a nearly impossible task. My initial go-between, Chief Gani, had broken completely with Adams and denounced the OPC-inspired violence. I decided to turn to the information highway. A friend in Dr. Fasehun's faction furnished me with an e-mail address used by Adams's lieutenants to publish their press releases. I dispatched a note requesting an interview, and three days later a response came that I should ring a number in Mushin. When I did, a man identifying himself only as Mike said he would do his best to set up a meeting but warned that it was improbable. Adams was in hiding, and Mike could not say whether or not his leader was even in Lagos. After a few more exchanges, I was given an address in the suburb of Ikeja.

As soon as I walked into the building for my meeting it became clear that Adams was not coming. My e-mail contact Mike turned out to be Razona Onajole, chairman of the OPC's political and ideology committee, and he had brought along two colleagues who identified themselves as the chairman of the research and strategy committee and the secretary in charge of press and publicity. This latter man had the irritating habit of beginning each of his points with a reference either to the Bible or to some obscure event in the nineteenth century. But Onajole, a businessman in his mid-fifties, was not the type of person I expected to be linked with the OPC. Poised and articulate, he hardly fit the image of an angry young man.

The issues of ethnic autonomy and a just distribution of the nation's resources originally raised by Isaac Boro and the Biafran civil war had not been resolved, he said. "This country is built on a false structure." The Yoruba southwest should be allowed to return to the conditions of the early postindependence days, when the region used the proceeds of its cocoa exports to fund free education. "What future lies for our children?" he asked. "What future lies for us?"

9

"This Animal Called Man"

The fundamental wrong in man is his Godlessness, his autonomous conduct, which is decided without reference to God.

OLUSEGUN OBASANJO

A DOZEN WOMEN dressed in flowing white robes rose as one and burst into song, singing "He Touched My Body, He Touched My Soul." A multitude of thousands scrunched together on wooden benches took up the verse, first in Yoruba and then in English, enveloping the open-walled church in the warmth of the human voice. A hundred ceiling fans twirled furiously but in vain to blow away the sticky midafternoon air flooding in from the street. The staggering heat lent an extra edge to the atmosphere. Church workers walked amid the mass with plastic tubs filled with fist-size plastic bags of water. They were the targets of a series of flying tackles by small groups of parched parishioners.

In the center of the building Pastor Temitope Balogun Joshua, a forty-year-old man dressed in white, strode purposefully around the red carpet of a circular altar, keeping time with the music by gently swinging a microphone in his hand. A sly grin creased his face. He was the man everyone had come to see—the prophet, the healer. A word, a simple touch from the pastor could heal anything that ailed, from criminal behavior and adultery to cancer and AIDS. Some said he was Jesus Christ himself. His fame for miracles and prophecies was surpassed in the slums of Lagos only by the notoriety of another young man, Ganiyu Adams, who also hailed from Arigidi, a sleepy town in Ondo State.

Pastor Joshua is the founder and general overseer of the Synagogue Church of All Nations, one of the literally hundreds of Pentecostal churches mushrooming through Lagos and much of the rest of coastal West Africa. Along the route to Pastor Joshua's church in the sprawling Ikotun-Egbi neighborhood on the outskirts of Lagos are dozens of billboards advertising a kaleidoscope of temples and tabernacles promising good health, ample wealth, and paradise on earth. Interpreting religious doctrine far more flexibly than does the traditional Christianity that was first brought by the European colonialists in the mid-nineteenth century, these modern-day pastors and so-called prophets practice faith healing and sometimes magic to prey upon the gullibility of their wealthier adherents and the desperation of the poor.

As the music of Pastor Joshua's choir died down, an Orwellian voice thundered enthusiastically over the loudspeaker system, "Look at your television screens now!" The eyes of thousands rose toward one hundred TV sets stationed in rows above the congregation. On-screen was the extraordinary sight of a heavyset man with a massive beard hobbling around in his underwear with the aid of a walking stick. The camera zoomed in on what appeared to be the badly burned left haunch of Nigerian super-heavyweight wrestler Armstrong Louis Okeke. The beloved warrior took a microphone from an attending church worker and testified that he had been the victim of a "spiritual burning." His career was finished. The doctors were powerless to help, so he had come to the pastor for divine healing.

Pastor Joshua stroked his trim Lenin-style beard and considered the case carefully. Soon he perked up, dramatically asking questions about the severity of the injuries and repeating the ghastly revelations for an audience already gasping with astonishment. To a wave of oohs and aahs, the camera continued to zoom in and out on the festering red wounds. Pastor Joshua descended from the altar and took a position ten feet away from the beleaguered champion. Glaring with exaggerated bulging eyes, he held Okeke in a trance, paralyzing the giant for several minutes with the sheer force of his spiritual gaze. Inching slowly forward, Pastor Joshua suddenly grabbed the walking stick and left Okeke tottering. For a moment, the crowd was certain that the gladiator would collapse. But he soon found a fragile balance, and the treatment began. The staring and glaring continued, as Pastor Joshua hunted down the demons.

Suddenly Armstrong fell to the earth and began writhing in the dirt. One of the pastor's aides ran over to the wrestler and stuck a microphone to his face. "I hand over my life to God," Armstrong proclaimed. He wiped the sweat from his brow. Even for a professional wrestler, it had been a worthy performance. When Pastor Joshua asked, "Who am I?" Armstrong responded breathlessly, "You are the prophet sent by God."

Commanded to rise, Armstrong stood, brushed himself off, and discovered to his utter amazement that he could walk easily. The hideous burn was still there but without the pain. At first he could not believe it, but after a minute he was jogging around the altar and doing exercises as if he were warming up for a match. The congregation, some of them fighting back tears, responded with excitement and roared their approval as Armstrong declared, "I hand over my life to God."

The next to speak was another wrestler, a cruiser weight whom Armstrong had brought to the Synagogue Church of All Nations to prepare for a recent match. Wearing his Nigerian championship belt around his waist, the young man narrated how Pastor Joshua had armed him with the necessary powers to defeat a notorious opponent who was clearly the stronger man. "Look at your television screens now!" the voice boomed over the public-address system. The video replay showed the young fighter held by his opponent in a seemingly inescapable headlock. Suddenly he broke free, slid to the floor, and pinned his adversary in a move so clearly contrived that it would have brought blushes to the organizers of the World Wrestling Federation. Several replays of the maneuver were punctuated by waves of "Amen" from the congregation.

The television screens and the loudspeakers went silent. Pastor Joshua dabbed his brow and paused for a moment to give his followers a chance to catch their breath. Then he announced it was confession time, during which he would remove "contrary spirits, witches, and wizards" from a whole gang of unfortunates, most of them young women, who were sitting glumly on the ground to the side of the altar awaiting the holy touch.

The first patient, a raggedly dressed woman in her twenties, scooted along the dirt until she reached one of the pastor's two camera crews. As soon as the microphone was put to her mouth she announced that she was possessed by "the power of destruction." The audience murmured. "All I have to do is start cursing people and they die!" she shouted, admitting she had killed her brother that way. The pastor asked how she had behaved when her brother died. The woman feigned crying for a moment and then broke into a mischievous smile.

"So no one knew you killed your brother?"

"No," she said, to more collective wails of protest. Pastor Joshua called for calm and asked the woman to describe her powers.

"I have negative powers in my mouth, in my eyes. I have negative power in my private parts," she said, adding quickly, "that is the strongest power." The audience groaned knowingly. She explained that she ran a beer parlor where she picked up men, followed them back to their apartments, and drugged and robbed them. She kept the sedative in a fake fingernail and administered it to the unsuspecting man's drink. If she fancied him, she might agree to make love. But if she did, usually a spirit in the form of a snake worked its way down from her chest and bit the man's penis, infecting him with the HIV virus or syphilis. In the meantime he would fall asleep, leaving her to ransack the house for valuables.

Pastor Joshua waited for a translation of the testimony into Yoruba over the loudspeaker, and when he tired of it, he tapped the microphone a couple of times and said "Amen" and "Praise the lord." It was time to heal. "Fire all over de body!" he commanded. The woman collapsed to the ground screaming "Fire" and holding her crotch, where, she had said, the strongest power lurked. "Fire all over de body!" Pastor Joshua's voice boomed, as the woman wriggled in the dust. "Fire all over de body," he continued while strutting around the altar. After several minutes, he ordered her to stop. One of his aides approached her with a microphone and she yelled, "I will give up my life for Jesus." With that she stood up and walked over to a bench to sit and watch the rest of the ceremony like any other worshiper.

On it went. The second patient, a heavyset man in his thirties, confessed that women actually paid him 2 hundred naira, about $2, for his sexual pleasures. "I have power in my eyes too," he said, explaining that with just a look he had caused crashes of *molues* and *danfos*, the rickety minibuses that rule Lagos's roads, and taken the lives of dozens. Again Pastor Joshua yelled, "Fire all over de body!" The man fell to the ground and squirmed for a few minutes until the pastor shouted. The man stood, pledged his life to Jesus, and ambled off to take his place among the cured.

Next was a nineteen-year-old girl, still in her blue-and-white school uniform, who confessed to harboring powers in her mouth, eyes, and inevitably, her private parts. Then a thirteen-year-old girl admitted that she was a witch who had used the power residing in her chest to kill her father and to render her aunt infertile.

A young woman claimed to be a witch and admitted to making a love potion from the sperm of her first husband. A fourteen-year-old boy used the power of his heart to drive his mother insane. She stepped forward to explain in Yoruba that indeed mental illness had prompted her to smash the family television and radio sets. Standing to the side, her husband and father shook their heads in despair.

It was all becoming too much for the prophet's sensibilities, and in mock frustration he bellowed, "Fire from heaven right now!" The group crashed to the floor and wriggled and rolled in the dust with such determination that the pastor had to shout several times to persuade them to stop. A collective sigh of relief went up from the congregation as confession time finally ended. Pastor Joshua marched around the altar with all of the smugness of a U.S. talk show host, as if he were the Jerry Springer of the tropics.

Like Springer, Pastor Joshua had his critics, and he was determined to let his followers know of the conspiracy against him. The camera lights were turned back on so that a man dressed in a suit and tie could testify to the plot. He was a deacon in a rival church, he explained, so desperate to destroy the Synagogue Church of All Nations that he had sent his own son as a spy to the church's Sunday school. The elders of his church had fasted for twenty-one days to bring down Pastor Joshua. "We wanted God to grant everybody the power to leave this place," he yelled, clearly distraught. But his son reported nothing out of the ordinary at Sunday school, and most of his church's workers had fallen on hard times. Some had lost their jobs, some their cars, and the church was in the process of dissolving. Now he had abandoned his "campaign of calumny" and regarded Pastor Joshua as "a second Jesus."

A pretty teenager followed the deacon to trash another rival house of assembly. A self-described "chronic fornicator," she revealed that her pastor was her lover. Pastor Joshua's jaw dropped.

"When was the first time?" he asked.

"When I was having my period," she said. The crowd groaned. "He approached me again, and when I said I didn't want to, he said since I had done it once, I could do it again."

"And where did these events take place?" Pastor Joshua asked, suddenly flabbergasted.

"In the church itself," she whimpered. The audience gasped. But that was not all. "I had four abortions, I had lesbian relationships," she said, raising her voice to overcome the uproar from the congregation, "and I even cheated on my exams!"

Shouts of "Fire!" erupted sporadically from the mass of onlookers. Pastor Joshua was mumbling into the microphone, letting the words *fornication* and *cheating* emerge audibly from time to time. He approached the girl. Slowly he raised his arms shoulder high, and he pulled invisible strings as if he were flying a kite. The girl rocked back and forth, increasingly unsteady, until she toppled over. "Fire! Fire! All over de body." Within minutes she too was cured, and after pledging her life to Jesus she walked calmly back to sit with the others.

The service was about to close, but before it did, Pastor Joshua asked if there were any more unidentified demonic spirits hiding in the audience. There were, of course. Two men in their early twenties came twirling out of their handily placed front-row seats as if pulled by some irresistible force. The camera crews focused first on a man wearing a Phoenix Suns basketball team shirt and a nasty-looking skull-and-cross-bones tattoo carved into his arm. Before the man had a chance to speak, Pastor Joshua urged the audience to listen carefully because "he is an armed robber." Apparently the prophet knew all. A spirit had possessed him, the man said, and had made his body impervious to bullets. "Even an atomic bomb wouldn't affect him," the pastor screamed. "If you shoot him, the bullet will not enter his body!" The young man said that in his last robbery he was shot at twelve times but the police were "wasting their bullets." The exorcism lasted only a few minutes before Pastor Joshua announced that "the power has finished and he's just a human being like you and me." The formerly invincible robber remained prostrate on the ground spitting up saliva.

The second youngster stepped forward and engaged Pastor Joshua with a defiant gaze. "What evil have you done?" the prophet asked.

"I have destroyed my brother, and the spirit made me steal money from my father," the boy said, with his mother standing behind him bemoaning her offspring's evil deed.

The pastor's response was quick and predictable. "Fire all over de body," he thundered. The ground apparently was afire, and the young man stumbled around the altar until he crashed into the bench where I was sitting. The imaginary blaze forced him to jump up immediately, and the congregation seemed bemused that the flames had not affected me. The boy gathered his wits and hid himself behind a pillar in front of the altar.

"Who am I?" Pastor Joshua asked with a chuckle.

"Jesus," the answer came in a whispered answer. "You are not a human being."

Someone sitting behind me slipped me a note from Pastor Joshua. Would an interview tomorrow morning be convenient? The choir resumed its beautiful song as the parishioners were urged to place their donations in the boxes scattered throughout the hall. As I got up to leave, I could not help but wonder when the pastor had found time to scribble the message.

ON MONDAY morning the church grounds were the picture of serenity. The 100-yard-long parking lot, which had been jammed with cars the day before, was empty. The low-lying Sunday school complex was eerily quiet, and a solitary woman swept the dusty grounds where a thousand boisterous children often played. The atmosphere inside the church itself was dark and cool, with only a handful of believers kneeling at the altar, deep in silent prayer. I headed for a door in the far wall, which, judging from the constant movement through it, was the gateway from the house of worship to the business offices. In charge of shepherding the human traffic was a stern teenager wearing a white head scarf who disappeared with my business card for a few minutes before she returned to motion me in.

The teenager led me through a small patio where fifty or so men, women, and children had gathered under the open sky for a chance to speak with the prophet. From there, we turned a corner, headed down the corridor of a ground-floor office block, and came into the television and radio production room. A bank of TV monitors and editing machines filled the far wall. Sitting behind me was a man wearing headphones who with great dexterity was cutting a cassette of music and the pastor's speeches. Across the room was another cubicle, where a woman was putting the finishing touches on a video relating the pastor's miracles.

A sense of efficiency, almost urgency, filled the room. Every few seconds someone rushed in or out of the door, always submitting to a brief body search by whoever else happened to be standing there—a surprising sign of paranoia. Invariably the church workers were eager youngsters in their early twenties, scurrying back forth with messages the prophet had scribbled on scraps of white paper.

A television in front of me came to life with a video about a tall, balding Swiss man who had traveled from Zurich in search of relief from Parkinson's disease. The voice-over explained that the man had been confined to a wheelchair for the past twelve years. After a few minutes of encouraging words from Pastor Joshua, the man rose and began walking unsteadily. It's a miracle, he said. Pastor Joshua beamed. That video was followed by another report about a heavyset German woman who had been beset for the past nine years by stomach cancer and by a back injury sustained in a car crash. After a few

minutes with the pastor, who raised his arms in the kite-flying position, the woman threw up and pronounced herself fit. "I feel released," she told the cameraman. "The pain is gone. I feel free."

Pastor Joshua claims to have cured two thousand people of AIDS,
both in Nigeria and in Ghana, where he has an office. In Lagos,
Sundays and Wednesdays were the days for treating AIDS, along with
barren women, and with the spread of HIV accelerating there was always a good turnout. Patients, I was told, arrived with a piece of paper
testifying to their infection, received treatment from Pastor Joshua,
and returned a week later with another piece of paper saying they
were clear of the virus.

A particularly gut-wrenching piece of video, a graphic depiction of
anal cancer, was playing as the door swung open and a rail-thin
woman told me it was time to meet Pastor Joshua. I followed her
through the corridor, past the families in the courtyard, and into a tiny
front room, where a dozen young women were jostling for position to
be the next. The surging pressure from aspiring visitors outside forced
the girl on guard to lean her full weight against the door.

The door to the inside room opened, spewing out a dozen young
people in white T-shirts and jeans. I entered and found the prophet in
urgent discussion with a team of aides. His black eyes darted from
face to face, and the subordinates hung on his every word. He looked
up, and we shook hands. Before we began, Pastor Joshua had a request. He asked to film our interview so there were no mistakes about
what he said. Before I could respond, the youths I had seen running
out of the office were piling back in with a full array of camera and
sound equipment.

Over the next forty-five minutes Pastor Joshua proved himself to
be an opaque subject. His answers often began with "As it was, so it is"
and usually ended with the explanation that everything was the result
of God's will. Typical was his response to the question of how he became a healer in the first place:

Man has two natures in one person—the human nature and divine nature. When you are talking of healing, you are talking of divine holiness. Divine holiness comes from God Almighty. The gift was given to me, not for the work of righteousness, which I have done. The gift of healing is given to me according to his grace. God chooses the grace rather than work as the Bible says in Titus 3:5. Since it is not the work of righteousness which I have done, then I think I am not a healer. God is the healer. I know the healer and I introduce people to the healer. Now what I am doing and what God is using me to do, you too can do the same, perhaps even greater because he said it's really by his example, and by obeying his commandments that we shall do greater things.

Answering questions of when, why, and how he received his special powers was problematic, he said, because God worked in mysterious ways. "Five years ago people realized the goodness, the potential in my life. But when God will minister to me, no one can say, because he says he will come like a thief in the night."

He would not even say whether his parents were religious. "As it was, so it is. You know Joseph and Mary, they were chasing Jesus when Jesus was four years old and he was going about preaching about God. Mary was chasing him all around. She was not happy about it. It showed that they were not religious. So my people, if I say they are religious, I am judging them. It is God that knows those who are religious."

The prophet said that as a boy he was an "obedient child," although one look at those dancing eyes suggested that obedience and the young Joshua were not close companions. He was said to have first drawn attention to himself as a child by successfully predicting the outcome of soccer matches. Before discovering his healing powers, he said he was a preacher, a teacher of the Lord's scriptures.

"People call you a prophet, a healer," I ventured.

"Everybody chooses to call me any name they want."

"How would you describe yourself?"

"I am just T. B. Joshua, and I think my work will explain my personality. The Bible said in the book of Matthew 7, verse 20, 'by their fruit we shall know them.' It means by their work we shall know them. I don't want to accept any title."

How did the prophet explain the existence of so many spirits and wizards in Nigeria?

"Oh, they were everywhere," he said, "in all nations. God simply had not yet chosen anyone to expose them."

And judging from the number of churches, Nigeria was the most religious country in the world, I suggested.

"One thing is for one to be religious before men. Another thing is for man to be religious before God. There can be a thousand churches. Are they really for the commandments? Are they really for God's work? Do they really live above sin?" Clearly he thought not.

But if everything boiled down to God's work, then why, I asked the pastor, did he use television cameras and videos to promote his church?

"Because I know my work is not for this generation alone; it's for the generation to come," he said proudly. "So to keep the record for the generation to come, one needs to employ sophisticated machines to keep the record up to date." Then he made an outrageous assertion. "It is God that is talking to you now. You hear the voice of God. But me, I am a human being like you, but it's the voice of God."

Not everyone agreed with Pastor Joshua's methods. He had been called a charlatan, a religious practitioner of "419" fraud. Pastor Joshua admitted to having his critics but insisted they only proved that he was doing God's work. "Without persecution, there is no progress. If you want to be the best among equals, you should expect persecution. The more the persecution, the greater the success."

I asked him about the financial side of the church, whether it survived from the donations of the congregation. Pastor Joshua clearly did not want to talk about the subject. "It is out of my hands. Money does not go well with the spirit of God. God says to look after today. Tomorrow will take care of itself."

Since he was said to be able to predict the future, I asked whether he could foresee if Nigeria would make it through this difficult time. "Yes. What is happening in Nigeria is what once happened in America. The America of old led to the great America of today. It once happened in Japan, and now Japan is great. So what is happening in Nigeria will soon lead to a great Nigeria." When I asked how soon, he said, "a matter of days." The pastor's optimism, like that of many of his countrymen, proved short-lived. At the end of 1999 Pastor Joshua foresaw imminent danger to the civilian government. Amid the widespread violence surrounding the OPC and the president's threat to impose a state of emergency on Lagos, Pastor Joshua issued a statement predicting that Obasanjo was in danger of being overthrown by a military coup.

———

IN THE EVER widening pool of Pentecostal churches in southern Nigeria, Pastor Joshua's outfit is, however colorful, only a medium-sized fish. Among the biggest is the Redeemed Christian Church of God, which regularly pulls in several million believers for its annual Holy Ghost Festival. The 1999 version was tagged as "Victory at Last."

Proof that religion is a thriving business in Nigeria can be found at Bishop David Oyedepo's Faith Tabernacle, an immense hexagonal structure in the town of Ota on the outskirts of Lagos. Completed in September 1999, just a year after it was started by Nigerian builders on a sprawling plot called Canaan Land, the red-roofed tabernacle can be seen for miles. In size it does not match the world's biggest church, the Roman Catholic basilica of Yamoussoukro in the Ivory Coast, but its official seating capacity of 50,400 ranks near the highest on earth. So well attended are its services that dozens of wardens are on hand to marshal the traffic, and an impromptu street market has developed fifty yards from the main entrance to sell food, drink, and church literature.

Whereas Pastor Joshua caters to society's losers—the ill and the downtrodden—Bishop Oyedepo gears his sermons to Nigeria's Christian elite. That some call Faith Tabernacle "the rich people's church" is an obvious source of pride. "We have quite a lot of middle-class followers, a notable number of high class people, and top government officials," he said in his sprawling office, where a band of young, well-dressed aides were busy designing an internet site on desktop computers and raced around with corporate efficiency. Less than a mile down the road is the farm of his good friend, President Obasanjo. Not surprisingly, the church's motto is "I am a winner," a slogan sported on bright red stickers adorning the cavalcade of cars and buses that bring in the multitudes twice a week. "It gives you an identity, that I am a winner," Bishop Oyedepo said. "It gives you a sense of conviction, that you are heading for something positive."

Career success, wealth, status in society, good marriages, plentiful children, even "miracle houses" all await those who accept Jesus through the Faith Tabernacle. The message is that the Lord expects his followers to enjoy material prosperity, and those who embrace the church, Oyedepo says, shall rise from "the dunghill to the palace." There is none of the admonitions about bad living or spirits and demons that reverberate in Pastor Joshua's church. Oyedepo's emphasis on the good life provides a powerful antidote to the despair that thrives in the society outside the hallowed walls of the cathedral. "In the year 2000," he told the faithful at a December service, "an earthquake is coming in your favor. An angel of the lord is descending with great power to roll away the stone that is blocking your destiny."

Oyedepo, a trained civil engineer, opened his first church in Kaduna in 1983. Today he claims a following in Kaduna of fifteen thousand. In the early 1980s the charismatic African churches were emerging from their humble origins in the university campus study groups of the preceding decade, and they were beginning to gain momentum. The messages of healing, miracles, and prosperity found sympathetic echoes among a populace that had seen the hope of the oil boom collapse into the spiral of economic decline and military rule. "That awakening was just a move of the spirit which was preparing Nigeria to able to go through the hours of hardships that we had to go through," Oyedepo said. "It required the endurance that Christian faith teaches, injecting hope into people even when everything looks hopeless."

This central belief in religion's role in strengthening the country's moral fiber has reached the political mainstream with the rise to power of Obasanjo, a born-again Christian. In his new book, *This Animal Called Man*, Obasanjo put it this way:

> One thing we must remember in our personal and national lives is that a nation without God is like a man without orientation, without memory, without plan and without hope, aimlessly drifting and being tossed up and down, back and forth. Whatever else we do as a nation to achieve our desirable objective of peace, unity and prosperity with development, we must return to God.[1]

Today, with churches of his Winners' Chapel spread across the breadth of Nigeria and some twenty-five other African countries, Oyedepo claims to be leading one of the world's fastest-growing religious movements, but he is clearly not satisfied. His next major project is to build a university, though not for religious instruction per se. Rather, in keeping with his message of prosperity, Oyedepo is planning to establish a college of business studies, with courses in administration, management, accountancy, and banking. "When they come in here, they are taught how to become productive, and by being productive their lifestyle begins to improve, and the environment begins to affect them," he told me. "This place is basically committed to improving people's standard of living." At a January 2000 service he praised those who had recently acquired property as sterling members of the congregation and called them to the front of the church. "All of you are landlords; give Jesus a big hand," he shouted.

Recruitment remains a top priority. February was dubbed "Multiplication Project," and the goal was "supernatural church growth" at a "wonder frequency." He exhorted each member of his flock to bring in four friends or relatives, anyone they could find. "This coming month, God makes you a super harvester in his temple," he boomed across the public-address system. "Identify the targets, identify their needs, and provide the Gospel solution." Find someone who was suffering from an illness, a family crisis, or depression, he suggested. "Show them the way to the church. Market your church." He clearly was. One of his handbills urged his harvesters to "constantly put evangelism pressure on your targets, until they finally bow this month."

The normal service is a two-hour affair. The bishop struts around the altar with a microphone clipped to his business suit expounding on the merits that a good Christian life will bring to career opportunities. He occasionally stands at his glass podium to consult the Scriptures. From time to time there are breaks when a live band strikes up religious tunes to a West African beat. Oyedepo leads the congregation in mass dances in which he and his believers twist and shake and keep time by whipping white handkerchiefs in the air, much as Ganiyu Adams's OPC followers do when waving off the harmful effects of police bullets. He calls these party interludes a "vigorous dance unto the Lord" and sometimes calls on church elders to engage the pastors in a dance competition.

He will shout "Hallelujah" or "In Jesus' precious name" as soon as he senses that the crowd is losing interest. "Do you see Jesus?" he asks as tens of thousands raise both arms in the air. A refrain of "Let me hear you shout you are a winner" brings a deafening roar. This is heady stuff in a country where the majority of people feel like anything but winners. It is especially attractive to Nigerians, who, probably more than most, live in the pursuit of instant gratification. As President Obasanjo wrote: "What matters to most Nigerians is the six P's, which are pursued at all cost—position, power, possession, plaudit, popularity and pleasure. Nothing else matters. With the six P's, he can buy anything and buy himself into anything. Honesty is disregarded, indolence is extolled, probity is derided, and waste and ostentation are paraded."[2]

As the service wound down, the bishop asked everyone to shake their neighbors' hands in an expression of common cause. Flanked by a gang of aides, Oyedepo moved out of the back of the church like a Hollywood star, occasionally stopping to shake hands with the faithful. As he reached his car, a black sport-utility vehicle with tinted windows, a crowd of men and women formed to receive his touch on their head, to some simply a benediction but to others a sort of divine touch to heal their ailments. As he climbed into the back seat for the short drive to his office, a young couple with a newborn child ran up for the bishop's blessing. After a short wait the window rolled down, and a hand emerged to briefly stroke the infant's head before the car spirited Oyedepo away to plan for his next conquest.

10

A Glass Cage

Igbos survive within the Nigerian state not because of the efforts of the government but because of the ingenious nature of the people to survive.

PROFESSOR OSY OKANYA

PERCHED IN A rickety wheelchair on the edge of a highway, Mazi Obinah Mmajah shouted to make himself heard over the roar of a truck belching dark clouds of exhaust in its wake. "We have been waiting for our government to do something," he said with a sardonic smile. "But they never come, so we live on charity." Nods of assent rolled down the row of a dozen middle-aged men sitting alongside Mazi in an odd assortment of ambulatory contraptions. Suddenly a minibus jammed with travelers skidded to a halt, and a young man jumped down from the passenger seat to be greeted by the collective wave of welcome from the men. He handed over a small wad of naira. "They stop to give us something to eat," said Mazi, "We survive thanks to people's generosity."

From the vantage point of an approaching vehicle, the thatched roadside lean-to where Mazi and his friends sat appeared to be one of dozens of impromptu taxi ranks positioned along the four-lane highway that links eastern Nigeria's staid political capital Enugu to the anarchic market town of Onitsha on the banks of the Niger river. Bus stops are as ubiquitous as police checkpoints and market stalls on this vital thoroughfare that carries on across the Niger, passes through the ancient kingdom of Benin, and leads to the metropolis of Lagos. The wheelchairs and the spontaneous military salutes that some of the men gave to passing cars hinted at the shelter's true purpose.

Mazi and his colleagues were veterans of the Biafran army, forgotten foot soldiers of the 1967–1970 struggle of the Igbos to secede from Nigeria and create their own nation. Thirty years after Gowon's promise of "No victors, no vanquished," they were still begging for a living. Some were paralyzed, others were missing a limb or two. All were haunting reminders of the human cost of civil war and unwitting prophets of a potentially frightful future should Nigeria's latest experiment with constitutional rule go badly wrong.

After receiving hospital treatment for their wounds at the war's end, hundreds of Biafra's disfigured soldiers were driven to the Oji River and deposited in a village called the War Disabled Veterans Camp. Promised instruction and work, they were literally put out to pasture. "We were told we were being sent for rehabilitation and training, but since then we have not seen anything," Mazi said. "We have petitioned the government so many times but it has been falling on deaf ears. No one knows why they don't listen to our call." Several hundred men still live in the camp, but age and ill health have taken their toll. "There used to be a lot more of us," Mazi said, reaching over to brush an insect off my shoulder. "But over the years we have been dying off." The village had no nurse, and although there was a hospital nearby, the men had neither the transport to reach it nor the money to buy the medicines the doctors prescribed.

Some of the men's families were with them. When I asked Mazi about his family, he fell into an embarrassed pause. "My wife is with my kinsmen because I cannot fend for her," he said finally. As for children, "there has been no issue yet." His home village of Olu, where his relatives live, is in a neighboring state and too distant for regular visits.

Mazi and his friends appeared to be in remarkably good humor, perhaps in part because of the warm support they receive from the public. The war was still in the mind of everyone in eastern Nigeria, even among the majority of the Igbos who were born after the guns fell silent. Igbos are taught from childhood that they are a special tribe like the Jews—industrious, clever, and persecuted. Survival requires hard work and communal solidarity. During the hour and a half I sat chatting with the men, a dozen vehicles stopped to donate money. Sometimes people handed it over in person, and other times they simply tossed wadded up balls of cash out the window. Local villagers also helped. They had cobbled together the shelter from wooden poles and bamboo, and the veterans paid young women from a nearby settlement to cook their meals for them.

Another group of war wounded sat under an identical cover across the highway. Each day new groups ambled up the dirt track from the camp at about 9:00 A.M. to man the stands. This road duty lasted until dusk. The donations were shared among the entire encampment. Mazi said he usually took his place on the road once or twice a week, though he would rather have been working. There had been a plan to produce polyethylene bags for the Onitsha market, but the veterans did not have enough money to purchase the necessary machinery. "Look at Nigeria now, everything broken," said Mazi. "Nigeria is like us, crippled."

Despite all that had happened, in Mazi's heart Biafran independence remained a valiant cause. After graduating from high school he was unemployed for a while before beginning to dabble in trading, a profession at which Igbos have proved themselves adept over the generations. For Mazi, however, trading prospects were grim. The approach of the war forced tens of thousands of Igbos from all over the country to return to the east. He ran off with a group of friends to join the army at the age of twenty-two without telling his parents.

"Our people were massacred in the north, so we had to believe in the Biafra cause," he said. "There was so much pressure on us from everywhere to fight, and when the bullet came, we were proud to take it." Mazi fought with the Sixty-First Brigade and rose to the rank of second lieutenant, with eighty men under his command. He felt almost invincible until a Nigerian bullet tore through his right leg in May 1968 and left him with a withered limb. For the remainder of the war, he stayed in a hospital bed in his village of Olu with dozens of other wounded soldiers.

He still remembers clearly the afternoon of January 12, 1970, when Major General Philip Effiong, to whom the separatist leader Ojukwu had handed power before fleeing to the Ivory Coast, went on the Biafran radio to announce the end of the war. "None of us was happy, because our aim was not achieved," Mazi recalled. "That day I heard the war was over, I realized that everything we had done was a complete failure." I asked Mazi about Ojukwu, a still popular but fading figure in Igbo politics. Ojukwu had returned from exile in 1982 and since then had spent his time traveling between Abuja, Enugu, and Lagos or abroad to the United States. At the entrance to his Lagos home in the fashionable Ikoyi neighborhood, there is a striking sign that reads "Beware of snakes."

I asked Mazi whether Ojukwu had ever passed by. He smiled. "Maybe our leaders drive by in their Mercedes Benz's with dark windows and we cannot see inside, but they never stop here. Ojukwu is living much better than us and he does not need us anymore." Ojukwu in Mazi's eyes was just another politician, and there was nothing worse than a politician, save perhaps for a military dictator. "The way we see it," he said, "politics is very big business. Politicians make a lot of empty promises that they never keep."

The alienation Mazi felt toward politicians of all stripes was similar to the enmity with which the Igbo people regard the rest of Nigeria. A conversation with almost any Igbo inevitably revealed a sense of being only a second-class citizen. Prejudice, said Professor Osy Okanya, the dean of the Faculty of Social Sciences at Enugu State University, lies at the heart of the Igbo problem. "Anytime you mention that you are an Igbo man you awake certain feelings. The Hausa man sees you and says, 'Ah, this man has come to grab.' The Yoruba man sees you as a *dankawaro*, an ant; the Igbos will get to places where it is thought no one can go. The other nationalities see the Igbos as people who will do the impossible," he said, adding with a wry smile, "by hook or by crook." Chinua Achebe, in *The Trouble with Nigeria*, put it this way: "Nigerians of all other ethnic groups will probably achieve consensus on no other matter than their common resentment of the Igbo. They would all describe them as aggressive, arrogant and clannish. Most would add grasping and greedy."[1]

And yet another thing almost all Nigerians agreed on was that Igbos were extremely hard workers. Although the major cities elsewhere in the country were filled with the downtrodden approaching motorists for a handout, they were a rare sight anywhere on Igbo land. Those Igbos who did pop their heads into one's vehicle almost always had something for sale. In every corner of Nigeria, from Kafanchan to Kano, from Wukari to Lagos, Igbos were prominent players in local commerce. Igbos have always been known for their entrepreneurial spirit, but as Professor Okanya explained to me in his office one morning, they have been forced to adopt a can-do business attitude almost as a religion because of their treatment since their defeat in the Biafran war. "It is to their credit that they have found a profession which no government can take away from them," he said. "It is part of the survival strategy to no longer count on the government."

In politics as in military affairs, the Igbos felt shortchanged. From independence until the revenge coup of 1966, they had held the commanding heights of the economy, they had dominated the officer corps, and their longtime nationalist leader Nnamdi Azikiwe had served as the country's then largely ceremonial president. Defeat in the civil war left the Igbos with little influence.

Clearly their leaders were partly to blame. For years Igbo politicians squabbled among themselves and were prepared to cast their lot with whichever power broker managed to secure Aso Rock. "Those who control power know that the Igbos at any time would be there for their bidding," said Okanya. "The Igbo elites have remained the military's willing tools."

In recent times the most visible Igbo presence at the national level was the spectacle of two former Biafran wartime propagandists, "Comrade" Uche Chukwumerije and Walter Ofonagoro, plying their trade on behalf of the Babangida and Abacha dictatorships. There was also Arthur Nzeribe's campaign to convince Babangida to scuttle the 1993 election process and the young pro-military campaigner Daniel Kanu's comical YEAA, for Youths Earnestly Ask for Abacha, or as Wole Soyinka once described the movement, "Youths Expire in the Abyss of Abasement."

Many Igbos were still smarting over Obasanjo's defeat of their political champion Alex Ekwueme for the PDP presidential nomination. "For the first time, the Igbos really came together under the Ekwueme banner," said Okanya, an admitted admirer of the man. Yet the magnanimous manner in which Ekwueme accepted his defeat and indeed went on to campaign for Obasanjo was also a source of pride.

As much as Igbos complained about their position in Nigerian society, few honestly contemplated another attempt at secession. "If you go to the markets the Igbo man, the Hausa, the Yoruba go about their business without knowing that there are differences," Professor Okanya said. "The embers of difference are found in the actions, or inactions, of the government." Nigeria's various ethnic groups were simply too interdependent. "Sixty percent of the food we eat here comes from the north. And over 60 or 70 percent of the food they eat in Lagos comes from the north. One hundred percent of the meat we eat here comes from the north. No one will feel comfortable leaving that relationship."

But again, like many observers, Okanya felt that much depended on the fate of the Obasanjo administration. "If anything happens to Obasanjo in the next one or two years I don't think this Nigerian federation will remain." When he heard the rumor of Obasanjo's death on May 17, Okanya said he called a friend in the security establishment. "The guy told me it was false, but that if it was true, he would be on the next available bus to his village because that would be the end of Nigeria."

When I told Okanya that the next morning I was leaving Enugu for Onitsha, the tempestuous market town on the banks of the Niger, he feigned shock. "Onitsha!" he said, pronouncing it sharply as in "Oneecha." "That place, no. It's too much. I could never live in that place. There is such commotion in Onitsha that sometimes it seems like the buildings are moving." The jokes about Onitsha were legendary. It was often touted as the biggest trading center in West Africa, which was saying something, given that raucous bargaining was a way of life up and down the Atlantic coast. At the market in Onitsha, went one story, you could purchase a used Boeing 747 jet engine in working order.

Onitsha's fame for outright lawlessness had earned it the reputation among some visitors as the worst city in the world, although of late the southeastern oil town of Warri, the scene of two years of violent ethnic clashes between Itsekirris and Ijaws, has probably stolen that dubious title. A BBC colleague had a rather unsettling experience in Onitsha one evening. He told the receptionist at his hotel that he was going to take a walk. "You can't do that," she said, "it's too dangerous." When he insisted that nevertheless, he was going out, she asked him with a straight face to settle the bill before he left. He refused and left the hotel but turned back almost immediately, after gunfire erupted just around the corner.

The sheer dilapidation of Onitsha's roads can take one's breath away. Jude Okafor, my taxi driver, and I entered Onitsha from the east in search of Port Harcourt Road, not to be confused with the road to Port Harcourt. We were looking for the offices of Caltech Ltd., an import-export company, where I was to meet Emeka Uzoatu, a former journalist turned businessman. Emeka was the friend of a friend and the brother of the Igbo writer Maxim Uzoatu, whom I once met in Lagos. During a brief telephone conversation he tried to offer me directions, but after consulting with Jude I assured him we would find our way easily enough. I should have listened to him and written down his instructions. Arriving in the center of Onitsha was to meet raw bedlam face to face. The pandemonium of cars, buses, and motorbikes, all with horns at full volume; occasionally a herd of cattle led by nomadic Fulanis; and a stifling heat quickly left one's head spinning. Drivers in Onitsha took quite literally the admonition on the traffic signs to "horn before overtaking" and they cut in and out of traffic, with razor-thin margins you could shave with. Markets of thousands of people spilled into the streets with no discernible rhyme or reason. Jude, an Igbo accustomed to the calmer realms of Enugu and Abuja, gripped the wheel in a spasm of panic and occasionally mumbled about how "uncivilized" the place was. By comparison, Lagos seemed rather placid.

We asked our way three times and received three different sets of directions, all provided with an air of total confidence. Finally we found the route. It involved reaching the road to Port Harcourt, doubling back down the far side, and turning right into Port Harcourt Road. Unfortunately it had rained within the past hour. Up ahead was a pool of water deep enough to submerge the engine of an average sedan. For a moment Jude froze. "My car! I can't go there," he said indignantly, before turning his head to look out the back window at a menacing onrush of traffic. "Okay, okay, we are going. We are going!" He shouted more than anything else to fortify his courage.

Quite ingeniously, he piloted our car onto the edge of an ad hoc garbage dump of overwhelming rankness. At its height, of at least 7 feet, it reached the bottom of a sign that warned against urinating, defecating, or dumping rubbish anywhere in the area. Jude revved the engine and roared into the pond, lifting his legs from the pedals as he did in case water rushed inside. For an instant there was the sensation that we were floating. As we hit dry land again, Jude exhaled and began wiping his brow with a white handkerchief. "Oneecha, hey!"

Emeka seemed somewhat surprised when I related the travails of our travel though the urban swamp. "The roads here are in poor condition, I suppose," he said with charming understatement. All in all, Emeka said, Onitsha was not such a bad place. It was full of business opportunities, and one just had to get used to its unique environment. Like most businessmen, he could cope with the driving challenges, the continual power outages, and the heat. In his view the biggest problem was the plague of gangsters and the police, who were often in cahoots with each other. A week before, a band of armed men had taken over the main road in town and shot up the markets on a looting spree. The police regularly mounted roadblocks and extorted money from traders bringing their goods to and from market. The practice was hampering business so severely that the new civilian governor said in his inauguration speech that one of his priorities was to remove the illegal police checkpoints.

I was interested in learning about the history of the city, so I headed off to see if I could arrange an audience with the traditional ruler of Onitsha, Obi Ofala Okecheukwu Okagbur. By now Jude had somewhat recovered his nerve, and refreshed by a plate of rice and beans washed down with a glass of water, he carefully negotiated his way around the potholes, many filled with water and most of them substantially broader than his car.

We reached the gates of the palace in downtown Onitsha and were quickly ushered into the parking lot. Unfortunately the Obi was indisposed; he was asleep. But one of the important six red-cap chiefs who form the OBI's inner council, B. C. Odiari, whose title was the "Osuma Affa of Onitsha" and the palace secretary, was prepared to answer my questions. Chief Odiari was an amiable fellow in his sixties and an expert on the history of Onitsha. In the dark coolness of his office, he told me of the birth of this extraordinary city.

As with most substantial settlements in West Africa, the story of the founding of Onitsha is of biblical proportions. Chief Odiari said it started several hundred years ago in the kingdom of Benin, the source of the great bronze sculptures that so enchanted the British conquerors that they carted the artwork off to the great museums of Europe and never returned them.

One day someone killed a staff member in the court of the Oba (the king), and his informants told him that the murderer was one of the settlers living on the outskirts of the kingdom. When sympathizers within the palace warned the settlers that the Oba's troops were preparing an attack, the settlers fled eastward on a long, hard journey. Many died on the way, and others grew so tired that they stopped to settle in what later became major towns such as Asaba. Eventually the leader of the emigrants perished, and his three sons took over.

When the column reached the Niger, it was decided that whoever first crossed the river and beat a traditional gong, an *ufie*, would be named the new Obi. The three brothers set off in their canoes. What two of the brothers did not know was that the third, clearly the cleverest, had hidden their father's *ufie* in his boat. The first brother to reach the shore ran up to a tree and began cutting wood to fashion a gong. Meanwhile, the second to reach the shore calmly stepped off his canoe and sounded the *ufie*. Although there was a dispute about the outcome of the contest, the race went not to the swiftest but to the wisest. On the bank of the river was born Onitsha, whose name means "endurance" in honor of the arduous pilgrimage.

Chief Odiari explained that his ancestors—Ibos—found the Igbo people living in scattered villages on the hills surrounding Onitsha. I told him I was under the impression that *Ibo* and *Igbo* were simply different spellings of the same word. "A common mistake," he said. "We are different. We speak a different language. We can understand a few words from what they are saying and they make meaning to you. But to have an actual conversation and follow what they are saying, no." The Ibos, although largely Christian now, had had their own traditional religion, Ominane, which centered on one God but involved a mild form of ancestor worship. Ibos had always had traditional rulers, the Obis. The Igbos had no such rulers until the British created them so they could more easily implement their system of indirect rule. Indeed, much divided the two peoples, Chief Odiari maintained in an example of the rather depressing Nigerian habit of always seeking to differentiate among even the smallest groups. "The Igbos have no culture," he said rather indelicately.

Chief Odiari estimated that the Ibos accounted for 5 percent of Onitsha's population and just 1 percent of the market traders who formed the backbone of the local economy. "Our greatest strength as a people is the maintenance of our culture, but our greatest weakness is the way we open our hands. It's not a weakness as such, but people capitalize on it. We allowed the Igbos into our fold, and before we knew it they overwhelmed us." I told him that the motto of my home state, Kentucky, was "United we stand, divided we fall," but for ethnic groups in Nigeria the national philosophy seemed to be, quite literally, the reverse.

One of the most powerful Igbo businessmen in Onitsha is Chief Sir Godwin Okeke, the former head of both the Anambra State and Onitsha traders' associations. When I walked in on him at his office at the G. U. Okeke Transport Company on the outskirts of town, he was sitting down with his banker and signing for a loan. Business, a word he pronounced with obvious relish in his booming voice, ran in his blood. Tall, graying, and wearing a traditional Igbo red cap, Okeke was an undying cheerleader for the Igbos in general and in particular for

Onitsha, which he considered the vibrant heart of Nigerian commerce. "Come down to Onitsha and you will see all the banks operating there. Why? Because they are doing business. It is mainly the Igbo-speaking people who are doing business in Lagos."

Okeke started trading out of the back of his beat-up car as a teenager, but the civil war interrupted his commercial ambitions. He returned to Onitsha in January 1970, a few days before the formal end of the conflict, to a scene of utter devastation. Some of the fiercest battles of the war took place in Onitsha. "It was like a ghost town," he remembered. "The city was completely destroyed. The whole of that main market was burned down during the war. Even the Niger River bridge was broken. We were crossing the river by canoes and ferries."

Over time, the people of Onitsha rebuilt their markets and restarted the trade for which they had become famous (some would say infamous). Okeke estimated that 70 percent of the people in Anambra State were involved in commerce. Down the road, south toward Port Harcourt, was another major trading town, Aba, that specialized in textiles. Ojukwu's home village of Nnewi, just east of the Niger River, has earned the nickname "Tai-Two," after Taiwan, because it manufactures spare motor parts for the entire West African subregion. Okeke was involved in trading, manufacturing, and transportation; his Okeke luxury buses ferried hundreds of passengers each day to Lagos. He had a factory in Lagos producing textiles for schoolchildren and mattress covers, and he had a retail store in Kano.

"Why," I asked, "were Igbos so irrepressibly dynamic?"

"Because we don't have anything here!" he roared. "We don't have enough land to farm. Our forefathers were sort of adventurers, so they moved about from one place to the other with their different trades. We are basically travelers, adventurers, like the Jews."

As we were talking, a sudden power outage sent the chief off on a diatribe about the neglect of the east. "You expect this type of thing for people who were defeated in war," he said with an air of resignation. "There is not much Igbo representation in the army, and the army has been in power for almost thirty years. They look after the north and the west. They forget that the wealth is coming from the east." He was particularly annoyed that the government had never expanded the two-lane road from Onitsha to Benin, which he claimed was the busiest in the country, into an expressway.

Things would have been different, he argued, if Biafra had succeeded in breaking away from Nigeria. The Yorubas would have also left to form their Odudua State, and "each one of us would have the opportunity to struggle for his or her area." The bloated center of the unified Nigeria that government had become, dispensing contracts and patronage, would never have developed. "Because of our selfish attitude, because of our idea to cheat, most people in Nigeria are not doing anything but collecting money from the so-called national cake. People make money without working for it. Useless contracts are being issued without anybody doing anything."

Okeke had had his own painful encounter with the military authorities in 1994 while he was the president of the Onitsha Amalgamated Traders' Association. The military administrator of Anambra State had offered him bribes to hand over control of market stalls, which in the central market cost up to 500,000 naira, about $5,000. Okeke had turned him down. "Paying me 1 to 2 million naira [$10,000–$20,000] to help them to build illegal stalls, mucking up the roads, is not worth it. My name is more important to me than 1 or 2 million." The authorities then declared the traders' association illegal, accused Okeke of theft, locked him up in chains in an army camp, and then burned down the market so that they could build a new one and sell off the stalls at a handsome profit. Five weeks later he was released after his lawyer challenged the detention in court.

Hopeful but not convinced by the Obasanjo administration's ability to bring about change, or improve matters, Okeke said the first thing the new government must do is recover some of the billions of dollars stashed in overseas bank accounts. "The poor people of this country are suffering because the wealth has been moved out of the country," he said. But however President Obasanjo performed, he said, it would be an improvement on the military.

"God is too kind to this country," he declared with a beaming smile. "If not for the death of Abacha, nobody knows what our fate might have been. The civilians were ruled out, the army was intimidated, and everyone was so afraid. So God said, 'Ah, I won't allow you to go to supper,' and he sent his angels to carry out the type of coup that we have never seen anywhere in the world. It was a coup from heaven."

When I returned to the car, Jude was stretched out on the back seat in a deep sweaty slumber. I awakened him gently, and after recovering consciousness he inquired with a trace of anxiety, "Can we leave for Enugu now?" We joined the highway and passed through a police checkpoint, where we saw a police officer standing in the middle of the road with a pistol in his right hand and his left extended toward the window of a truck. Another driver was handing over a few bills to the forces of law and order. "About the price we arranged for the trip..." Jude started to say slowly.

I knew where this was going and said, "But Jude, we had a deal. You're not trying to renegotiate at the end of the trip?"

"Noooo!" he said. "But Oneecha, hey!"

Back at the war veterans' station on the highway, sitting at the opposite end from Mazi, Nwoho Benson hunkered down in an incredible tricycle made from cannibalized bicycle parts. "Our local technology," he said with an ironic chuckle. Benson, who said he was "about fifty," leaned over to show me a hole in the top of his head about a half-inch deep and an inch long in the shape of a teardrop. A bullet had skimmed his skull during a battle in 1968, and he has suffered partial paralysis in both legs ever since. He came from a village near Enugu called Ngwo, and unlike Mazi he had regular visits from his wife. His three-year-old son Onu, or miracle, was proof of that. Benson politely asked whether I minded if he finished his lunch of pounded yam and meat in a red plastic bowl while we talked.

Benson's goal was to complete his master's degree in education at the University of Ibadan so he could become a teacher. He had earned his bachelor's degree in 1992, but since then he had not found the money to take the next step. From a box he kept under his legs he pulled out a stack of papers, mainly correspondence from the university, and rifled through them until he found the one he was looking for. It was a letter on University of Ibadan stationary informing him that because of lack of payment, he had forfeited his place in the master's program but was welcome to reapply next year. "Are there any institutions for the crippled in your country which might be able to help us here?" he asked. I said I was not sure but perhaps he could send a letter to the embassy. They would know if there were any such institutions.

"What about the government, now that the civilians are in control?" I asked.

"The government? I don't think so," he said, bouncing with a laugh.

After making a donation to the group, I bade farewell, and all the men waved and saluted in return. "Whatever we get, we eat," shouted Benson, still chewing his pounded yam. "Whenever you return, we will be here."

———

THIRTY YEARS to the month after the end of the civil war that was supposed to free his people from the shackles of Nigeria, Chukwuemeka Ojukwu sat on a couch in his comfortable home in Enugu and complained that the Igbos were so traumatized by the experience that they are caught in a sort of time warp. "Part of our problem is that we don't realize that we have survived," he said in the impeccable upper-class English accent he had picked up at Oxford University. "People are still doing things to secure their survival. I try to tell them, you have to live, you are back, I am here."

He said that symptoms of the trauma were everywhere, that politicians had no principles and supported the government of the day, military or civilian, whether or not it was good for the Igbo people. "People who have made money are preeminent in society, and generally the real authentic leaders can only be heard if they can somehow tag onto one of those." He said that youngsters readily abandoned school and turned to market trading to make quick money. "Even in the bush, the deepest villages, young men are thinking how to make their millions overnight. With the total breakdown of our administration, the morals we were taught as youngsters are not being taught anymore."

Blame for the Igbo mind-set, according to Ojukwu, falls on the policies adopted by Gowon's government immediately after Biafra's surrender. Coupled with Gowon's directive that there would be "No victors, no vanquished" was a decision to wipe out the savings of an entire people with the stroke of pen. No matter how much anyone had had in the bank during the war, after the war the then finance minister Obafemi Awolowo limited each person to recovering the equivalent of £20. "You can imagine the frenzy with which the Igbo people went into the struggle for survival, and after so many years, it has become almost a reflex."

According to Ojukwu the Igbo people are still treated as second-class citizens, with little representation in government or the military, just as they were when he led the Biafran rebellion as a thirty-three-year-old army colonel. He described them as living "in a glass cage below a glass ceiling." Under both the British and the Nigerian rulers ever since, the Igbos have been regarded as too pushy, too industrious, and with too much wanderlust to be afforded equal treatment. "The problem with Nigeria has always been how to accommodate these very energetic Igbos," he said. "Under the British, it was how to accommodate the uppity Igbos. Then after independence, it was how to accommodate these Igbos who don't stay in their area but wander around everywhere. That is why it was easy to think that the answer was to kill them off and prevent them from ever coming back." The Igbos survived, however, and they returned to occupy an integral part of the economies of cities such as Kano where they had been slaughtered thirty years ago.

Since his return from exile in the Ivory Coast in 1982, Ojukwu has occupied a unique place in his beloved Igboland—a former rebel leader who now calls for Nigerian unity, a man widely admired by Igbo commoners but who has proved unable to translate that esteem into political weight, a sort of political gadfly without an audience. Gowon, his enemy in war, he now regards as a friend, and Obasanjo, the man who accepted Biafra's surrender, he speaks of with respect.

Today, Ojukwu refuses to renounce his decision to declare Biafran independence. Tens of thousands of Igbos had been murdered by rampaging northern mobs, and he had had no choice but to establish a refuge for his people. "It had to be done. Biafra was really not so much that this is our sovereign territory but rather it was a beacon. It was something our people no matter where they were would look at with hope. If I can only get to that line, I am safe."

Biafra is still close to his heart, and he regards the three years of separation from Nigeria as "probably the only period that an African group has been totally free." The fledgling state had attracted support in some quarters, from maverick mercenaries to Charles de Gaulle and the British novelist Frederick Forsyth, with whom Ojukwu seriously discussed staging a coup in the tiny nearby nation of Equatorial Guinea to establish an Igbo state there. But what Ojukwu called an "international conspiracy" to help Nigeria put down the rebellion, a conspiracy led by Britain and including the United States and the Soviet Union, ultimately doomed Biafra. The odd mix of international supporters for his cause can be seen in his driveway, where a Mercedes Benz 600 limousine sits gathering dust. It was a gift from the right-wing German politician Franz Josef Strauss, but it was appropriated and used by various military governments until Babangida returned it on the eve of his departure from office in 1993.

Ojukwu recalls fondly the incredible innovation and resilience the Igbos demonstrated during the war years in coping with shortages of food and medicine and designing makeshift weapons. "It did not matter when they bombed our airfield because we had it functioning in three hours," he said proudly. "One day I was called out of a cabinet meeting to see the first attempt at testing a rocket. The test was in the garden; it took off and landed in the garden. But by the end of the war we had a homing device that was accurate at six and a half miles. It was exciting for anyone."

Ojukwu freely admits he is a tribalist—"the very circumstances of Nigeria only permit an idiot to be 'detribalized'"—and says that what he calls "ethnic sovereignties" should be the building blocks of a more just society. "The natural order is a development of your ethnic sovereignty." In that analysis, he shares much with the likes of the OPC and the Ijaws in the Niger delta. "Here in Nigeria you must first recognize the primordial sovereignties and then negotiate their position within the amalgamation starting from that recognition that they are sovereign. In that case, the sky is the limit," he said. "The issue is not whether you want a unified government for the entire country but what accommodation within that unity do you give to the various ethnic sovereignties that you cannot just paper over?"

Since independence, however, the pertinent questions of how the various ethnic groups can live together amicably have not been addressed. "Everywhere we go we tell people we are independent," he said, slapping his chest. "But we haven't done anything with it." Nigerians still do not have a constitution that they can call their own; the laws of the land were first written by the British colonialists and were later amended and replaced by military juntas seeking to justify their own rule. "Our development has been arrested first by the coming of the British and postcolonial governments—because we have done just as much to ourselves as others have done to us," he said. "We have not been allowed to breathe—locked together and there you will stay."

Once again, ethnic tensions are at a boiling point, the economy is in worse shape than ever before, and even within Igboland, communal strife has reared its divisive head in the ongoing conflict over land between two neighboring clans, the Umuleri and Aguleri. The structural problems that have bedeviled Nigeria since Lord Lugard's amalgamation in the name of the British Crown have not been resolved. Politicians, Ojukwu believes, are stirring up ethnic hatred because they have little else to offer. "The more empty the leadership, the more reliance on primordial forces," he said.

Part of Nigeria's current instability, he continued, is due to the increasing dominance of the Yoruba people. As evidence he cites Obasanjo's rise to power and the growing unrest in the southwest. "We are going through a creeping revolution at the moment because the initiative in Nigerian society is in the hands of a people, the Yorubas, who thrive in anarchy. But because it is in their hands I don't think immediately that Nigeria will collapse. Somehow they manage anarchy."

There is certainly much anarchy to be managed in Nigeria, but just doing that—if it can be done—is not enough. The tragedy of the future is that Nigerians refuse to learn from their own past. "We are far more anxious to dismiss what happened than anything else. Nobody wants to get to the bottom of anything. So you are confronted with asking yourself, was it [Biafra] worth it?" He clearly thinks not; ultimately, the rebellion was in vain. "I am a soldier and anything that brings about war, that brings about killing, I regret," he said in a lowered voice. "The mere fact that I am discussing the war with you right now clearly underlines the fact that the whole thing was a monumental waste."

Epilogue

———

If we want to climb out of the hole we are in,
it is a job for all the people.

CHINUA ACHEBE

O N OCCASION, Semiu Aremu said, he forgets that he is no longer
in uniform. It might happen when he is addressing his seven
children or the customers who board his *danfo* minibus taxi for a journey through the frenetic streets of Lagos. "Sometimes I yell at my passengers, 'Get inside!' Or I yell at them that we are not moving unless
they are well-seated. Then, one of them usually says, 'Driver, you have
a very high commanding tone.' That's when I realize that I have to remember I am a civilian now, and I apologize to them."

Aremu and I were chatting in the front room of his depressingly
run-down cement-block house that looked out on a mud alleyway re-
verberating with the constant commotion of joyously screeching children. The army generals had left power, Obasanjo was in office, and I
had come to see Aremu to discuss his own transition from military to

civilian life. My old guide Kayode Sukoya drove me to his home in the Abule-Ijesha area of Yaba, not far from the University of Lagos campus.

Aremu served in the army for twenty-eight years and rose to the rank of warrant officer before finally leaving in December 1998. The hardest part of adapting to his new life was switching mental gears and taking personal initiative again. "Everything we did was under command, and so you adapt yourself to that," he said. "I never expected that one day I would do something on my own again." He still had to report back from time to time to collect his pension, but he was starting to value the independence of civilian life. "Yes, the freedom is good. It is nice to spend time with the family again. I can now sleep on my own time. If I wake up early, fine, and if not, it is not a problem."

Tired bones had convinced him it was time to quit the army. He had had an inkling that the military would soon be returning to the barracks, and he reckoned that if that happened the army would get back to the business of serious exercise. "I can't really run anymore, and if they started real training, I might not be able to cope with it." Although Aremu looked fighting fit, his legs betrayed a certain sluggishness as he shuffled around the room. "I wanted to get out before reaching an age where I cannot do any hard work again. I had exhausted all of my energy in the military."

Well, not quite all. He had to make a living. By the time he left, his monthly wage in the army was only 4,000 naira, about $40, and his savings were a bit thin, bolstered only by the profits his wife made trading in the market. Though a trained electrician with a specialty in air conditioners and refrigerators, jobs were so scarce that Aremu opted to do what thousands of others had: get into the transport business. For a while he assumed the arduous task of driver, but then he purchased an old *danfo* and hired a neighbor to drive it. Piloting a *danfo* through the streets of Lagos—which resemble an amusement park bumper car ride—is a young person's business, far too taxing for a man of forty-nine, and besides, as he said, he did not really have the patience for it.

As he continued to ponder the question of why he left the army, he said, "there is another point." Though its generals have been in power for most of the country's independence, and though Babangida, Danjuma, Abacha, and many other officers had become fabulously wealthy, the Nigerian Army itself is in awful shape. Pay is terrible, the barracks are often the equivalent of decrepit slums, and morale and discipline are woefully low. Aremu was a proud defender of the military's reputation, but he admitted that things had changed. "All these young boys are coming in with the idea of making money. As a soldier, you should come into the service to serve your nation with all your strength. You don't join the army because you want to become a millionaire."

As he recalled it, when he enlisted in 1969, discipline and morale were high and soldiers were proud to wear the uniform. He joined the army mainly because job prospects were dim, the country was in the midst of civil war, and a lot of young people his age were signing up. He tricked his parents, he said, by telling his father that he was going to town for a job interview. When I asked why he had resorted to deception, he looked at me in astonishment. "Because no one wants their children to join the army, especially when there was a war on." It was the same today. Because his home was near the main military hospital, he and his neighbors routinely witnessed the arrival of wounded troopers from the battlefields of Sierra Leone, where they were serving with the West African intervention force, ECOMOG. "Every day we see soldiers being brought into the hospital with mutilated bodies. Do you think parents want their children to experience that? War is a terrible business."

Aremu began as an infantryman, but after his training as an electrician he worked in the maintenance department of his unit. Initially stationed at Defense Headquarters on Lagos Island, he eventually moved to Bonny Camp on Victoria Island. All the while he lived in his parents' home, traveling to work each morning on public transport. He married and fathered a flock of children.

The army started its steep slide downward when Babangida took power in 1985. "It is not easy to mix the military with a civilian administration," he said with a shake of the head. "It's like having two wives; you can't satisfy them both. The army cannot please both the military and the civilians at the same time. Under Babangida, the government had very little time for the soldiers and for training. The standards were very low." But he bridled at suggestions that the coups of the 1980s were solely the fault of the military. "The politicians were not acting fine. They brought in the army. Politicians who were out of power used the military to remove the politicians who were in power."

Aremu paused and sent out for a couple of soft drinks. On the wall was a blackboard, on which was scribbled:

> sixty seconds make one minute
> 24 hours make one day
> 7 days make one week
> 4 weeks make one month
> 52 weeks make one year
> 365 days make one year
> 366 days make one leap year
> 12 calendar months make one year

I asked him what it was for. "I teach the children during my free time," he said. "Education is so bad now. The teachers are always on strike, and the schools are useless. The children learn nothing. Someone who only went to primary school in my day has the equivalent of a secondary school certificate today, and a certificate in my day is the same as a university degree now." The only alternative was to hire tutors, but he could not afford them, so he conducted his own classes. "I cannot let them look for a job with this education." He tapped his foot and said with a depressed air, "Nigeria."

The military had become scapegoats, he felt, for the mess Nigeria was in, when in fact, "We are all to blame, civilians and military, everyone." Take the case of the 1999 presidential elections, when the mainly Yoruba voters in the western part of the country opposed Obasanjo because he was a former general. "The people don't understand," he said. "They wanted the military to go but during the council elections there were many former soldiers elected. Then they supported Falae, but Falae had worked for a military government even more recently than Obasanjo. If you are in a military government, whether a soldier or a civilian, you are part of that administration."

But the military had absolutely no respect for civilians, I said. I recalled the incident I had witnessed on Victoria Island when I had watched soldiers beating the faces of two drivers, whom they forced to crawl along the road on their knees. "Doubling," Aremu said matter-of-factly. "It's a common punishment in the barracks." One had to see it from the soldiers' point of view, he explained. "Most drivers do not observe the regulations, and they believe when it comes to the police, well, they can pay them off. You must understand what happens to an army driver when he brings a damaged vehicle to the barracks. The officers get so furious. A driver that has an accident, no matter what the cause, will be punished and will have to pay for the damages. A soldier knows that a civilian driver will bribe the police, so he will punish him. Next time he drives more carefully." Perhaps "doubling" was a metaphor for how the military have dealt with civilian society: Since you do not play by the rules, neither will we.

Aremu doubted that the military would return to politics anytime soon. As an institution, the army was in deep crisis, and it had enough problems of its own to deal with. It had been too discredited to make a comeback, at least for the time being. But he was certain that there were ambitious soldiers and politicians willing to use the army to achieve their goals. "I can imagine right now the politicians in government sitting around a table and wondering how they are going to fatten their bank accounts while the people are starving," he said. "The politicians out of power might come to the military and say, 'can't you just help us push those people out?' The future of this country is in the hands of the civilians now, not the military. Let's see how they deal with it."

———

AREMU'S belief that the military was too discredited and demoralized to pose a threat to the civilian government was a common one in the early months after Obasanjo's inauguration. Given Nigeria's history of military rule, however, such confidence would appear premature in the extreme. If Babangida's career was any guide, someone in the armed forces would be lurking out there waiting for an opportunity.

In his first few months in office, Obasanjo surprised Nigerians with the speed with which he moved on several fronts. He retired 100 officers who had held political office in previous military regimes. The government was committed to reducing the size of the armed forces and to rebuilding and retraining the military with help from the United States. If completed, the four-year program would mark the biggest reform of the armed forces since the aftermath of the Biafran civil war.

Obasanjo also introduced anticorruption legislation and suspended controversial oil contracts awarded by the Abubakar government on the eve of its departure from office. Miraculously, the fuel shortages that had plagued Nigeria for years disappeared, though they had already begun doing so in the final days of the Abubakar government. The Nigerian National Petroleum Corporation issued new guidelines barring middlemen from obtaining contracts for oil sales, effectively eliminating commissions that in the past had been worth up to 15 cents per barrel and had cost the country hundreds of millions of dollars. A new government committee was to investigate shady business deals under military rule.

Envoys were dispatched to London, Washington, and other Western capitals to seek access to bank accounts where the government believed Abacha, his family, and his business associates had squirreled away several billion dollars. In October, Switzerland announced it had frozen four such accounts, three in Geneva and one in Zurich. Enrico Monfrini, a Genevan lawyer representing the Obasanjo government, claimed to have documentary evidence that Abacha and his associates had stolen $2.2 billion from the Central Bank. "Funds were diverted on a daily basis," he said. "It was child's play."

A reinvigorated civil society quickly made its voice heard too, with the press forcing the speaker of the House of Representatives, Salisu Buhari, to resign and demanding an investigation into the Senate president, Evan Enwerem. Buhari had no option but to step down after a press campaign led by *The News* magazine revealed that he had lied about his age and about having earned a degree from the University of Toronto. One thousand protesters organized by the Nigeria Labor Congress besieged the National Assembly in mid-August to protest the government's decision to provide between $25,000 and $35,000 in furniture allowances for each of the 469 members of the National Assembly at a time when the minimum monthly wage stood at approximately $30.

A human rights panel, which was headed by the respected former Supreme Court justice Chukwudifu Oputa and included Father Mathew Kukah, was to begin investigating abuses since the January Boys coup in 1966. "You will help us scale over an unprecedented wicked and oppressive era in our history," Obasanjo said while inaugurating the commission. The panel was to provide Nigerians with a healing process of the sort pioneered by South Africa's Truth and

Reconciliation Commission by airing significant human rights cases with both victims and the alleged perpetrators testifying in public. The most sensational development in the human rights field, however, occurred in mid-October, when Abacha's son Mohammed, his chief security officer, Major Hamza al-Mustapha, and several other security officials were arraigned on charges of murder relating to a series of still unexplained assassinations of prominent opposition figures, including Abiola's wife Kudirat. Mustapha and Lieutenant Colonel Yakassi were also charged with the murder of Yar'Adua.

But by early 2000 Nigerians were disappointed at how slowly Obasanjo and the National Assembly were moving to address the burning issues of the day. In the first seven months of civilian rule, the assembly did not pass one major bill, including the budget. That left the human rights panel effectively paralyzed by a lack of funds. A report by another commission looking into corruption under the Abubakar government had not been published, presumably because it was too sensitive. Enthusiasm for Obasanjo's Universal Basic Education program was dampened by the knowledge that it would be carried out by the very people who had presided over the collapse of the country's schools.

Ethnic and political violence continued to spiral beyond anyone's control. In his first year in government, Obasanjo witnessed a series of local upheavals in which thousands died. The polarization nurtured in the years of military rule continued its relentless spread. Obasanjo's responses gave little reason for cheer. Orders to shoot rioters on sight in Lagos and the razing of the Niger delta village of Odi by army troops bore the hallmarks of a military ruler rather than of a civilian leader seeking to promote peaceful dialogue. Following the Kaduna riots over Sharia, a growing minority of people were wondering if military rule might be more stable than civilian government after all. As one columnist put it, Nigerian democracy had gone "democrazy."[1]

In 2000 and beyond, Obasanjo faces conflicting demands from the

Nigerian people and international creditors, whom he repeatedly urged to help establish Nigerian democracy by wiping off at least some of the country's $34 billion foreign debt. The IMF, whose stamp of approval Nigeria needed to begin talks with Western creditors, said it was prepared to reach a new loan agreement worth $1 billion provided the government moved quickly to introduce market reforms. These would include cutting the budget deficit and privatizing ailing publicly owned companies, on which the state is spending some $2 billion in annual subsidies.

A planned sell-off of state-owned companies provided a major test for Obasanjo, since his previous administration had acquired many of the companies during the 1970s when the ideology of state capitalism was in vogue. Several of his ministers, including power and steel minister Bola Ige, had in the recent past voiced hostility to selling what they considered to be the nation's patrimony to Nigerian businessmen who they believed had acquired their wealth by illegal means. "You see the people who are now mouthing 'privatize,' they are looking for ways in which they can invest their stolen money," Ige told me in December 1998. "It is not that they are anxious that those things should work better. It is that they want to buy government-established companies at lower rates than they should be. They just want to invest their ill-got gains there. So it is not privatization; it is looting."

Nevertheless, government officials took pains to declare their commitment to privatization and to reform. Finance minister Adamu Ciroma said in August 1999 that all new macroeconomic policies would be designed to establish free market economics and that the notorious NEPA electricity company and Nigerian Telecommunications Ltd. would be sold off. Unless Nigeria accomplishes these critical goals quickly, it will fall further behind. Without an efficient information sector, Nigeria will remain locked into the ranks of the underdeveloped nations. "If we don't get this telecoms business right, we have ended the possibility that we will ever become a developed country, or even just move from underdeveloped to developing," said Dr. Folarin Gbadebo-Smith, a dentist and businessman involved in the telecommunications business.

Individual initiative is seen by the powers that be not as a resource but as a threat. "It is still this mentality of scarcity," Dr. Gbadebo-Smith, a graduate of Ohio State University, told me in his Lagos office. "There is a question they ask in this country: Who is behind you? They are looking to see who is the power behind this man. You have to be somebody in the system—the son of an emir. If not, then no matter how brilliant your idea, to hell with it. Your only way out of that problem is to bribe somebody."

It was a lesson Dr. Gbadebo-Smith learned in 1995 when his Telepoint Company attempted to set up a system of pay phones that would accept credit cards. After five months of operations, the state telephone monopoly Nitel cut all of Telepoint's lines. Telepoint was unable to operate for the next nine months until Nitel had completed its own system of pay phones. "After that, when I wrote to apply for a line at a certain address, the next day a Nitel line would appear. Then they told me that since they had a phone there, they could grant me a line."

The trouble with Nigeria, he said, is simply a state of mind. In Nigeria the people are expected to work for the government, not the other way around. "It derives from the master-servant relationship that is still entrenched in this culture," he said. "My driver is not human in the same sense that my children are; my domestic help, my house girl, she is not allowed to go out on Sundays. It is basically a form of slavery, and it is the same way that those in government look at the population. Until the day we break this mind-set, when people realize that the house help is as human as they are, we will not see a change in this society."

The new government's moves to reshuffle the army high command and to investigate corruption and human rights abuses provided some necessary breathing space, as did the unexpectedly high oil prices on the economic front. But unless the economy improves and there is quick movement to end the sharpening strife in the Niger delta, Obasanjo could face an intensification of demands to restructure Nigeria into a confederation of regions or, even more worrying, into independent nations.

Decentralization is an idea whose time has come in Nigeria. Its principal supporters are advocates of "ethnic sovereignty," including a wide range of people from Ijaw activists in the Niger delta and the former Igbo secessionist leader Chief Ojukwu to the human rights activist Dr. Beko Ransome-Kuti, who believes his Yoruba people "simply need some space" to govern themselves and plan their own economic development free from Abuja. But they are not the only supporters.

One of the most eloquent arguments for redrawing Nigeria's political map to collapse the currently unworkable federation of thirty-six states into six powerful regions comes from an unlikely source: wealthy northern businessmen. Their fundamental premise is that simplification would be more efficient; six regions would mean leaner, more effective government. "With thirty-six states, we have thirty-six governors, thirty-six deputy governments, an infinite number of permanent secretaries, political advisers, members of the state assemblies, to the point that 90 percent of the states' entire income goes to service these people, who all live in the state capital and constitute an insignificant part of the population," said Abba Kyari, the managing director of the United Bank of Africa. "This state structure is literally taking all the money for itself and [that] means that there is no education, no health services, and an abundance of illiteracy and poverty. As long as you keep that structure going, you are going to have problems in Nigeria. It translates into social and political instability and it is thrown into ethnic and religious fault lines."

In the meantime, the challenge for the Obasanjo administration is to use its limited resources wisely. Faced with severely deteriorating roads, electrical power systems, health facilities, and schools at all levels, it needs to spend to rebuild a shattered economic infrastructure and improve the living standards of its people. Education is critical. As Abba Kyari put it: "If we do not solve the educational problem in the next fifteen years, we are just going to be slaves and nothing else, perhaps not with chains but it's just as good as slaves."

Obasanjo's agenda necessarily involved tackling many issues at once—the legacy of military corruption and human rights abuses, economic collapse, ethnic conflict, and reform of the armed forces—all the while trying to maintain good relations with international creditors and to attract badly needed foreign investment. However daunting the challenge appears, Nigeria has the best chance at any time in nearly twenty years to begin to realize its vast potential and to bring a very dark period in its short history to a close. Most Nigerians believe, and I tend to agree, that Obasanjo's administration represents the last chance to establish enough economic and political stability to avoid the breakup of the country.

So Nigeria stands at a crossroads with three probable scenarios in front of it, two of which would produce severe consequences. The most productive scenario would demand Herculean efforts by the current administration to throttle corruption and mismanagement, strengthen the judiciary and parliament, and revive the economy, giving confidence to foreigners and Nigerians alike to invest in the economy. On the political front, the government should initiate a constitutional conference to allow a wide range of representatives from ethnic, religious, labor, women's, political, and business groups to decide how they want to live. The results should then be put to a nationwide referendum, which might create enough space for Nigerians to start talking and listening to one another. And ultimately, to fashion a political and economic order in which they feel they have a true stake.

Should such an attempt at national dialogue be stymied, a second scenario would see the perpetuation of the status quo, with a civilian government lurching from crisis to crisis, the economy remaining gripped by stagnation, and the legitimacy of the state in constant question. Nigeria would continue to bleed away its abundant natural and human resources, living standards would spiral ever downward, sporadic religious and ethnic clashes would claim more lives, and the remnants of the professional class would follow millions of their country men and women to positions abroad.

In the third scenario, one of disaster, the civilian administration would fail to deal with Nigeria's myriad social and economic problems, opening the door to a return of military dictatorship. That could spark an outbreak of ethnic and regional violence not seen since the Biafran civil war and possibly leading to the breakup of the country.

By early 2000 there appeared to be scant reason for optimism. There were simply too many problems, too much anger, and too little time. Nigeria seemed to be an approaching tropical firestorm, and there was nothing the new civilian government, however honorable its intentions, could do to stop it.

While the international community readied thousands of UN troops and millions of dollars to go into peacekeeping operations in the failed states of Sierra Leone and Congo, it would have been wise to embark on preventive diplomacy in Nigeria by fashioning a multilateral plan to help ease the foreign debt burden and to target funds and expertise to rebuild the country's education system. Those two measures alone might just make a difference.

But just when despair about the future becomes overwhelming, one meets or recalls someone who restores one's faith that Nigeria just might turn itself around after all. One such person is Bilikisu Yusuf, the tall, elegant, sometimes fiery, and highly articulate Muslim woman who is one of the prime movers in Nigeria of Transparency International, the anticorruption organization. Although she said she hoped the return to civilian government would mark a vast improvement over the succession of military regimes, Bilikisu was far more concerned with the public's responsibility for the mess Nigeria was in.

Nigerians, she seemed to be saying, got the government they deserved. "The whole thing starts from the people themselves and their expectations," she said. "A minister's family will expect him to do things that are impossible on a minister's salary; they make spurious demands such as expecting them to buy a new car or take them on trips. Where does the money come from? When an honest aspirant for public office comes along, his village and his family will say, 'No, not that one because he won't eat and he won't let us eat.'"

As a result, Nigeria lived in a dog-eat-dog world in which the elite robbed the country's future generations to satisfy their present desires. It was not always this way, she said. In the early postindependence years, education, for example, received ample state investment. Standards and morality were higher. "Now there is bribing, and if you don't buy handouts from the teacher he will fail you. It just permeates right through to the students, to the teachers, to the principals, to the vice chancellors. A society that fails to invest in education is in decline. And with all the unemployment, by the time students finish school, there isn't much for them to do. So we are creating an army of restless youth, angry, hungry, restless youth."

Bilikisu was working with grassroots Muslim groups, which Transparency International was organizing to work in local communities for justice and against corruption. In conservative northern Nigeria, this was a revolutionary concept. The effort was part of a larger campaign in which activists such as retired General Ishola Williams set up committees in every local government to monitor the performance of government at all levels. "We are the majority, and the elite who manipulate all these things are a tiny minority, powerful yes, but they can't compete with us," she said. "Civil society must hold them to account and refuse to let them get away with it."

Corruption—"the degree of insanity," she called it—had reached down to the lowest levels, to the local government and even the village. "It's very un-African in the sense of traditional society. There is supposed to be this moral suasion which stops you from misbehaving in your locality. But now we have Nigerians looting money from their own people. It's not enough for us to say, 'Ah, the leadership is corrupt, government is corrupt.' We have not internalized the message of probity, accountability, and transparency. If we are going to hold people to account and really make meaningful change in Nigeria, we must first begin with ourselves."

Notes

———

The following citations refer only to text drawn from other sources. All other direct quotes are based on the author's personal interviews and are not cited here.

PREFACE

1. John de St. Jorre, *The Nigerian Civil War* (London: Hodder and Stoughton, 1972), 404.
2. Chinua Achebe, *The Trouble with Nigeria* (Oxford: Heinemann, 1983), 1.
3. Wole Soyinka, *The Open Sore of a Continent: A Personal Narrative of the Nigerian Crisis* (Oxford: Oxford University Press, 1996).

CHAPTER 1: A COUP FROM HEAVEN

1. Michael Crowder, *The Story of Nigeria* (London: Faber and Faber, 1978), fourth edition, 23.
2. Thomas Pakenham, *The Scramble for Africa* (Parklands: Jonathan Ball, 1991), 413.
3. Ibid., 11.
4. Eghosa E. Osaghae, *Crippled Giant* (London: Hurst and Company, 1998), 5.
5. Keith Richburg, "Decay 101: The Lesson of 'Africa's Harvard.'" *The Washington Post*, August 11, 1994.
6. Charles R. Babcock and Susan Schmidt, "Man with Nigeria Ties Was at Clinton Dinner," *The Washington Post*, November 22, 1997.

CHAPTER 2: VOTING DAY

   1. Janet Mba-Afolabi, "Cannibals in their Midst," *Newswatch* (Lagos), February 22, 1999.

CHAPTER 3: ARMY ARRANGEMENT

   1. Maggie Black, *A Cause for Our Times—Oxfam: The First Fifty Years*, 1992; cited in Alex DeWaal, *Famine Crimes, Politics and the Disaster Relief Industry in Africa* (Oxford: James Currey) and (Bloomington & Indianapolis: Indiana University Press, 1997), 75.

CHAPTER 4: THE OGONI WARS

   1. Nick Ashton-Jones, *The ERA Handbook to the Niger Delta* (Environmental Rights Action, 1998), 203.
   2. Ken Saro-Wiwa, *A Month and a Day: A Detention Diary* (London: Penguin Books, 1995), 73.
   3. Ken Saro-Wiwa, *Similia: Essays on Anomic Nigeria* (Port Harcourt: Saros International Publishers, 1991), 47.
   4. Saro-Wiwa, *A Month and a Day*, 52–54.
   5. *Genocide in Nigeria: The Ogoni Tragedy* (Port Harcourt: Saros International Publishers, 1992), as found in www.prairienet.org/acas/genoch5.html.
   6. John de St. Jorre, *The Nigerian Civil War* (London: Hodder and Stoughton, 1972), 116.
   7. Ibid.
   8. Ken Saro-Wiwa, *On a Darkling Plain: An Account of the Nigerian Civil War* (Port Harcourt: Saros International Publishers, 1989), 10.
   9. Saro-Wiwa, *A Month and a Day*, 63.
  10. Ibid., 65.
  11. Saro-Wiwa, *Similia*, 75.
  12. Ibid., 137.
  13. Saro-Wiwa, *Similia*, 168–170.
  14. Saro-Wiwa, *A Month and a Day*, 76.
  15. Human Rights Watch/Africa, *Nigeria—The Ogoni Crisis: A Case Study of Military Repression in Southeastern Nigeria* (New York: Human Rights Watch, July 1995), vol. 7, no. 5.
  16. Saro-Wiwa, *A Month and a Day*, 80.
  17. Ken Saro-Wiwa, *Defence Statement* (1995).
  18. Saro-Wiwa, *A Month and a Day*, 89–92.
  19. Saro-Wiwa, *A Month and a Day*, 102.
  20. Steve Kretzmann, "Hired Guns," *In These Times Magazine*, February 3–16, 1997.
  21. Ibid., 121.

22. Ibid., 126.

23. "Shell-Shocked: The Environmental and Social Costs of Living with Shell in Nigeria" (Amsterdam: Greenpeace International, 1994), found at www.greenpeace.org.

24. SPDC Press Release, "Statement by SPDC Managing Director Brian Anderson," November 14, 1995.

25. Shell Environment Brief, London, 1998.

26. "Oil Spills," Shell Environment Brief, London, 1998. Available at www.shellnigeria.com.

27. U.S. Department of Energy, Energy Information Administration, Nigeria (Washington: September 1996), 62.

28. Saro-Wiwa, *A Month and a Day*, 158–159.

29. Karl Maier, "An Unpleasant Situation in Ogoniland," *The Independent* (London), August 15, 1993.

30. Saro-Wiwa, *A Month and a Day*, 76.

31. Chris McGreal, "Ken Saro-Wiwa Not Entirely Innocent?," *Mail and Guardian* (Johannesburg), April 4 to 11, 1996.

32. Ibid.

33. Dominic Midgely, "The Man Who Fooled the World," *Punch*, March 1998, 28.

34. Human Rights Watch/Africa, *Nigeria—The Ogoni Crisis*, 13.

35. Ibid.

36. RSIS/MILAD/LOO/94.004. "Restricted." Also published as Appendix, "Ogoni—The Struggle Continues" (Geneva: World Council of Churches, December 1996), 96–97.

37. Ibid.

38. Human Rights Watch/Africa, *Nigeria—The Ogoni Crisis*, 14 and press conference on May 22, 1994.

39. Human Rights Watch/Africa, *Nigeria—The Ogoni Crisis*, 15.

40. Ibid.

41. World Council of Churches, "Ogoni—The Struggle Continues."

42. McGreal, "Ken Saro-Wiwa: Not Entirely Innocent?," *Mail and Guardian*.

43. Michael Birnbaum, QC, *Nigeria: Fundamental Rights Denied. Report of the Trial of Ken Saro-Wiwa and Others* (London: Article 19, in association with the Bar Human Rights Committee of England and Wales and the Law Society of England and Wales, June 1995), 9.

44. Michael Birnbaum, QC, *A Travesty of Law and Justice* (London: Article 19, December 1995), 2.

45. "Saro-Wiwa's Last Public Statements," Association of Concerned African Scholars, ACAS Alerts and Related Material on Ken Saro-Wiwa and Nigeria, www.prairienet.org/ACAS/Lastword.html.

46. "Why the General Killed," Wole Soyinka [statement] available through the Association of Concerned African Scholars website, www.prairienet.org/ACAS/Soyinka.html.

CHAPTER 5: THE JOURNEY OF A THOUSAND MILES ...

1. Michael Crowder, *The Story of Nigeria*, fourth edition (London: Faber and Faber, 1978), 159.
2. Quoted in Thomas Pakenham, *The Scramble for Africa* (Johannesburg: Jonathan Ball, 1991), 464.
3. Oronto Douglas, personal communication.
4. *Nigeria: Report of the Commission Appointed to Enquire into the Fears of Minorities and the Means of Allaying Them* (London: Her Majesty's Stationery Office, 1958), 50.
5. Ibid., 42.
6. Ibid., 95.
7. Major Isaac Boro, *The Twelve-Day Revolution* (Benin City: Idodo Umeh Publishers, 1982), 87.
8. Ibid., 94.
9. Ibid., 131.
10. The Kaiama Declaration, "Being the communiqué issued at the end of the all Ijaw Youths Conference, which was held in the town of Kaiama this 11th Day of December 1998." Found at www.seen.org/kaiama.
11. Mike Osunde (reporting from Benin City), "Ijaw Youths Council Dissociates from Pact with Obasanjo," *The Guardian* (Lagos), January 5, 1999.
12. Ibid.
13. Statement issued January 4, 1998, by the Niger Delta Human and Environmental Rights Organisation (ND-HERO), signed by President Azibaola Robert.
14. Weekly Roundup No. 2 of Main Events for West Africa, UN Office for the Coordination of Humanitarian Affairs, Integration Regional Information Network for West Africa, January 8–14, 1999.
15. UN IRIN Humanitarian Information Unit, *Nigerian Kidnappings Worry Oil Firms*, Item: irin-english–1165 (Lagos, July 5, 1999).
16. "One of Five Kidnapped Britons Released in Nigeria," *Reuters*, Lagos, August 11, 1999.
17. "Angry Nigerian Youths Attack Texaco Office," *Reuters*, Lagos, August 19, 1999.

NOTES

CHAPTER 6: THE FAITHFUL

1. "Nigerian bishops warn of 'national suicide,'" *Reuters*, Lagos, February 28, 2000.
2. "Obasanjo says Nigeria will overcome unrest cycle," *Reuters*, Abuja, March 1, 2000.
3. Wole Soyinka, "This is Prelude to War," *The News* (Lagos), February 29, 2000.
4. Peter Cunliffe-Jones, "Nigerian governor sticks by Islamic code, but willing to compromise," *Agence France Presse*, (Gusau, Nigeria), March 8, 2000.
5. Muyiwa Akintunde, "This Isn't the Sharia We Know," *Africa Today*, December 1999.
6. Interview between Governor Sani and Peter Cunliffe-Jones (of *Agence France Presse*), Richard Dowden (of *The Economist*), and Koert Lindijer (of *NRC Handelsblad*), Gusau, December 7, 1999.

CHAPTER 7: CHILDREN OF HAM

1. Abdulsalam Isa, "Ethnic Cleansing in Takum, Taraba," *The Guardian on Sunday* (Lagos), August 30, 1998.
2. Frank Willett, *African Art*, revised edition (London: Thames and Hudson, 1993), 69.
3. Ibid., 73.
4. "Kafanchan Crisis: Victims Blame Government," *Weekly Trust* (Kaduna), July 16, 1999.

CHAPTER 8: THE SPIRIT OF ODÙDUWÀ

1. Michael Crowder, *The Story of Nigeria*, fourth edition (London: Faber and Faber, 1978), 94.
2. Mcnezer Fasehun, "Obasanjo Woos Oodua Leader," *P.M. News*, December 8, 1998.
3. Joke Hassan and Tokunbo Fakeye, "At daggers drawn," *Tempo* magazine (Lagos), March 11, 1999.
4. According to a letter he wrote while in detention to NADECO deputy chairman Chief Abraham Adesanya, June 1999.
5. Mike Odoh, "Yorubas Flee Northern Nigerian City After Riots," *Reuters*, Kano, July 27, 1999.
6. William Wallis, "Nigerians Flee Ethnic Violence," *The Financial Times* (Kano), July 30, 1999.

CHAPTER 9: "THIS ANIMAL CALLED MAN"

1. Olusegun Obasanjo, *This Animal Called Man* (Abeokuta: ALF Publications, 1999), 205.
2. Ibid., 191.

CHAPTER 10: A GLASS CAGE

1. Chinua Achebe, *The Trouble with Nigeria* (Oxford: Heinemann, 1983), 45.

EPILOGUE

1. Ben Ejiogu, "Nigeria at the crossroads," *The Guardian* (Lagos), March 20, 2000.

Further Reading

Achebe, C. *A Man of the People*. Oxford: Heinemann, 1966.

———. *The Trouble with Nigeria*. Oxford: Heinemann, 1983.

———. *Anthills of the Savannah*. New York: Doubleday, 1988.

———. *Things Fall Apart*. New York: Fawcett, 1985.

Beckett, Paul A., and Young, Crawford, eds. *Dilemmas of Democracy in Nigeria*. Rochester: University of Rochester Press, 1997.

Coleman, James S. *Nigeria: Background to Nationalism*. Berkeley & Los Angeles: University of California Press, 1958.

Crowder, M. *The Story of Nigeria*. 4th Edition, London: Faber and Faber, 1978.

de St. Jorre, John. *The Nigerian Civil War*. London: Hodder and Stoughton, 1972.

Falola, T. and Ihonvbere, J. *The Rise and Fall of Nigeria's Second Republic 1979–84*. London: Zed Press, 1985.

Forrest, T. *The Advance of African Capital—The Growth of Nigerian Private Enterprise*. Edinburgh: Edinburgh University Press, 1994.

Human Rights Watch/Africa. *Nigeria—Threats to a New Democracy: Human Rights Concerns at Election Time*. New York: Human Rights Watch, June 1993.

———. *The Dawn of a New Dark Age*. New York: Human Rights Watch, October 1994.

———. *The Ogoni Crisis: A Case-Study of Military Repression in Southeastern Nigeria*. New York: Human Rights Watch, July 1995.

———. *The Price of Oil: Corporate Responsibility and Human Rights Violations in Nigeria's Oil Producing Communities*. New York: Human Rights Watch, February 1999.

Ihonvbere, Julius, & Shaw, Timothy. *Illusions of Power: Nigeria in Transition,* Trenton, NJ: Africa World Press, Inc, 1998.

Joseph, R. *Democracy and Prebendal Politics in Nigeria: The Rise and Fall of the Second Republic.* Cambridge: Cambridge University Press, 1987.

Kukah, Mathew Hassan. *Religion, Politics and Power in Northern Nigeria.* Ibadan: Spectrum, 1993.

———. *Democracy and Civil Society in Nigeria.* Ibadan: Spectrum Books, 1999.

Luckham, R. *The Nigerian Military—A Sociological Analysis of Authority and Revolt, 1960–67.* African Studies Series No. 4, Cambridge University Press, 1971.

Obasanjo, O. *My Command: An Account of the Nigerian Civil War 1967–70.* London: Heinemann, 1981.

———. *This Animal Called Man.* Abeokuta: ALF Publications, 1999.

Okri, Ben. *The Famished Road.* London: Vintage, 1991.

Omotoso, Kole, *Just Before Dawn,* Ibadan: Spectrum Books Ltd., 1988.

Osaghae, Ighosa, E., *Crippled Giant: Nigeria since Independence.* London: Hurst, 1998.

Paden, J.N. *Religion and Political Culture in Kano,* Berkeley: University of California Press, 1973.

———. *Ahmadu Bello, Sardauna of Sokoto.* Zaria: Hudahuda Publishing Company, 1986.

Pakenham, Thomas. *The Scramble for Africa.* Johannesburg: Jonathan Ball Publishers, 1991.

Saro-Wiwa, Ken. *On a Darkling Plain: An Account of the Nigerian Civil War.* Port Harcourt: Saros International Publishers, 1989.

———. *A Month and a Day, A Detention Diary,* London: Penguin books, 1995.

Soyinka, Wole. *Aké, The Years of Childhood.* Ibadan: Spectrum Books, 1991.

———. *The Man Died.* London: Vintage, 1994.

———. *The Open Sore of a Continent, A Personal Narrative of the Nigerian Crisis.* Oxford University Press, Oxford, 1996.

Usman, Yusufu Bala. *The Manipulation of Religion in Nigeria 1977–87.* Kaduna: Vanguard Printers and Publishers, April 1987.

Willett, Frank, *African Art.* Rev. ed. London: Thames & Hudson, 1993.

Index

Aba, 146–147

Abacha, Ibrahim, 67, 156

Abacha, Maryam, 48, 156

Abacha, Mohammed, 144, 296

Abacha, Sani
  Abiola, jailing of, 28
  corruption, 42–43, 295
  coups, 16, 61–62, 67, 72–73
  death of, 5
  and the elections of 1993, 72
  military college, 51
  Muslim-Christian conflict, 163
  opponents, actions against, 156–
    159, 171, 228, 239
  rule of, 3–4, 17–19, 73
  and Saro-Wiwa, 86–87, 102–103,
    107, 109–110
  and the United States, xix

Abiola, Kudirat, 28, 232, 296

Abiola, Moshood
  and Babangida, 60, 63–64, 69–72
  biographical sketch, 27–28
  coups, involvement in, 60

and Dasuki, 159
  electoral campaign of, 17, 26–27
  incarceration of, 229
  Obasanjo, inauguration of, 3
  return, release and death of, 4–5,
    28, 73
  as southern Muslim, 170
  and the Yorubas, 231–233,
    242–243

Abubakar, Abdullahi, 182

Abubakar, Abdulsalami
  assumption and relinquishment of
    power, 4–7, 233–234
  and Babangida, 46, 50
  and the Ijaws, 126–128
  release of prisoners, 110
  scarcity of fuel, 42–43

Abubakar, Atiku, xxii, 147–148

Abudu, Ganiyu, 37

Abuja, 1
  Abiola's death, 5
  construction contracts, 47, 116
  Sharia, 180

Abu, Sully, xxxii, 1

Achebe, Chinua, xxv-xxvi, 56, 79, 273, 289

Action Group Party, 12, 233

AD. *See* Alliance for Democracy Party

Ada George, Rufus, 87, 94, 97

Adams, Ganiyu, 234–235, 237, 239–248, 252, 266

Ade, King Sunny, xxv

Adou, Atari, 128

Afenifere, 229–230

Afonja, 233

Afuwaj, Yaned, 217, 220–221

Agip, 80, 112, 115, 118, 138

Agwam Baju, the, 221–222

Agwatyap I, 222

Agwey, Haruna, 214–215

Ahmadu Bello University, 154, 172–173

Ahmed, Farouk, 225

Akaluka, Gideon, 169

Akassa
  community discussion of concerns, 135–138
  conflict with oil companies, 138–140
  health program in, 133–135
  and the impact of oil, 130–133
  tour of, 128–139
  See also Ijaws

Akassa Community Development Council, 133, 136

Akassa Community Development Program, 132–138

Ake, Claude, xv, 101

Akeh, Jubril, xxiv

Akilu, Halilu, 63–64, 70

Akintola, S. L., 233

Aku Uka, the, 197, 200–203, 206–207

Alagoa, Chris, 111, 113–115, 117–118, 132, 139

Alamieyeseigha, Diepreye, 140–141

Alhaji, Alhaji Abubakar, 98

Alliance for Democracy (AD) Party, 29–30, 234

All People's Party (APP), 29, 33, 188

al-Mustapha, Hamza, 28, 102, 157, 187, 296

Al-Tukri, Aliyu Ibrahim (Tukur Tukur), 167–168, 175

Amnesty International, 91–92

Anderson, Brian, 95

Andonis, alleged violence against Ogonis, 100–102

Annan, Kofi, 4, 243

Anyaoku, Emeka, 4, 243

APC. *See* Arewa People's Congress

APP. *See* All People's Party

Archibald, Thomas, 219

Aremu, Semiu, 289–294

Arewa People's Congress (APC), 247

Aribaba, Toyin, 32–33, 35–38

Asmau, Nana, 151

Association for a Better Nigeria, 70

Awolowo, Obafemi
  description of Nigeria, 8
  electoral candidate, 57–58, 60, 229
  finance minister, 284
  Yoruba activism, 12
  Yoruba infighting, 233

Ayadi, Adeoye, 31

Ayetoba, Felix, 34–36

Ayin, Kolai, 219

Azikiwe, Nnamdi, 12, 57, 274

Babangida, Ibrahim
  and Abacha, 3, 73

and Abiola, 3, 27, 29, 69–72
attempted coup against, 66–68
the Biafran war, 53
and Buhari, 61–62
career and character sketch of, 43–45
coups on the way to power, 58–62
on Fawehinmi, 238
government under, 16–17, 44–45, 62–65, 68–72
interview with, 50–74
and the military, 292
and the Mobile Police, 199
Muslim-Christian conflict, 164
Obasanjo, inauguration of, 2
Ojukwu's Mercedes, 286
prelude to an interview with, 45–50
and Saro-Wiwa, 88, 91, 98
Tiv-Jukun conflict, 207
and Yar'Adua, 156
Babangida, Maryam, 47–49, 66
Badey, Albert, 105
Bagobiri, Bishop Joseph, 209, 224–225
Baikie, W. B., 197–198
Bako, Sabo, 172–173
Balatima, 117
Bamaiyi, Ishaya, 104, 187
Bank of Commerce and Credit International, 157
Bantaji, Galadima Adamu, 204–205
Bantaji, Rabin, 203–204
Bature, Nuhu, 221–222
Bekederemo-Clark, Chief Edwin Kiagbodo, 126
Bello, Ahmadu, Saradauna of Sokoto, 13, 50–51, 151, 154
Bello, Joseph Olalekan, 24
Bello, Muhammadu, 150

Bello, U. K., 66–67
Benson, Nwoho, 282–283
Better Life for Rural Women, 47
Biafra, 285
civil war, xxvi, 13, 53, 84–86, 271–272
Birnbaum, Michael, 108
Bishut, Kaka, 219
Bissalla, I. D., 57
Bitiyong, Tagama, 219
Bolou II, Thunder Efeke, 141
Bonnke, Reinhard, 162, 164, 178
Boro, Georgina, 125
Boro, Isaac, 123–128, 249
Boutros-Ghali, Boutros, 4
Boyd, William, 92
British colonialism
background of Tiv-Jukun conflict, 197, 201, 206
founding of Nigeria, 9–11
in Kafanchan, 219–220
Ogoniland, 82
palm oil, 120–123, 130
and the Sokoto Caliphate, 151–153
Brown, Bobo, xvii–xviii
Buhari, Muhammadu, 2–3, 16, 60–62, 148
Buhari, Salisu, 295

Campaign for Democracy, 229
Beko Ransome-Kuti, 68
Ganiyu Adams, 243
Oodua People's Congress, 230
CAN. See Christian Association of Nigeria
Carter, Gilbert, 233
Carter, Jimmy, 29, 38

Catholic Bishops Conference of
    Nigeria, 147
Central Bank of Nigeria, 186
Chafe, Bala Umar, 189–191
Chagoury, Gilbert, 6, 18, 87
Charles (Charles Philip Arthur George,
    Prince of Wales), 2
Chevron, 93, 112
Christian Association of Nigeria (CAN),
    146, 177
Christians
    conflict with Muslims. *See* Muslim-
        Christian conflict
    faith healing, 251–263
    missionaries in the middle belt,
        219–221
    Pentecostal churches, 263–267
Chukwumerije, Uche, 274
Ciroma, Adamu, 69, 297
Civil Disturbances Special Tribunal,
    107–109
Civil Liberties Organization, 65
Claude-Eze, Chief J. E., 136
Clinton, Bill, xix, 18
Conference of Ogoni Traditional
    Rulers, 104
Constitution
    drafted during Obasanjo's military
        rule, 57
    Gani Fawehinmi's challenge to,
        238–239
    origin of crisis, 13
    and religion, 145
    set in place by the British, 11
    and Sharia, 14–15, 166–167
Constitutional Rights Project, 65
Consul, Gowon, 113–114, 116–118
Corruption
    Abacha, recovering funds siphoned
        off by, 295

bribing of journalists, 202–203
    by Nigeria's leaders, xxiii-xxiv
    con artists, xxiv
    and contractors, 47
    and fuel, 40–43
    Obasanjo, actions taken by, 294
    Obasanjo on, 20
    Ogoniland, fleecing motorists in,
        78–79
    payoff at the airport, xxxiii-xxxvii
    and public responsibility for
        Nigeria's condition, 301–303
    and Sharia, 184–185
    under Babangida, 45, 68–69
    and the West, xxii
Crowther, Samuel, 129, 197–198

Dambatta, Kabiru Isa, 164
Danbazau, Lawal, 152
dan Fodio, Abdullahi, 150
dan Fodio, Shehu Usman, 150–151, 175,
    194, 209, 218
Danjuma, Theophilus Yakubu, 52, 55,
    57, 86
Dankabo, Alhaji, 161
Danwi, Charles, 108
Dasuki, Ahmad, 158
Dasuki, Aliyu, 157–158
Dasuki, Ibrahim, 73, 157–159, 195
Dasuki, Sambo, 157
Daufa, Chief Ombu, 116
Davidson, Basil, xxi
Decentralization, 299
Decree 2, 16
Deedat, Ahmed, 164
de Gaulle, Charles, 285
Delta, the. *See* Niger delta
Dick, Nottingham, 123, 125

Digitemie, Esther, 133–136
Digitemie, Justina, 132–133, 136
Dikko, Umaru, 16
Dimka, Bukar, 57
Directorate of Mass Mobilization for
      Self-Reliance, Social Justice, and
      Economic Recovery, 88, 91
Diya, Oladipo, 19, 232
Dosara, Ibrahim, 180–182, 188–189
dos Santos, Ana Paula, 48
Douglas, Oronto, 127
Dungs, John, 126
Durbar, 152–154

Eagle Square, 1–2, 6
Economy
      at the time of independence, 12
      in contemporary northern Nigeria,
            155–156
      contemporary policies, 297–298
      under Babangida, 65
      of underdeveloping nation, xxi–xxii
      under Gowon, 54
      under Obasanjo (military), 15
      under Shagari, 15–16
Education
      Ahmadu Bello University, 154, 172–
            173
      at the time of independence, 11–12
      contemporary state of, 155–156
      corruption in, 302
      government neglect of in the mid-
            dle belt, 220
      need to solve problem of, 299–300
      Universal Basic Education program,
            296
Eduok, Nsikak, 127
Effiong, Philip, 272

Ehuwa, Kolawole Bright, 38
Ehuwa, Chief Simeon, 36
Ekwueme, Alex, 29–30, 274
Elections
      in Ayetoro, 31–38
      candidates in 1999, 28–30
      held under Obasanjo, 57–58
      history of, 23
      of 1983, 58–59
      of 1993, 69–72
Elf, 80
Enough is Enough, 139–140
Environment, oil and the destruction
            of, 94–96, 111
Enwerem, Evan, 295
Enyaosu, Fabulous, 246
Epebu, 111–118
Eretan, Thompson, 34–35
Eriga, Chief G. T. Digitemie, 136
Ethnic politics
      and the Biafran war, 13
      in Nigeria and the world, xx
      Obasanjo and contemporary, 296
      roots of, 7–9, 11–13
      tribalism and contemporary
            Nigeria, 286–287
      See also names of ethnic groups

Fagbuagun, Bayo, 32–33, 35–38
Faith healing, 251–263
Faith Tabernacle, 263–267
Falae, Olu
      as electoral candidate, 28–29, 38,
            234
      as member of military government,
            22–23, 29, 34, 293
      picture of as prisoner, 227
Farrakhan, Louis, 164

Fasehun, Frederick, 227–236, 239, 241, 246

Fawehinmi, Gani, 73, 107, 232, 235, 237–241, 248

Federal Electoral Commission, 58

Forsyth, Frederick, 285

Fuel, shortages in Nigeria, 40–43, 294–295

Fulanis, 150–151, 217–221

Garba, Idris, 163

Garba, Joseph, 55

Gbadebo-Smith, Folarin, xxii, 298

Gezo, 233

Giwa, Dele, 16, 63–64

Goldie Taubman, George Dashwood, 9–10, 120–121

Gooden, Tomoworio ("Mecks"), 128–130, 132–133, 135, 138

Gora, Bala Ade Dauke, 222–224

Government regimes
  Abacha, 3–4, 17–19, 73
  Babangida, 16–17, 44–45, 62–65, 68–72
  Buhari, 16, 60–62
  from Abacha to Obasanjo (civilian), overview of events, 3–6
  Gowon, 52–54
  Ironsi, 51–54
  Mohammed, 56–57
  Obasanjo (military), 14–15, 57
  Shagari, 15–16, 58
  Shonekan, 17, 72, 102–103
    Tafawa Balewa, 11–13, 51

Gowon, Yakubu, 13, 50, 52–54, 84–85, 270, 284–285

Greenpeace, 92

Gusau, Aliyu Mohammed, 29

Gwadabe, Lawal, 157

Habib, Nuuman, 164

Haruna, Mohammed, 40, 43–44, 46–49, 64

Hausas
  Muslim-Christian conflict in Kano, 160–165, 169
  perceptions of, 220–221
  precolonial history, 149–151
  Tiv-Jukun conflict, 204
  Yorubas, violent clashes with, 245–249
  Zango Kataf, violence in, 222–224

Health, program in Akassa, 133–135

Hewett, Edward, 120–121

History
  British colonialism. See British colonialism
  of elections, 23
  from Abacha to Obasanjo (civilian), overview of events, 3–6
  inauguration of Obasanjo (civilian), 1–3, 6–7, 19–22
  independence to onset of military rule, 11–13
  of Islam in Nigeria, 148–154
  Kafanchan, 217–220
  the middle belt, 193–194
  military rule, after Shagari, 16–19
  military rule, initial period, 13–15
  Onitsha, 278
  pre-colonial, 7–9
  Tiv-Jukun conflict, 197–198, 201–202, 206–207
  of Zango Kataf, 211

See also Babangida, Ibrahim, interview with

Holland Jacques, 120

Human rights, investigating abuses, 295–296

Human Rights Watch/Africa, 102, 106

Hussein, Imam, 173

Iaregh, Francis, 198

IBB. *See* Babangida, Ibrahim

Ibos, and Igbos, 278–279

Ibru, Alex, 187

Idiagbon, Tunde, 16, 61

Idowu, Omogbemi, 33–36

Igbos
   Biafran war, 13, 53, 84–86
   and Ibos, 278–279
   and the Ijaws, 119
   industriousness of, 279–281
   legacy of the Biafran war, 269–72, 282–287
   Muslim-Christian conflict, 146–147, 160–165, 169
   and Ogonis, 84, 89
   Onitsha, 275–278
   perceptions of and by, 273–275

Ige, Bola, 155, 297

Ijaws
   Boro and the secessionist effort, 123–125
   and British colonialism, 121–123
   protests against oil companies, 112, 125–128
   and the slave trade, 119
   Yorubas, clashes with, 141–142
   See also Akassa

Ijaw Youth Council, 127, 141, 244

Ikena, Ndubusi, 165

Ikonibo I, Chief I. N. Antony, 117, 130–32, 137–139
   See also, Akassa

IMF. *See* International Monetary Fund

Independent National Electoral Commission (INEC), 26, 31

INEC. *See* Independent National Electoral Commission

Integral WXYZ, 123–124

Internal Security Task Force, 105–106

International Monetary Fund (IMF), 41, 63, 297

International Telegraph and Telephone, 27–28

Ironsi, John Aguiyi, 51–52, 54, 57

Islam
   origins in Nigeria, 148–154
   radical/militant, 165–176
   See also Muslim-Christian conflict

Isoun, Turner, 142

Itsekiris, 84, 112, 126, 275

IYC. *See* Ijaw Youth Council

Ja'amutu Tajidmul Islami ("Movement for Islamic Revival"), 166, 168–171, 175

Jackson, Jesse, 2

Jaja, King, 121

Jangebe, Buba, 148

Jibril, Mallam, 150

Joint Action Committee, 239

Joint Aid Monitoring Group, 184–185, 188–191

Jos, 169, 195
   Obasanjo's inauguration, 29

Joshua, Temitope Balogun, 251–264

Journalists, avoidance of Nigeria, xviii
Juju, 228–229, 235–236, 244
Jukuns
    Aka Uka, the, 197, 200–203, 206–207
    background of Tiv-Jukun conflict, 197–198, 201–202, 206–207
    fighting with Tivs, 195
    Tiv-Jukun conflict and trip to Taraba, 198–208
Julius Berger Plc., 47

Kaa, massacre at, 100–101
Kaduna, 42
    Babangida's university, 74
    Maitastine uprising, 58
    military training college, 50
    Muslim-Christian violence, 65
    Sharia crisis, 145–47
Kafanchan, 208–210, 217–220, 225
Kamalu, Olua, 101
Kano, 160–165, 167, 169–171
Kanu, Daniel, 274
Kanu, Nwankwo, xxv-xxvi
Katafs, 223–224
Katsina, Hassan, 52
Kehinde, Seye, xxx
Kemedi, Dimueari von, 141
Kennedy, John F., xxviii
Khatami, Mohammad, 171
Khomeini, Ayatollah, 170, 174
Knight, Bill, 114, 132–133, 138
    See also Akassa
Kobani, Edward, 87, 90, 93–94, 97–100, 104–105
Kobani, Mohammed, 105
Kogbara, Ignatius, 96

Koko, William, 121–122
Komo, Dauda Musa, 103–105
Kude, James (Atomic), 222–224
Kukah, Mathew, 193, 209–212, 221, 295
Kumbe, Barry, 87, 99, 103–104
Kumo, Suleimanu, 45, 169–171, 178, 184
Kuti, Fela, xxv, 24, 27–28, 55
Kyari, Abba, 148, 299–300

Lagos, xvii, xx, 19, 24–26
    airport, Murtala Mohammed, xxxi-xxxvii
    British protectorate, 233
    election results, 38
    ethnic riots, 19, 246–48, 296
    life expectancy, 181
    Pentacostal churches, 252
    population projection, xxii
    press, 155
    pro-democracy protests, 231
    University of, 290
Land Use Decree of 1978, 15
Largema, Abogo, 51
Lawal, Awawu, 24
Lekwot, Zamani, 223
Leton, Garrick, 87, 91, 93–94, 97–100, 104, 108
Liberia, cost of civil war, xx
Lugard, Frederick, 10–11, 122, 151–152, 197, 219
Lukman, Alhaji Rilwanu, 89

Maccido, Mohammed, 157
Mahadi, Abdullahi, 154–156, 168

Maimalari, Zakariya, 51
Major, John, 195
Makoko, 26, 30–31
Mandela, Nelson, xxv, 2, 29
Marwa, Muhammed, 58
Meabe, Celestine, 105, 108
Mecks. *See* Gooden, Tomoworio
Mesuadebari, Adolphus, 101
Middle belt, the
    explosive politics of, 193–195
    Kafanchan, 208–210, 217–220, 225
    Nok, 212–215, 220–221
    perceptions from, 221
    Taraba, trip to and Tiv-Jukun conflict, 195–208
    Zango Kataf, violence in, 222–224
Military, the
    Babangida, attempted coup against, 66–68
    Babangida, coups involving, 44, 58–62
    Babangida, interview with, 50–74
    Babangida on political meddling, 55
    coups following independence, 13–16
    and elections, 23, 70–71
    and Islam, 154
    northern elite, relationship with, 156
    Obasanjo, inauguration of, 6–7, 20–21
    Obasanjo on, 20
    under contemporary civilian rule, xxii, 289–294
Minna, xxix, 45–46, 208
Mitee, Ledum, 87, 97, 100, 102, 104–107
Mmajah, Mazi Obinah, 269–272

Mobil, 112
Mobile Police, 199–200, 203, 205
Mohammed, Aliyu, 98, 158, 209
Mohammed, Kur, 51
Mohammed, Murtala, 14, 27, 52, 55–56
Mohammed, Tanko, 198
Monfrini, Enrico, 295
MOSOP. *See* Movement for the Survival of the Ogoni People
Movement for the Survival of the Ogoni People (MOSOP), 81, 83–84, 87, 90–105
Muhammadu, Isa, Jr., 224
Mujahid, Abubakar, 165–172, 175
Musa, Mallam, 174
Musa, Mansa, 149
Muslim-Christian conflict
    in Kaduna, 208–209
    in Kano, 160–165, 167, 169
    lack of in Nok, 217
    Sharia. *See* Sharia
    violence, 65, 146–147

Nana, Chief, 121
National African Company, 120
National Democratic Coalition (NADECO), 229
National Electric Power Company (NEPA), 31
National Party of Nigeria (NPN), 57–58, 60
National Republican Convention (NRC), 69, 98
National Security Organization, 56
National Youth Council of the Ogoni People (NYCOP), 96, 99, 104–105, 110

Ndokis, alleged violence with Odonis, 102

Nieweigha, Ken, 140–141

Niger delta

Akassa. *See* Akassa

Epebu, trip to, 111–118

and the government, 115–116

Ijaws. *See* Ijaws

kidnappings of oil company employees, 139–140

Ogonis. *See* Ogonis

palm oil and British colonialism, 118–123

violence in, 112, 117–118, 140–142

Niger Delta Development Commission, 140

Niger Delta Oil Council, 124

Niger Delta Volunteer Service, 124–125, 128

Niger Delta Wetlands Center, 132

Nigeria Labor Congress, 295

Nigerian Bar Association, 68

Nigerian National Petroleum Corporation (NNPC), 80, 93–94, 294–295

Nigerian Red Cross, 142

Nigerian Television Authority, xxx

Nitel, Nigerian Telecommunications Ltd., 298

Nkpah, Naayone, 108

NNPC. *See* Nigerian National Petroleum Corporation

Nok, 212–215

Nok, Ibrahim, 213–217

NPN. *See* National Party of Nigeria

Nwodo, John, 6

NYCOP. *See* National Youth Council of the Ogoni People

Nzeogwu, Chukwuma, 51

Nzeribe, Arthur, 274

Obadina, Tunde, 160–163

Obasanjo, Olusegun

arrest of, 18, 73, 157

Biafran war, 13, 53

and conflict in the Delta, 139–141

consultation regarding coup, 55

contemporary challenges and disenchantment with, xxii–xxiii, 296–300

electoral candidate, 23, 28–30, 33–34, 38

human rights, 295

and the Igbos, 274–275, 281–282, 285

inauguration of, 1–3, 19–22

military reform, 294

as military ruler, 14–15, 57–58, 293

and Mujahid, 169

Nigerians, what matters to them, 267

prediction of great future for Nigeria, 241

release and election of, 5

and religious conflict, 143–147, 177–178, 179, 191

religious faith of, 264–265

and Saro-Wiwa, 86, 89

and Yar'Adua, 156

Yoruba-Hausa violence, 246, 248

and the Yorubas, 233–234, 240, 244–245

Obi, Paul, 128

O'Brien, Michael, 70

Ochi, Sunday Akolo, 191
Odi, 141–142
Odiari, Chief B. C., 278–279
Ofoebu, Hyginus, 165
Ofonagoro, Walter, 274
Ogonis
    and the Biafran war, 84–86
    conflict within the, 96–100,
        104–105
    execution of Saro-Wiwa, 110
    history of, 82
    Internal Security Task Force action
        against, 106–107
    massacres of and alleged ethnic vi-
        olence, 100–102
    Ogoni Bill of Rights, 90, 92
    Ogoni Day, 93–94, 96
    oil and government failure, 80–83,
        89–90
    Saro-Wiwa, activism of, 91–94
    Saro-Wiwa's participation in poli-
        tics, 87
    Wiwa, interview with, 75–78
Ogundamasi, Kayode, 229, 235–236,
    239
Oil
    Akassa, impact of on, 130–133,
        138–140
    corruption associated with, 40–43,
        79
    discovery of, 12
    and environmental destruction,
        94–96, 111
    and the Ogonis, 76–77, 80–84,
        89–90, 93–96, 103–104
    palm, 118–122, 130
    protests against in the Delta, 112
    supplier to U.S., xx, 18, 42
Oil Minerals Producing Areas

Development Commission (OM-
    PADEC), 127, 140
Ojukwu, Chukwuemeka Odumegwu,
    13, 53, 272, 283–287, 299
Okadigbo, Chuba, 142
Okafor, Jude, 276–277, 282
Okagbur, Obi Ofala Okeheukwu, 277
Okanya, Osy, 269, 273–275
Okeke, Armstrong Louis, 252–253
Okeke, Godwin, 279–282
Okigbo, Pius, 68
Okoli, Udoka, 71
Okri, Ben, xxv, 79
Okuntimo, Paul, 102–104, 106–107
Olujawon, Akeem, xxv
OMPADEC. See Oil Minerals
    Producing Areas Development
    Commission
Onajole, Razona, 248–249
Onitsha, 275–282
Onitsha Amalgamated Traders'
    Association, 281
Oodua People's Congress (OPC), 228–
    231, 233–236, 239, 244, 246–249
OPC. See Oodua People's Congress
Operation Araba, 52
Operation Climate Change, 127
Oputa, Chkwudifu, 295
Orage, Chief Samuel, 105
Orage, Chief Theophilus, 105
Organization of Islamic Countries,
    65
Orji, Clifford, 24–25
Orkar, Gideon, 66
Orubebe, Bello, 128
Otu, Agbarator Friday, 96
Owonaru, Sam, 123, 125
Oxfam, 53
Oyedepo, David, 263–267

Pajeane, 165
Pakenham, Thomas, 10
Palm oil, 118–122, 130
Pam, Yakubu, 51
PDP. *See* People's Democratic Party
People's Democratic Party (PDP), 29,
  33, 274
Pickering, Thomas, 4
Police
  fleecing motorists in Ogoniland,
    78–79
  killings at Umuechem, 91
  Mobile, 199–200
  at Obasanjo's inauguration, 21–22
  Port Harcourt, encounter at, xvi-xvii
Pro Natura International, 132

Ransome-Kuti, Beko
  arrest of, 68, 229
  birthplace of, 27
  decentralization, 299
  elections and the military, 70
  juju, 236
  optimistic predictions for Nigeria,
    241
Ransome-Kuti, Olikoye, 27
Rapid Response Squad, 247
Rasaki, Raji, 67
Religion
  Aka Uka, the, 197, 200–203,
    206–207
  Durbar, the, 152–154
  faith healing, 251–263
  Islam. *See* Islam
  Muslim-Christian conflict. *See*
    Muslim-Christian conflict

Pentecostal churches, 263–267
  politicization of, 14–15
  riots, 58
Rewane, Pa Alfred, 232
Rice, Susan, xix
Royal Dutch/Shell, 76, 131. *See also*
  Shell Petroleum Development
  Corporation
Royal Niger Expedition, 197

Sade, xxv
St. Jorre, John de, xxvi
Sanda, Bashir, 180, 183
Sani, Ahmed, 148, 176–188
  See Sharia
  See Zamfara
Sankara. *See* Ogundamasi, Kayode
Sankara, Thomas, 229
SAP. *See* Structural Adjustment
  Program
Saro-Wiwa, Ken
  arrest, trial, and execution of, xxix,
    3, 18, 76, 105–110, 125
  Atomic, meeting in prison with,
    224
  biography, 76–94
  interview with his father, 77–78
  MOSOP and political activism, 96–
    105
Saro-Wiwa, Maria, 85
Schmidt, Helmut, 2
SDP. *See* Social Democratic Party
Seal, xxv
Shagari, Shehu, 2, 15–16, 23, 57–60,
  148, 156
Sharia
  arrival of, 150

constitution, inclusion in, 14–15,
  166–167
  Muslim-Christian conflict, 144–148
  in Zamfara, 176–192
Shaw, Flora, 10
Shell. *See* Shell Petroleum
  Development Corporation
Shell Petroleum Development
  Corporation (SPDC)
  discovery of oil in the Niger delta,
    123
  financing of security forces, 125, 138
  headquarters, xv
  in Ogoniland, 80, 90–97, 103–104
  sabotage in the delta, 112
  and Saro-Wiwa, 110
  Shell Club, xvii-xviii
  subcontractor crew held hostage,
    139–140
Shinkafi, Umar, 49, 69
Shonekan, Ernest, 17, 72, 102–103
Slave trade, 119–120, 151, 194
Social Democratic Party (SPD), 69, 98,
  164
Sorajee, Soli, 77
Soyinka, Wole
  description of Nigeria, xxx-xxi
  Nobel Laureate, xxv, 79
  on Obasanjo, 147
  Saro-Wiwa, execution of, 109
  Yoruba religion, 231
  on Youths Earnestly Ask for
    Abacha, 274
Springer, Jerry, 256
SSS. *See* State Security Service
Stanley Oninabharobasi, Ezekiel,
  115–116
State Security Service (SSS), 182, 189
Statoil-BP, 132

Strauss, Franz Josef, 285
Structural Adjustment Program (SAP),
  63, 65
Sukoya, Kayode, 26, 290
Sule, Maitama, 170–171
Synagogue Church of All Nations, 252–
  258

Tafawa Balewa, Abubakar, 11–13, 23,
  51, 124
Telepoint Company, 298
Texaco, 112, 136, 138, 140
Thatcher, Margaret, 64
Third Eye, 70
Thomas, Biyi Bandele, xxv, 209
Tinubu, Bola, 247–248
Tivs
  background of Tiv-Jukun conflict,
    197–198, 201–202, 206–207
  fighting with Jukuns, 195
  Tiv-Jukun conflict and a trip to
    Taraba, 198–208
  Tor Tiv, the, 205–207
Tofa, Bashir, 17, 69–70
Torkula, Alfred Akawe, 206–207
Tor Tiv, the, 205–207
Transparency International, xxvii, 178,
  301–302
Tukur, Bamanga, 30
Tukur, Tukur. *See* Al-Tukri, Aliyu
  Ibrahim
Tutuola, Amos, 79

UAC. *See* United Africa Company
United Africa Company (UAC), 120,
  128–129

United Bank of Africa, 148

United Nations, xxi-xxii, xxv, 77, 301

United Nations Development Program, Human Development Report of 1993, 181

United Party of Nigeria, 60

United States
and Abacha, xix, 3, 18–19
and Biafra, 285
oil, consumption of Nigerian, xx, 18, 42
Saro-Wiwa, visit of, 91

Universal Basic Education program, 296

Unrepresented Nations and Peoples Organization, 92

Usman, Bala, 179

Uzoatu, Emeka, 276–277

Uzoatu, Maxim, 276

Victoria, Queen Alexandrina, 153

Waribungo, Sabina, 137

Weeks, Mike, 136–137

Wilbros, 96

Williams, Ishola, xxvii, 47, 302

Willink Commission, 122–123

Willink, Henry, 122

Wilson, Hitler, 135

Wiwa, Jim Beeson, 75–78

Wiwa, Ken, Jr., 84–86, 91, 104, 109–110

World Bank, xxi, 65

Yaji b Tsamia, Ali, 149

Yakassi, Ibrahim, 157, 296

Yak, Nyet, 215

Yakubu, Jibril Bala, 187

Yar'Adua, Shehu Musa
and Abacha, 156–157
arrest of, 18, 73
coups, involvement in, 55, 57
electoral candidate, 69
murder of, 3, 73, 296
Obasanjo's deputy, 14

Yohanna, Simon, 211–212, 217

Yorubas
and Abiola, 28–29, 231–233
Adams on the, 242–245
divisiveness of, 232–236
Hausas, violent clashes with, 245–249
Igbo perception of, 287
Ijaws, clashes with, 141–142
opinion of Obasanjo, 58
pre-colonial, 8–9, 232–233
self-perception and experience, 231–232
separatism and the Oodua People's Congress, 228–231, 239–240

Young, Andrew, 29

Youths Earnestly Ask for Abacha, 274

Yusuf, Bilikisu, 178–179, 189–190, 301–303

Yusuf, Kabiru, 195–196, 198–203, 206

Yusufu, M. D., 45, 56, 144

Zakzaky, Ibrahim
arrest of, 171

emirs, 152, 154
interview with, 174–176
as Islamic radical, 173
and Mujahid, 165–169
and Sharia, 178, 188

Zamfara, 176–192
Zango Kataf, 210–211,
    222–224
Zaria, 42, 149–74, 201, 211, 218
Zimbabwe, xxxii